# DAILY

—

# DEVOTIONS

—

## from

—

# PSALMS

# DAILY

—

# DEVOTIONS

—

# from

—

# PSALMS

## 365 DAILY INSPIRATIONS

## JOYCE MEYER

New York • Nashville

FaithWords
Hachette Book Group
1290 Avenue of the Americas, New York, NY 10104
faithwords.com
twitter.com/faithwords

First Edition: October 2022

FaithWords is a division of Hachette Book Group, Inc. The FaithWords name and logo are trademarks of Hachette Book Group, Inc.

The publisher is not responsible for websites (or their content) that are not owned by the publisher.

The Hachette Speakers Bureau provides a wide range of authors for speaking events. To find out more, go to www.hachettespeakersbureau.com or call (866) 376-6591.

Library of Congress Cataloging-in-Publication Data
Names: Meyer, Joyce, 1943- author.
Title: Daily devotions from Psalms : 365 devotions / Joyce Meyer.
Description: First edition. | New York, NY : FaithWords, 2022.
Identifiers: LCCN 2022019458 | ISBN 9781546016168 (paper over board) | ISBN
    9781546002574 (leather) | ISBN 9781546016151 (ebook)
Subjects: LCSH: Bible. Psalms—Devotional use. | Devotional calendars.
Classification: LCC BS1430.54 .M49 2022 | DDC 242/.5—dc23/eng/20220606
LC record available at https://lccn.loc.gov/2022019458

ISBNs: 978-1-5460-1616-8 (paper over board), 978-1-5460-0257-4 (leather),
978-1-5460-1615-1 (ebook)

Printed in the United States of America

LSC-C

Printing 1, 2022

# INTRODUCTION

The Book of Psalms is amazing. It helps us know and understand God, it teaches us how to worship Him, it instructs us in wisdom, it encourages us, and it offers practical advice for our everyday life. It also shows us that we can be completely honest with God about how we feel, because we see the psalm writers pouring out their hearts to Him in its pages, whether they felt joyful, confident, hopeful, angry, frightened, discouraged, lonely, or depressed. As they expressed their hearts to God, they received strength and comfort, they realized that He is utterly trustworthy, they reaffirmed their faith in Him, and they gave Him thanks and praise. Biblestudytools.com defines praise as "a description of value or worth." So when we praise God, we let Him know how much He means to us, which is more than we could ever express.

I hope this devotional will help you relate to God as the psalmists did and that you will share your heart with Him freely and in new ways while you go through it and for the rest of your life. As you do, I believe you will discover fresh and wonderful qualities about Him and be strengthened in your faith and trust in Him. No matter what you face in life, God wants to be involved in it. He wants you to tell Him how you feel, and He wants to help you.

Psalms is the longest book of the Bible, with 150 chapters that were originally written as worship songs or poems during the time period from 1000 to 300 BC. The Old Testament shepherd who became King David wrote most of the Book of Psalms, and others, including Moses, Asaph, and the sons of Korah, wrote psalms as well.

I pray that the Book of Psalms will comfort you and that you will grow closer to God and understand His love for you in a whole new way as this devotional leads you through the year ahead of you.

# CHOOSE YOUR FRIENDS CAREFULLY

*Blessed is the one who does not walk in step with the wicked.*

**PSALM 1:1**

The company we keep is important because we tend to take on the traits of those with whom we spend a lot of time. Choose to spend time with people who will make you a better person, not with those who tempt you to lower your standards or compromise your morals.

Ask God to arrange divine connections for you, so you will continually be influenced by the very best of people. Don't choose your friends based merely on a desire to be in the most popular social group or because you think they can help you climb the ladder of success. Choose people with proven godly character.

Getting to know people takes time, and we need to see them in all kinds of situations and watch how they respond. How do they treat other people—especially those they might consider to be "unimportant"? Everyone is equally important to God, and each person should be important to us also.

As you begin this new year, take an inventory of the people who are influencing you. If they are not helping you be a better person, you may need to pray about whether or not spending so much time with them is wise.

*Father, help me make good choices about the people I allow to influence my life, and help me be a good influence on everyone I am around.*

# DELIGHT IN THE WORD OF GOD

*Blessed is the one...whose delight is in the law of the Lord, and who meditates on his law day and night.*

PSALM 1:1-2

God wants us to delight in His ways and to think about His Word over and over in order to understand it fully. The more we study, think about, and talk about God's Word, the more we will benefit from it. People who give God's Word a place of importance in their lives will be like trees planted by a stream of water, trees that never stop yielding good fruit, no matter how things are going in their life (Psalm 1:3). They will be steadfast and steady.

God's Word is food for our spirit, and it keeps us strong. It enables us to go through difficulties yet continue walking in love and doing what we should be doing. It is important for us to not allow our circumstances to rule our behavior. We should always be guided by the Holy Spirit. Psalm 1 teaches us that this type of person will prosper in whatever they do. But the wicked are like chaff that blows away in the storms of life (vv. 3–4). They have no strength to stand firm when they are inconvenienced or suffering.

*Father, I want to be a strong, spiritually mature Christian who brings glory and honor to Your name through my behavior. Help me stay strong in Your Word and keep You first in my life.*

# GOD LAUGHS

*The One enthroned in heaven laughs; the Lord scoffs at them.*

**PSALM 2:4**

The first part of Psalm 2 says that people and nations come together and rise up against the Lord, determined to walk in their own ways instead of following His ways. They are rebellious and resist God's authority in their lives. The Bible teaches us that God laughs at this. He doesn't laugh because He thinks their behavior is funny; He laughs because their actions are futile. God rules and always wins in the end.

God is not an angry God, but He can become angry and rebuke those who refuse to walk in His ways. He will give us the nations as our inheritance (v. 8) and make our lives wonderful if we will simply love and obey Him. But if we choose not to obey, our lives will be unhappy, and we will be like a piece of pottery dashed against the ground and broken in many pieces (v. 9).

We should have a reverential (respectful) fear and awe of God, knowing that although He is good, there are consequences for continued disobedience. People and nations who love and serve God will be blessed as they take refuge in Him.

*Father, I believe that everything You tell me to do is for my benefit. Help me be wise and promptly obedient to You at all times.*

# GOD IS OUR DELIVERER

*I call out to the Lord, and he answers me from his holy mountain.*

**PSALM 3:4**

No matter how many people come against us, God is our deliverer. Our enemies try to tell us that God will not deliver us, but He always does. This may not happen in the way we expect, or when we wish it would, but He will not leave us helpless when we cry out to Him and place our trust in Him.

God is a shield around us, and when we are discouraged, He is the lifter of our heads. Even when we could worry about things, God helps us sleep well at night, and when we awaken, we are refreshed and ready to face another day.

We do not need to fear, no matter how many people or things come against us, because God is greater than them all. He will fight our battles for us while we rest in Him. He deals with all our enemies, and our deliverance comes from Him. Be encouraged today that you are not alone and that God is fighting for you.

*Father, thank You that You are with me and fighting for me. Help me not to worry or believe the lies of my enemies.*

# I WILL NOT FEAR

*I lie down and sleep; I wake again, because the Lord sustains me. I will not fear though tens of thousands assail me on every side.*

**PSALM 3:5–6**

Fear is one of the biggest problems people face, yet God's Word encourages us frequently not to fear. One of the biggest reasons we do not need to fear is that God is with us. He will never fail us or forsake us (Deuteronomy 31:8), and just as He sustained the psalmist David, He sustains us. Therefore, we can say with David, "I will not fear."

Can you try to imagine your life without any fear? I find myself responding in fear much more often than I wish I did, and, perhaps like you, I am still studying God's Word and praying about this area of my life because I want to live by faith and not allow fear to steal my joy. Fear brings torment (1 John 4:18 NKJV), and God does not want us tormented. He sent Jesus to earth so we could have an abundant quality of life and enjoy it (John 10:10).

At one time, I lived with great fears constantly. I am thankful that I have been delivered from most of them, but I want total victory in this area, and I am sure you do too. Don't despair. God delivers us from our enemies "little by little" (Deuteronomy 7:22). Every day, you can get better and better in every way. Keep pressing in, and remember that God sustains you and that you can trust Him.

*Father, I trust You, and I trust that You are sustaining me, working in me, and delivering me from all my fears. I will not fear because I believe You are with me. Thank You.*

# GOD'S RIGHTEOUSNESS

*Answer me when I call, God of my righteousness! You have relieved me
in my distress; be gracious to me and hear my prayer.*

**PSALM 4:1 (NASB)**

In today's verse, David calls upon the Lord as "God of my righteousness." The Bible mentions two types of righteousness. I think
most people view righteousness as a quality that comes from right
behavior, but a totally different kind of righteousness is available
to us as believers in Jesus Christ.

God's righteousness can be simply defined as "right standing
with Him," and it is a gift He gives to us when we receive Christ as
Lord and Savior. It is a gift of His grace, which we receive through
faith. We cannot do anything to earn it or make ourselves worthy
of it; it has already been paid for through Jesus' suffering, death,
and resurrection.

God views us as righteous in Christ because Jesus has taken
our sin and given us His righteousness. Because of this act of
love and mercy, God now thinks of us as right with Him in every
way. We do not have to think of ourselves as "wrong," but we can
be confident that we are in right relationship with God through
Christ.

*Father, thank You for sending Your Son to die for my sin and to give
me His righteousness.*

# SLEEP WELL AT NIGHT

*In peace I will lie down and sleep, for you alone, Lord, make me dwell in safety.*

**PSALM 4:8**

Many people have difficulty sleeping at night, but the psalmist David tells us that our sleep can be sweet, no matter what kind of difficulty we face. Don't ever try to solve your problems by thinking about them over and over; instead, take the time you would spend worrying and pray for what you need while giving thanks to God for all the wonderful things He has already done for you.

As you lie in bed thinking about the goodness of God, you will soon drift off to sleep. God answers prayers, but He doesn't answer worries and complaints. The Lord has set you apart for Himself, and He hears you when you call to Him. He gives us release from our distress and has mercy on us when we pray.

If you are not sleeping well, search your heart and ask God to show you if you have done anything for which you need to repent. If so, then repent and go to sleep with a clean conscience. We are not able to hide anything from the Lord, so it is best not to try to do so. Talk to Him openly and honestly about whatever is on your mind, receive His forgiveness and mercy, and don't worry about it any longer.

*God, You are so good and merciful, and I am grateful for Your forgiveness and for all the ways You help me. Thank You.*

# MORNINGS WITH GOD

*In the morning, Lord, you hear my voice; in the morning I lay my requests before you and wait expectantly.*

**PSALM 5:3**

No matter how much you have to do in the mornings, it is good to spend some time with the Lord before doing other things. Start your day with Him, and the rest of the day will go much better than it would otherwise. Pray and ask God to help you with all that is in front of you each day and wait expectantly for His help.

James 4:2 says, "You do not have because you do not ask God." Ask God to lead you in righteousness and spread His protection over you. Psalm 5:12 says that God promises to surround the righteous with His favor "as with a shield." Just imagine how exciting this day will be as God gives you favor everywhere you go. Watch for it and thank Him for it.

I believe that God will make difficult things easy for you and that His favor will bring promotion in your life as you love, praise, and worship Him. God loves you and waits to hear your voice in the morning, and He delights in answering your requests. Watch for His answers, for they will surely come.

*Father, I am excited about this day because I know You are with me and I trust that You will guide me and give me favor in all I do. Thank You.*

# YOU PUT A SMILE
# ON GOD'S FACE

*Lead me, Lord, in your righteousness because of my enemies—make your way straight before me.*

**PSALM 5:8**

In Psalm 5, David makes clear that God is not pleased with the wicked, with evil people, or with the arrogant. But, because of His great love, those who love Him and seek righteousness can enter His presence and bow before Him.

I feel certain that God is pleased with you as you spend time with Him and desire to learn His ways. It surely must put a smile on His face when we seek Him. We are not perfect, but at least we are seeking to grow in our relationship with Him, and He delights in those who do so.

When Jesus was baptized, "A voice from heaven said, 'This is my Son, whom I love; with him I am well pleased'" (Matthew 3:17). Then, on the mount of transfiguration, God spoke these words again (Matthew 17:5). Our temptation would be to think, *That is only because it was Jesus*, but I think our loving Father also speaks this over us as we seek Him and desire to know and follow His ways.

Don't be afraid to think that God is pleased with you. It will give you the confidence you need to do the things He asks you to do. Just keep growing in Him, letting Him take you from one measure of spiritual maturity to the next. Always remember that even though your behavior is not perfect, God sees your heart and knows that you want to please Him.

*Father, I will take a step of faith and believe that You are pleased with me even though I am not perfect in all my ways. I love You and I want Your will in my life, and I believe that pleases You. Thank You.*

# TELL GOD HOW YOU FEEL

*Have mercy on me, Lord, for I am faint; heal me, Lord, for my bones are in agony.*

PSALM 6:2

In Psalm 6, David is completely honest with God about how he feels. He says he is worn out from his groaning, and that all night he floods his bed with tears (v. 6). He is exhausted from dealing with his enemies, and he cries out to God to have mercy on him (v. 2). He wants to know how long the Lord will make him wait for deliverance (v. 3). It is good to know we can tell God how we feel, because sometimes we simply need to vent our feelings, and it is best to do so with God. Although David had problems, he filled this psalm with confessions of faith.

He says, "Turn, Lord, and deliver me; save me because of your unfailing love" (v. 4). He infers that the dead don't praise God (v. 5), but he does. David confesses that he believes the Lord has heard his cry for mercy and has accepted his prayer (v. 9) and that all his "enemies will be overwhelmed with shame and anguish" (v. 10). I love the honesty of this psalm concerning how David feels, and yet his faith is in the goodness and integrity of the Lord.

We might feel better about some of our problems if we would follow David's example and, instead of trying to impress God with our prayers, be totally honest yet full of faith at the same time.

*Father, I am so grateful that I can come to You honestly and without pretense. Even though my faith is in You, I still feel overwhelmed and weak at times. Even then, I trust that You will deliver me and make me strong again.*

# THE ANTIDOTE FOR WORRY

*My soul also is greatly troubled; but You, O Lord—how long?*

**PSALM 6:3 NKJV**

Today's scripture speaks of a troubled soul. Someone whose soul is troubled usually feels worried and anxious. Jesus tells us not to worry about tomorrow because each day has worries of its own (Matthew 6:34). We probably could find something to worry about every day, but we don't have to worry about anything. When we go through troubles, we can cast our anxiety on the Lord, and He will comfort us and lift our burden. Philippians 4:6–7 tells us not to be anxious or worried about anything but instead to pray and be thankful, and then we will have God's peace that transcends understanding.

Prayer is the antidote for worry. We can worry, or we can give our problems to God in prayer and enjoy our lives while He takes care of our troubles. Worry can give us a headache, but it cannot solve a problem, so why would we waste our time doing something that does no good?

All of us, including me, have wasted many hours in our lives worrying about things that either never happened or were resolved in due time. Worry takes its toll on us in many ways; it ages us, causes pain in various parts of our body, makes us unhappy and difficult to get along with, and can even cause us to begin to resent people who don't seem to have any problems. But none of this has to happen. All we need to do is to trust God with everything that concerns us, one day at a time.

*Father, forgive me for the time I have wasted worrying when I could have trusted You and let You solve my problems. Help me trust You more in the future.*

# COUNT YOUR BLESSINGS

*I am worn out from my groaning. All night long I flood my bed with weeping and drench my couch with tears.*

**PSALM 6:6**

I think we could agree that the psalmist David was feeling sorry for himself when he wrote today's scripture. We can all feel that way at times. The best way to break free from self-pity is to count your blessings, and I mean literally count them. Get some paper or a notebook and write down your blessings. Now write down why you feel sorry for yourself, and look at both lists. I am sure your blessings will far outnumber your problems. Love is not self-seeking, and that's what self-pity is—it focuses entirely on self.

Self-pity, like many other negative emotions, is a waste of time. I had a serious case of self-pity for many years. Anytime I didn't get my way I felt sorry for myself. If Dave played golf and I was home alone, I felt sorry for myself. If I had any kind of problem, I felt sorry for myself. I am so glad God has set me free from self-pity, because it is miserable.

Self-pity doesn't make anything better; it only makes people feel worse. God spoke to my heart one day and said, "Joyce, you can be pitiful or powerful, but you cannot be both." I knew I had a choice to make, and thankfully I decided I would rather have power.

God will enable you to overcome feeling sorry for yourself by helping you remember all the blessings in your life if you simply ask Him.

*Father, I don't want to feel sorry for myself. I know that doing so is disrespectful to You because You have blessed me so much. Help me avoid this negative emotion. Thank You.*

# BE WILLING TO FACE
# YOUR FAULTS

*Lord my God, if I have done this and there is guilt on my hands—if I
have repaid my ally with evil or without cause have robbed my foe—
then let my enemy pursue and overtake me; let him trample my life to
the ground and make me sleep in the dust.*

**PSALM 7:3–5**

In today's scriptures, David is being pursued by his enemies, and
he boldly prays that if he has mistreated anyone, he would be
justly punished and that his enemies would indeed overtake him.
David is not afraid to face truth, for it is only truth that makes us
free (John 8:32). David had not mistreated his allies, but I love
the fact that he was willing to face it if he had.

In this same psalm, David also asks God to arise in His anger
and rise up against the rage of his enemies and decree justice for
him (v. 6). Then he boldly says, "Vindicate me, Lord, according
to my righteousness, according to my integrity, O Most High"
(v. 8). Some people could consider his reminding the Lord that
he is righteous and a man of integrity to be prideful, but I believe
David speaks this way because of his great confidence in God.

He was willing to be corrected if he had done wrong, and this
gave him faith to claim God's promises of deliverance from his
enemies.

*Father, thank You that I can depend on You to correct me when
I need it, but also to help me when I am in trouble.*

# WHAT GOES AROUND COMES AROUND

*Whoever digs a hole and scoops it out falls into the pit they have made.*

**PSALM 7:15**

Today's scripture teaches us an important lesson: When we cause trouble for others, it will recoil back on us, and when a person causes violence, it will come down on their own head. This is the principle of sowing and reaping.

In Genesis 8:22, we find that as long as the earth remains, there will be "seedtime and harvest"—sowing and reaping. Although this verse speaks of harvesting plants that will provide food for us, we can see that seed sown does bring a harvest, according to the type of seed that was planted.

Paul teaches that we should not be deceived by thinking we won't reap what we have sown. He says God is not mocked, "for whatever a man sows, that and that only is what he will reap" (Galatians 6:7 AMPC). Matthew 7:1–2 says, "Do not judge, or you too will be judged. For in the same way you judge others, you will be judged, and with the measure you use, it will be measured to you." And Luke 6:31 says, "Do to others as you would have them do to you," which is also called the Golden Rule. Just imagine how wonderful the world would be if we all treated others exactly as we would like to be treated.

Let's start today applying the principle of sowing and reaping in a greater way than ever before and get ready for an abundant harvest of good things.

*Father, I repent for any time I have mistreated others, and I ask for forgiveness. I want to start fresh and, with Your help, sow what I would like to reap.*

# PRAISE DEFEATS
# OUR ENEMIES

*Through the praise of children and infants you have established a
stronghold against your enemies, to silence the foe and the avenger.*

**PSALM 8:2**

There is great power in praise. When we praise God, it confuses
the enemy. We see an example of this in 2 Chronicles 20:22, when
Jehoshaphat prepared to fight a battle: "As they began to sing and
praise, the Lord set ambushes against the men of Ammon and
Moab and Mount Seir who were invading Judah, and they were
defeated."

When the devil brings adverse circumstances into our lives,
he expects us to get upset and be afraid. But if we praise, worship, and thank God instead, the devil's plans are thwarted, and
he is defeated. Our praise silences the foe and the avenger, just as
today's scripture says it will. We are praising God anytime we talk
or sing about His goodness and the mighty things He has done.

You may be in a battle right now, wondering what to do. I
suggest that you praise God by remembering and thanking Him
for all the good things He has done for you in the past. While you
wait on Him to give you victory in your current situation, your
praise will push back the enemy while simultaneously increasing
your joy.

*Father, I have many reasons to praise You. I am thankful for all Your
mighty works and for all the victories You have given me in the past,
and I am expecting a breakthrough once again. I praise You for this
victory before I even see it.*

# CREATED TO RULE

*You made them rulers over the works of your hands; you put everything under their feet.*

**PSALM 8:6**

When David considers the heavens, the moon, and the stars that God has set in place and how majestic they are, he says, "What is mankind that you are mindful of them, human beings that you care for them?" (Psalm 8:4).

As human beings, we have been made "a little lower than the angels" and are crowned with "glory and honor" (Hebrews 2:7). We have also been given a position of authority over all other created things, and God expects us to be bold and use our authority to resist the devil and all his evil works. James 4:7 teaches us: "Submit yourselves, then, to God. Resist the devil, and he will flee from you."

In Christ, you are "the head, not the tail," and when you follow the Lord's commands, you "will always be at the top, never at the bottom" (Deuteronomy 28:13). You have been given the name of Jesus, which is above every other name (Philippians 2:9–11). If you know who you are and what it means to be God's child, then you will hold your head high and be confident that you can do whatever you need to do through Christ, who gives you strength (Philippians 4:13).

God is watching over you, and He cares for you intimately, so you need not be afraid.

*Father, thank You for creating me and accepting me as Your child. Thank You for giving me authority, power, and the name of Jesus.*

# THE IMPORTANCE OF A THANKFUL HEART

*I will give thanks to you, Lord, with all my heart; I will tell of all your wonderful deeds.*

**PSALM 9:1**

Often throughout the Book of Psalms, we find David giving thanks to God. Perhaps this is one of the main reasons that God calls David a man after His own heart (1 Samuel 13:14; Acts 13:22). David was humble, and he revered and respected God. He was repentant, he trusted God, he loved Him, and he was devoted to Him. He was faithful and obedient, and he gave God the glory and recognition He deserved. Yet David was not perfect; we know from Scripture that in a time of weakness he committed adultery and murder. He did repent of his sins (2 Samuel 11:3–5, 14–17; 12:9, 13), and God still calls him a man after His own heart.

This should be encouraging to all of us. I think the fact that David was thankful was one of his best character traits, for when a person has a grateful heart, it tells us a lot about them. One can easily complain, because we usually have plenty of unpleasant circumstances and people in our lives to irritate us, but at the same time we have much more to be thankful for than we have to complain about.

I recommend beginning each day with thanksgiving and developing the habit of thanking God throughout the day for the many things He does for you. Thanksgiving is part of praise, and in Psalm 9:3, after David declares praise to God in verses 1–2, he says that his enemies turned back; they stumbled and perished before God. He gave thanks with all his heart and his enemies were defeated.

*Father, I repent for all the times I have complained when I should have been giving You thanks for all Your goodness. Help me develop the habit of being thankful at all times, in all things.*

# BE GLAD AND REJOICE

*I will be glad and rejoice in you; I will sing the praises of your name, O Most High.*

**PSALM 9:2**

Today's scripture encourages us to be glad, rejoice, and praise God, as the psalmist David did. This reminds me of Philippians 4:4, where the apostle Paul tells us to rejoice. He then urges us to not worry or be anxious about anything, but to pray and give thanks to God *in* every circumstance and *in* everything—not *after* everything works out well for us (Philippians 4:6).

When I first started my ministry, I depended on my circumstances for my happiness. Finally, the Lord showed me the doorway to joy by teaching me that fullness of joy is found in His *presence*, not in His *presents*, meaning what He does for us (Psalm 16:11).

If we wait until everything in our lives is perfect before we rejoice and praise God, we won't ever have consistent joy. Learning to enjoy life and be glad even in the midst of difficult circumstances is one way we develop spiritual maturity.

Paul also writes that we "are progressively being transformed into His image from [one degree of] glory to [even more] glory" (2 Corinthians 3:18 AMP). Glory represents spiritual maturity, and it is important for us to learn how to enjoy the spiritual maturity we experience at each level of our development as believers.

Choose today to rejoice and be glad in the Lord, enjoying His presence and giving Him praise, regardless of your circumstances.

*Help me to find my joy in Your presence, Lord, and to rejoice and to be glad in each day.*

# THE LORD HELPS THOSE WHO ARE OPPRESSED

*The Lord is a refuge for the oppressed, a stronghold in times of trouble.*
**PSALM 9:9**

Oppression occurs when one person exercises authority over another in an abusive and unfair way, or when someone is needlessly controlling. Throughout God's Word, we are promised that God will help, protect, and deliver those who are oppressed. He is a shelter for the oppressed, and He executes righteous judgment for them. I was abused sexually by my father, and I have experienced the deliverance of God and seen Him deal with those who hurt me.

In order to receive God's help when we are being oppressed, we need to forgive our oppressors and trust God to bring a recompense (reward) in our life. If you are being treated unfairly, don't try to take revenge on those who are or have hurt you; instead, give the situation to God, and He will repay you. He'll even give you a double blessing for your former trouble (Isaiah 61:7).

If you have been or are currently being oppressed, tell God about your situation, cast your care on Him, forgive your oppressors, and pray for those who have hurt you. You may need to separate yourself from the situation for your own protection, but don't let what other people have done to you ruin your life by filling you with hatred and unforgiveness.

*Father, I forgive all those who have treated me unfairly, and I trust You to repay me and bring a recompense in my life.*

# TRUSTING WHEN YOU CANNOT SEE

*Those who know your name trust in you, for you, Lord, have never forsaken those who seek you.*

**PSALM 9:10**

We can expect to face various tests as God trains us in spiritual maturity. One of them is the "trust test." We must learn to trust God in all things, even—and especially—when we do not understand what is happening in our lives.

I'm sure you have at times asked God, "Why am I going through this?" or "Lord, what are You doing in my life through these circumstances?" You may have said, "God, I just don't understand!" Growing in spiritual maturity means not allowing situations you do not understand to cause you to give up on God or to doubt His love for you. It means learning to say, "This must be a test. God is teaching me to trust Him."

One lesson I have learned through the years is this: There is no such thing as trusting God without unanswered questions. If we had all the answers to all the questions that run through our minds, we would not need to trust God, because we would know everything. There will always be things we simply do not understand. This is why we need to learn to say, "Lord, I don't understand this, but I trust You."

*Father, help me to trust You always, especially when I do not understand what You are doing. I choose to believe that You are always working for my good.*

# THE JUSTICE OF GOD

*The Lord is known by his acts of justice; the wicked are ensnared by the work of their hands.*

**PSALM 9:16**

One of my favorite characteristics of God is that He is a God of justice. This means that He makes wrong things right if we put our trust in Him. We waste too much time worrying about and being upset by the wicked. We should pray for them, because if they don't repent of their wrong behavior and change their ways, they will be ensnared by the work of their own hands.

When Jesus was on the cross paying for our sins and suffering more than we can imagine, He asked His Father to forgive those who treated Him unjustly. He said, "Father, forgive them, for they do not know what they are doing" (Luke 23:34). Jesus sets an example for us to follow regarding how to deal with people who hurt us. When we forgive, we do ourselves—not our enemies—a favor. We set ourselves free from any anger or bitterness and release them to God, who is the only One who can successfully deal with them.

If someone has hurt you, don't let them continue hurting you day after day by harboring ill feelings toward them. Let go and let God show Himself strong in your life. Hurting people hurt people, and remembering this often makes it easier to forgive them. God is not only a God of justice, but He is also merciful. Let us follow His example and enjoy the peace that only He can give.

*Father, grant me the grace to forgive anyone who has hurt me or treated me unjustly. I want to be merciful, as You are.*

# WHY DOES GOD HIDE HIMSELF IN TIMES OF TROUBLE?

*Why, Lord, do you stand far off? Why do you hide yourself in times of trouble?*

**PSALM 10:1**

We may feel at times as though God doesn't care about us. We have a problem and we cry out to Him, but it seems He is asleep or hiding Himself. Why? One reason God hides is to provoke us to seek Him, and another is to stretch our faith. Faith only grows as we use it, and if we get everything we want the minute we want it, our faith will never grow. Faith and patience work together to bring us to the victory He promises (Hebrews 6:12). As difficult as waiting is, it is good for us, because it helps us grow spiritually.

God wants us to trust that His timing is perfect, that He has heard our prayers, and that He will bring the answer at just the right time. You are not alone. God is with you, and He is watching over the situation you are in right now. We spend most of our time in life waiting on God to do something, so we may as well learn to "wait well." Whatever you are waiting on now, the wait may soon be over, but after that you will want or need something else and will need to begin waiting again.

I am waiting on God to do several things right now, and I have learned by experience that being impatient won't get Him to hurry. We may as well enjoy ourselves while we wait. God may not be early, but He is never late. His timing is perfect.

*Father, help me be patient as I wait on You to bring the answer to my prayer and provide what I need. Thank You.*

# WHEN WILL GOD DEAL WITH THE WICKED?

*Why does the wicked man revile God? Why does he say to himself, "He won't call me to account"?*

**PSALM 10:13**

Wicked, evil people are arrogant. They think only of the moment they are in and fail to realize that one day God will call them to account for their deeds. God is extraordinarily patient, and I am sure that while the wicked seem to be getting away with their evil deeds without punishment, God is trying to deal with them and bring them to face truth and repent of their actions.

We should pray for those who do evil instead of judging or criticizing them, because if they don't repent, their end will not be good. The psalmist David writes that the thoughts of the wicked have "no room for God" (Psalm 10:4). And Psalm 14:1 says that only a fool believes there is no God. He boasts of his ways and takes advantage of the weak, but God will arise. He will not forget the oppressed, the fatherless, or the helpless. God hears the prayers of the afflicted and oppressed, and He will come to their rescue.

Let me encourage you today to remember that God is just, and He always makes wrong things right in the end. Don't become weary in doing good, because in due time you will reap the reward of your faithfulness (Galatians 6:9). Our God is the King of kings and the Lord of lords. All power belongs to Him, and He will not leave you helpless.

*Father, help me not to resent the wicked, but to pray for them and be patient while I wait on You to deliver me.*

# IS YOUR FOUNDATION STRONG?

*When the foundations are being destroyed, what can the righteous do?*
**PSALM 11:3**

Foundations may not seem exciting, but they are important. When Dave and I built our first home, we didn't invite anyone over to see the foundation; we only wanted to show them the finished house. But it turned out that we had a crack in the foundation that caused problems; repairing it took a lot of work and extra money.

We should make sure our foundations in life are strong. Our spiritual foundation can only remain strong if we spend time in God's Word and time with Him in prayer and fellowship on a regular basis. We should never take a vacation from this. We need God's Word to feed our spirit daily, just as we need food for our physical body every day.

The foundation of a strong, long-lasting marriage must be the Word of God. Dave and I have been married since 1967. This is not because we agree about everything, but because we choose to obey God's Word when issues arise between us.

A solid foundation and a life built on God's Word will stand strong through the storms of life and give glory to God. Build your life on God's Word, and you'll have a life you can enjoy.

*Father, help me build my life on Your Word and always put You first in everything I do.*

# GOD SEES EVERYTHING

*The Lord is in his holy temple; the Lord is on his heavenly throne. He observes everyone on earth; his eyes examine them.*

PSALM 11:4

The thought that God sees everything we do is sobering. Nothing is hidden from Him. He knows all our thoughts before we even think them, and He knows all the words we will speak before we say them. He knows all our needs, and He wants to meet them in the right way at the right time.

God's Word tells us in Revelation 22:12 that each of us will be rewarded according to the works we have done during our earthly lives. Our salvation is not based on our works, but our rewards are. I found forty-six Bible verses on the topic of the rewards of God. I am excited to see what surprises God has planned for us when our time on earth is over and we go to our heavenly home.

Also in Revelation 22:12, He says, "Look, I am coming soon! My reward is with me, and I will give to each person according to what they have done." I don't want to miss any of my rewards, and I doubt that you do either, so keep in mind that nothing is hidden from God.

Children often behave better when they know a parent is watching them, and as children of God, we may tend to do the same. We should behave with excellence because we love God, and not merely to get a reward, but rewards are promised. Let's live a righteous life so we can receive a righteous person's reward.

*Father, I understand from Your Word that You have rewards prepared for Your children. I ask You to help me live in such a way that when I get to heaven, I will be able to receive the full reward You have for me.*

# THE IMPORTANCE OF FAITHFULNESS

*Help, Lord, for no one is faithful anymore; those who are loyal have vanished from the human race.*

**PSALM 12:1**

Perhaps you have felt at times as David did when he wrote Psalm 12:1—that no one around him was faithful or loyal. You may also have a hard time finding faithful friends—people who will stick with you when they realize you are not perfect or when you go through hard times.

The ultimate example of faithfulness is God. Second Timothy 2:13 says that even "if we are faithless, he remains faithful." We are to imitate Him, which means we are to be loyal, even if people around us are not.

You may feel at times as though you are the only one who is loyal, the only one who is being nice, the only one who tries to do the right thing, or the only one who apologizes or forgives. If so, keep on doing these things. Be a faithful person, and you will eventually experience the blessings of faithfulness.

You cannot control how other people behave, but you can determine that you will be faithful, no matter what. First, commit to being faithful to God, because this is the most important expression of faithfulness you can show. Also, commit to being faithful in your relationships with other people. As you are loyal to God and others, you will discover and reap the great rewards of a faithful life.

*Father, thank You for being faithful to me, even when I am not faithful to You. I pray that You would help me to be faithful to You in every situation and to be loyal to the people You have placed in my life. I pray also that You will surround me with people who are faithful friends to me.*

# BEING IN THE WORLD, BUT NOT LIKE THE WORLD

*Help, Lord, for no one is faithful anymore; those who are loyal have vanished from the human race. Everyone lies to their neighbor; they flatter with their lips but harbor deception in their hearts.*

**PSALM 12:1-2**

Psalm 12 was penned about a thousand years before Christ came to earth, yet the condition of the world in David's day seems similar to the world in which we live now. Jesus says that we are in the world but should not be like it (John 15:18–19). We cannot look to the world as an example of how we should behave; instead we must look to God's Word.

No matter what people around us do, God gives us grace to do what is right if we are willing to do it. You may be the only Christian where you work, in the neighborhood where you live, or at the school you attend. Instead of viewing your situation as something difficult, consider it a privilege that God has chosen you to represent Him and be a light in a dark place.

People often tell me that they are the only Christian in their family. They lament how hard it is and speak of all the temptations they face. I know this can be challenging, but if you walk in love with the lost souls around you and show them Jesus through your behavior, you can have a powerful impact on their life and may have the opportunity to lead them into a relationship with Him.

God has chosen you and me to be alive at this time in history, and each of us should seek Him concerning how He wants to use us. God will always give us grace for our place if we ask Him for it.

*Father, I want to be used by You to be a blessing to other people and to lead them to You. I don't ask You to put me where I can be comfortable, but to put me where You need me.*

# GOD WILL KEEP
# THE NEEDY SAFE

*"Because the poor are plundered and the needy groan, I will now arise," says the Lord. "I will protect them from those who malign them."*

**PSALM 12:5**

It is very difficult when we are being mistreated or are in need and feel we have no one to help us. But we are not alone, and our needs will be met because we have God's promise of protection. The Lord "will keep the needy safe and will protect us forever from the wicked" (Psalm 12:7).

We receive God's promises by faith. Hebrews 11:6 says, "Without faith it is impossible to please God" because He wants us to "believe that he exists and that he rewards those who earnestly seek him." If you are in a difficult situation right now, I urge you to believe God's promises and believe that He is working on your behalf, even though you may not see the results yet.

Faith is the substance of things we do not see (Hebrews 11:1), but that substance can be more real to us than something we can see and feel if we put our trust in God. By faith we can see realities that are yet to come. Our destiny in life can change depending on our faith in God. If faith can move mountains (Matthew 17:20), then surely faith can move our problems, because nothing is impossible with God (Luke 1:37).

*Father, when doubt floods my thoughts, I pray that my faith in You will be strong enough to move them out of the way. I know You are good, and I believe You will meet my needs. Thank You.*

# TRUSTING GOD IN DIFFICULT TIMES

*How long, Lord? Will you forget me forever? How long will you hide your face from me? How long must I wrestle with my thoughts and day after day have sorrow in my heart? How long will my enemy triumph over me?*

**PSALM 13:1-2**

We have all asked questions such as the ones David asks the Lord in today's scriptures. Perhaps, as was the case with David, God didn't answer us. Job asked God why he was in his situation, but God never gave him an answer either. Without unanswered questions, we wouldn't need to trust God, and that is what He wants us to do—to trust Him, His ways, and His timing.

The Bible uses language such as "in due time," "at the appointed time," and "in the fullness of time." None of these phrases tell us what we would like to know, but they do tell us that God has a perfect timing for our deliverance and breakthrough.

David must have been distraught when he wrote Psalm 13, because he goes on to say that if God doesn't give him light, then he may die, and his enemies will rejoice (vv. 3–4). But, as we have seen before, David boldly shares his thoughts and feelings with the Lord and then declares that he trusts in His unfailing love and will continue to sing His praise (vv. 5–6).

We can all relate to David in his questioning, and hopefully we can also relate to his decision to trust God in the midst of all his questions. We may not understand why things are happening in our lives, but at the same time, we can trust that God will help us at just the right moment.

*Father, waiting on You for breakthrough is difficult, and I am tired of suffering, but I do put my trust in You and know that You will deliver me. Thank You.*

# WE LEARN BY DOING

*But I have trusted and relied on and been confident in Your loving-kindness and faithfulness; my heart shall rejoice and delight in Your salvation.*

**PSALM 13:5 AMP**

I particularly like the Amplified Bible's rendering of today's scripture, and I hope you will pay close attention to it. Notice that the psalmist David says to the Lord, "I *have trusted* and *relied on* and *been confident in* Your loving-kindness and faithfulness" (italics mine). This tells me that God had proven Himself to David in many situations. The only way David could look back and say that he had trusted, relied on, and been confident in God was for him to have done it and realized that God never failed him.

God will never fail you either. You can trust Him completely. Yet, many times, human nature will prompt you to take matters into your own hands and see if you can solve your problems instead of trusting God to handle them.

Many of us have spent our lives trying to take care of ourselves, and it takes time to learn how to trust God in every situation. But we learn by doing, as David did. We have to step out in faith, and as we do, we will experience God's faithfulness, which makes it easier to trust Him the next time.

*Father, You are completely trustworthy. Help me to remember the times You have been faithful to me and to trust You to be faithful again and again and again.*

# WE SEE GOD EVERYWHERE

*The fool says in his heart, "There is no God."*

**PSALM 14:1**

Those of us who believe in God find it difficult to understand how anyone could look around and not believe in Him. God upholds and maintains the universe with His mighty Word (Hebrews 1:3). Think about it: What or who keeps the planets, moon, sun, and stars in the sky? Why don't they fall on us? How does the earth rotate perfectly in its orbit day after day?

How can anyone watch the formation and birth of a baby and not believe in God? I admit that I find not believing in God difficult to understand, yet many people do not believe, and we should pray for them diligently. I am thankful that I can believe in God, and I am sure you are also.

A monk named Brother Lawrence (1614–1691) came to faith in God one day as he saw a tree that had been dead in the winter blossom again in the spring. He said that he knew that only God could cause that to happen year after year. Some would call this nature, but then where did nature come from, and who causes it to keep working perfectly?

God always has been and always will be. Anything else that exists does so only because He desires it to be so. Brother Lawrence wrote a classic book titled *The Practice of the Presence of God.* He saw God everywhere and in everything, and he dedicated his life to enjoying His presence.

*Father, I believe in You and I pray for all those who don't. I ask that You reveal Yourself to them in a way they cannot deny.*

# A BURDEN FOR THE LOST

*The Lord looks down from heaven on all mankind to see if there are any who understand, any who seek God.*

**PSALM 14:2**

In Psalm 14, David laments how corrupt people have become. They devour people, never call on God, and are "overwhelmed with dread" (vv. 4–5). Corrupt people "frustrate the plans of the poor," but God is the refuge for those who are oppressed or poor (v. 6), and He is present with the righteous (v. 5). David cries out for the salvation of Israel and asks that the Lord would restore His people (v. 7).

God invites us to pray for anything we want and need (Philippians 4:6), and praying for others should be first on our list. Many people don't know how to pray for themselves, but as intercessors, we can stand in the gap between them and God, and we can pray for them. Jesus is at the right hand of God, interceding for us (Romans 8:34), and we can and should be doing the same for those poor souls who don't believe in God and whose works are evil.

It is never too late for a person to receive Christ as their Savior. My father was eighty-three years old when he finally gave his heart to Jesus. He died at eighty-six, and he missed so much that he could have had in life. I know he died with many regrets about the way he had lived. I never gave up praying for him and finally saw a breakthrough, and I encourage you to continue praying for people you love and know who need Jesus but continue rejecting Him.

*Father, I want to have the same compassion You have for people who are lost without You. Fill my heart with a desire to pray for them regularly so they can have the joy of knowing You and spend eternity with You.*

# THE POWER OF WORDS

*Lord, who may dwell in your sacred tent? Who may live on your holy mountain?*

**PSALM 15:1**

In Psalm 15, as David answers his own question about who may live close to God, he not only mentions those who are blameless and do what is right, but he also mentions several things about the type of words we speak.

Verses 2–4 of this psalm teach us that those "whose walk is blameless" speak truth from the heart, do not slander or cast slurs on others, and keep their word. They keep their commitments and follow through on what they say they will do, even if doing it hurts them. This is integrity, and it is something our society today lacks greatly. Being a person of integrity is extremely important. God always keeps His Word, and He expects us to keep ours.

If you tell someone you will call them back, be sure you do it. If you make an appointment with someone, keep it unless you have an emergency and can't go—and in that case, at least communicate with them, so they are not waiting for you, not understanding why you didn't come. If you commit to work in the nursery at church twice a month, then be sure you show up to do it. Anytime we don't keep our word, someone else suffers because of our negligence, and this is wrong.

We are called to be excellent in all our ways, and integrity is part of excellence.

*Father, help me use my words in ways that build people up, and help me always do what I say I will do. Thank You.*

# GOD WILL KEEP YOU SAFE

*Keep me safe, my God, for in you I take refuge.*

**PSALM 16:1**

Violence is all around us these days, and people are often concerned about their safety when they go out. We should always use wisdom in our choices, but we can trust God to keep us safe. If you go to a store alone at night, keep a watchful eye regarding what is going on around you. If you are going for a run, daytime might be better than nighttime, especially if you are running alone. God gives us wisdom, and He expects us to use it.

Not only does God Himself keep us safe, but He sends us ministering angels to help us and watch over us (Psalm 91:11; Hebrews 1:14). It is comforting to remember that we have angels with us all the time. I am prone to forget this because I can't see them with my natural eyes, and you may be also. But I am sure that angels keep us safe, often at times when we don't even realize they are working.

Hebrews 13:2 says, "Do not forget to show hospitality to strangers, for by so doing some people have shown hospitality to angels without knowing it." Angels can take on human form, so they may be with us more frequently than we imagine. Keeping this in mind will help dispel any fear you have for your safety. If you want to build your faith in the knowledge that angels are all around, just search the Bible for the word *angel* and you will find at least a hundred scriptures about them.

*Father, help me use wisdom in all that I do. Thank You for keeping me safe, and for sending angels to watch over me.*

# GOD IS YOUR PORTION

*Lord, you alone are my portion and my cup; you make my lot secure.*

**PSALM 16:5**

I remember a time when I was working hard and became frustrated because nobody seemed to appreciate my hard work. I asked the Lord, "Father, what do I get out of this?" I admit my question was foolish, but God did answer me. He spoke to my heart and said, "You get Me." I've thought about that a lot over the years and have since found various scriptures, such as our verse for today, that say God is our portion. Saying God is our portion is the same as saying He is our inheritance, reward, or allotment in life.

God does, of course, do many things for us, but having *Him* is our greatest blessing and should always be enough to satisfy us. As a matter of fact, no matter what else we have, if we don't have His presence in our lives, nothing else we have means anything. God is our all-sufficient One; He's all we will ever need.

In the Old Testament, all the tribes of Israel received an inheritance or allotment of land except the priestly tribe of Levi; God told them that He was their portion (Deuteronomy 18:1–2; Joshua 13:33). They had the privilege of serving Him as priests. Jesus is our high priest (Hebrews 4:14), and we are co-heirs with Him (Romans 8:17), so our portion is also the Lord. And the Holy Spirit who lives in us is the guarantee of this eternal inheritance that we have received (Ephesians 1:13–14; Hebrews 9:15).

*Father, I am grateful that You are my portion, my inheritance. There is nothing I desire more than I desire You. You are all I need, my all-sufficient One.*

# INTIMACY WITH GOD

*I will praise the Lord, who counsels me; even at night my heart instructs me.*

**PSALM 16:7**

Having a close, personal, intimate relationship with God is wonderful. It is obvious from Psalms that David had this kind of relationship with the Lord, and we can have it too. David wrote that even during the night God spoke to and counseled him. Most of us wake up at some time during the night, and even then, God is with us, watching us, and He may well speak to us if we are listening.

David said his eyes were "always on the Lord" (Psalm 16:8), and we can form the habit of always having one ear turned toward the Lord no matter what we are doing. We can always be watching and waiting for God to speak to us. This kind of intimate relationship with God gives us great confidence that no matter what happens, we will stand firm and not be upset or disturbed.

Even in difficult times our hearts can rejoice and be glad, and we can rest secure in God's love for us. You can be assured that God will not abandon you. He shows us the path of life, and in His presence, we are filled with joy (Psalm 16:9–11). Always keep God first in your life, and He will take care of everything else you need.

*Father, I am grateful that I can have an intimate relationship with You. Draw me to You and help me keep You in my mind and heart at all times. You are more important to me than anything else.*

# HAVING A CLEAN CONSCIENCE

*Hear me, Lord, my plea is just; listen to my cry. Hear my prayer—it does not rise from deceitful lips.*

**PSALM 17:1**

The importance of maintaining a clean conscience before God cannot be overstated. Paul spoke about his conscience confirming through the Holy Spirit that he was doing the right thing (Romans 9:1). We should be careful not to sin against our own conscience, because this becomes a heavy burden to carry. David invited God to examine and test him, for he was sure he had committed no evil, nor had he transgressed (sinned) with his mouth (Psalm 17:2–3).

We can see from today's scripture that David felt sure he had held firmly to the Word of God and that God would answer him when he called on Him (Psalm 17:4–6). Sadly, too often we try to operate in faith while having a guilty conscience, so we can't bear good fruit. We are to be led by peace, and Paul writes that anything we do that is not done in faith is sin (Romans 14:23).

When we repent of sin, God not only forgives our sins, but He removes the guilt that comes with them; therefore, we can always walk before God with a clean conscience if we pursue purity of life and are quick to repent when we do sin.

*Father, I love You, and I appreciate what Jesus has done for me. Forgive all my sin and cleanse me of all guilt and condemnation. I want to walk with You with a clean conscience at all times.*

# THE APPLE OF GOD'S EYE

*Keep me as the apple of your eye; hide me in the shadow of your wings.*
**PSALM 17:8**

The phrase "the apple of my eye" originally referred to the pupil of the eye. If you think about it, we are very protective of our pupils. If anything potentially damaging comes near the eye, we immediately close the eyelid to protect it. God protects us in the same way.

Today, the "apple" of the eye would refer to something chosen above others. If you were to go to the grocery store to get an apple, you would look at all the apples and choose the one that looked best to you. God chooses each of us as the apple of His eye. We are all special to Him, and He is especially fond of us. We are His children, and all His plans for us are good. We should not feel that we are better than anyone else, but we should have the confidence to believe that we are special to God and that we are indeed the apple of His eye.

You can be assured that God is with you today, watching over you at all times. He is protecting you as one would guard the pupil of the eye, and you can rest in His loving care. God created you to enjoy life, so be sure you enjoy yours today and don't waste it worrying, because God has everything under control.

*Father, thank You that I am the apple of Your eye and that You love me and have promised to protect me. Help me rest in You and not be afraid.*

# I LOVE YOU, LORD

*I love you, Lord, my strength. The Lord is my rock, my fortress and my deliverer; my God is my rock, in whom I take refuge, my shield and the horn of my salvation, my stronghold.*

**PSALM 18:1–2**

What God wants more than anything else is for us to love Him. When a teacher of the Jewish law asked Jesus what the most important commandment is, He replied: "Love the Lord your God with all your heart and with all your soul and with all your mind and with all your strength" (Mark 12:30). Jesus also said, "If you love me, keep my commands" (John 14:15).

Notice that He did not say, "If you obey Me, I will love you." God's love for us is unconditional, and we can love Him only because He first loved us (1 John 4:19). He wants us to receive His love as a gift and then respond by obeying Him gladly, knowing that everything He asks us to do is always and only for our good.

Sometimes we struggle to obey God in areas where it is hard for us to obey, but instead of simply trying harder, perhaps we should focus on loving Him more. The more we love Him, the easier it is to obey Him. We want to please God, and any sacrifice we need to make in order to do it is worth it. If you struggle with a weakness or a particular sin, spend more time with the Lord and in His Word. You will find that to be more successful than human effort and struggle. Tell the Lord several times each day that you love Him, and thank Him for loving you.

*Father, I do love You, and I want to love You more and more. Thank You for loving me. Help me be obedient to You in all things.*

# GOD WILL MEET YOU
# WHERE YOU ARE

*He reached down from on high and took hold of me.*

PSALM 18:16

The slightest cry from our heart to God catches His attention, and He comes down from on high and takes hold of us, as He did for the psalmist David. I am glad we don't have to try to get to Him, but He comes to us and rescues and helps us. Psalm 18:9 states that "He parted the heavens and came down." Just think of how awesome it is that God came down and thank Him for it.

You can be in the middle of the biggest mess you have ever been in, and God will meet you where you are. He will meet you, lift you up, and set your feet on solid ground. Don't make the mistake of thinking you must be a better person in order for God to help you. Jesus said He came for those who are sick in their soul, not those who are well; He didn't come for "the righteous," He came for "sinners" (Mark 2:17). This is the good news of the gospel.

The apostle James writes, "If any of you lacks wisdom, you should ask God, who gives generously to all without finding fault, and it will be given to you" (James 1:5). I am so glad that God meets us where we are and helps us get to where we need to be.

If you are struggling with sin or weakness in any area of your life today, simply cry out to the Lord. He will come down and meet you where you are, and He will help you.

*Father, I cry out to You today and ask for Your help. Meet me where I am, Lord, and strengthen me in my weakness. Thank You.*

# LIVING LARGE

*He brought me forth also into a large place; He was delivering me because He was pleased with me and delighted in me.*

**PSALM 18:19 AMPC**

I believe we should have a large vision for our lives. Today's scripture backs that up. We serve a big God, who does big things. He "is able to do exceedingly abundantly above all that we ask or think" (Ephesians 3:20 NKJV).

I would rather ask for a lot and get some of it than ask for a little and get all of it. Don't be afraid to ask God for big things. Be confident and bold, as the psalmist David was. In 1 Corinthians 2:9 (NKJV), Paul writes that "eye has not seen, nor ear heard, nor have entered into the heart of man" all the good things God keeps ready for those who love Him.

Even though we are imperfect, God wants us to be blessed. He shows us His mercy and goodness even in the midst of our weaknesses. However, if we don't ask Him for anything, we won't receive anything.

I love the boldness of David in Psalms. The writer of Hebrews also encourages boldness, saying that we should come boldly to the throne of grace because we have a High Priest who understands our weaknesses, meaning Jesus (Hebrews 4:15–16).

Love God with your whole heart, be quick to repent when you sin, and pray boldly, unafraid to ask God to bring you into a large place.

*Father, thank You for Your amazing goodness in my life. I ask You to do great things in my life.*

# GOD GIVES YOU STRENGTH AND KEEPS YOU SECURE

*For by you I can run against a troop, and by my God I can leap over a wall. This God—his way is perfect; the word of the Lord proves true; he is a shield for all those who take refuge in him. For who is God, but the Lord? And who is a rock, except our God?—the God who equipped me with strength and made my way blameless. He made my feet like the feet of a deer and set me secure on the heights.*

**PSALM 18:29–33 ESV**

All storms are not in the weather forecast; sometimes they take us by surprise. Life is the same way. We never know from one day to the next exactly what may come up, and this is one reason we should be glad that God promises to be our strength. His Word tells us that we can do whatever we need to do through Christ, who is our strength (Philippians 4:13).

It is amazing the things we can go through with God's help. We may not always understand why something has happened to us or when it will be over, but Psalm 18 tells us that God's way is perfect (v. 30), and this truth should give us comfort. Habakkuk 3:19 says that God makes our feet like those of a deer, and a deer has the ability to climb steep mountains and remain stable.

Always remember that you don't need to live in fear, because God can handle anything that comes up in your life. He will be a shield around you and keep you safe and stable.

*Father, thank You that I can go through life without fear and know that no matter what comes up, You will give me the strength to handle it.*

# GOD'S CARE IS ALL AROUND YOU

*The heavens declare the glory of God; the skies proclaim the work of his hands.*

**PSALM 19:1**

Today's scripture teaches us that even the skies, which we see each day, speak of God's glory. In fact, I believe you will see evidence of Him and of His care for you all around if you simply look for it. In addition to seeing it in nature, you may see it in the smile of a loved one, in the grace He gives you in a difficult situation, in a breakthrough of healing or financial provision, or in a circumstance you could never orchestrate in your own strength, which leaves you saying, "Only God could do this!" If you will make a point to be aware of God's hand working in your life, you will see it, even in ways that may seem common, ordinary, or not very spiritual.

In Luke 12:24–28, Jesus speaks of birds and flowers, observing that God feeds the birds without their having to plant or harvest their own food and that the flowers "do not labor or spin" to make themselves beautiful. Nothing in the natural world works to take care of itself or worries about whether it will be cared for. Everything in God's creation depends on Him and His faithful care, which we see season after season, year after year.

Today, take a look outside and notice what you see. God is taking care of it all, and He is taking care of you.

*Thank You, God, that all around me, I see evidence of the fact that You care about me.*

# NATURE PROVES
# THE EXISTENCE OF GOD

*The heavens declare the glory of God; the skies proclaim the work of his hands. Day after day they pour forth speech; night after night they reveal knowledge. They have no speech, they use no words; no sound is heard from them. Yet their voice goes out into all the earth, their words to the ends of the world. In the heavens God has pitched a tent for the sun.*

**PSALM 19:1-4**

It is difficult to seriously ponder the universe and the beauty of what God has created and still not believe in Him. For example, I read that experts once thought that there are about 10,000 species of birds, but now they believe that figure may be doubled. There are 45,000 various kinds of spiders, 900,000 different kinds of insects now known, and these numbers are always increasing. The list of these types of things is endless and awe-inspiring.

God's creativity is beyond imagination. Every human that has ever existed has different fingerprints and DNA. When we think of how unique we all are, it is hard to imagine that there is no God.

Paul wrote that nature itself leaves us without any excuse for not believing in God. "For since the creation of the world God's invisible qualities—his eternal power and divine nature—have been clearly seen, being understood from what has been made, so that people are without excuse" (Romans 1:20).

I enjoy watching videos about nature and the animal kingdom because seeing what God has done and how everything in the universe works together always amazes me. I often literally shake my head in astonishment when I watch them. Let's not take nature for granted but instead seriously ponder how brilliant and amazing it is, remembering that God created it all.

*Father, thank You for all the beautiful and amazing things that You created for our enjoyment and pleasure. Your creation leaves me in awe.*

# HIDDEN FAULTS

*But who can discern their own errors? Forgive my hidden faults. Keep your servant also from willful sins.*

**PSALM 19:12-13**

Truly knowing oneself may be one of life's biggest challenges. We are good at seeing other people's faults, but not always as good at recognizing our own. Paul mentioned that he didn't know of anything against himself and that his conscience was clear, but even that didn't mean he was innocent (1 Corinthians 4:4). Only God judges accurately, and He will bring hidden things into the light (1 Corinthians 4:5).

I pray that God will forgive my unconscious and hidden faults, as well as the things I am aware of and repent for. I encourage you to do the same. It is always best to keep our heart clean and pure before God and to have a humble attitude, knowing that God sees things we do not see.

Paul asked the Christians in Rome why they judged others for things they also did: "Therefore you have no excuse or defense or justification, O man, whoever you are who judges and condemns another. For in posing as judge and passing sentence on another, you condemn yourself, because you who judge are habitually practicing the very same things [that you censure and denounce]" (Romans 2:1 AMPC).

We do as Romans 2:1 describes because we make excuses for our faults but think there is no excuse for others' faults. The minute we make an excuse for sin, we have said in our heart that even though the action was wrong, our reason for doing it makes it acceptable. This is deception, and as Romans 2:1 notes, we have "no excuse."

*Father, help me not to judge others, realizing that I sin myself and may even do things wrong that I am totally unaware of. Help me see truth and not be deceived.*

# WORDS AND THOUGHTS

*May these words of my mouth and this meditation of my heart be
pleasing in your sight, Lord, my Rock and my Redeemer.*

**PSALM 19:14**

Our thoughts and words are powerful. They affect not only other
people, but us as well. No one can "tame the tongue," according
to James 3:8, so we definitely need to pray about this on a regular
basis.

How much would your thoughts and words have to change
for all of them to be pleasing to God? This is a sobering question,
and if I ask it of myself, I have to say they would probably need
to change more than I realize. God wants all our words to be in
agreement with His Words. They should be uplifting, encouraging, positive, and truthful.

Our conversation should be filled with gratitude toward
God and people, and it should not be haughty, but humble. We
should not be judgmental or critical, nor should we gossip or
repeat other people's secrets. The Bible has much to say about
both our thoughts and our words, and we should pay close attention to them. God's Word teaches us that we should think before
we speak (Proverbs 29:20), and that our words should be few
(Ecclesiastes 5:2).

I think about and meditate on these scriptures regularly, and
they help me discipline my thoughts and words.

*Father, I want to please You with all my thoughts and words. I need
Your help because I cannot do it alone.*

# ANSWERED PRAYER

*May he give you the desire of your heart and make all your plans succeed.*

Psalm 20 is very encouraging. God wants to answer our prayers, give us the desires of our heart, and make all our plans succeed. How exciting and refreshing it is to think about the good life God has planned for us and how He wants us to be blessed in all we do.

If you are going through a difficult season in your life right now, you can be encouraged that God has better things in store for you. Keep praying and asking God to give you victory, help, and protection.

You are God's anointed (Hebrews 1:9; 1 John 2:20, 27), and He promises to give "victory to his anointed" (Psalm 20:6). Psalm 20 reminds us that some people put their trust in horses and chariots (that is, other things), but we trust in the name of the Lord our God. Your enemies will be brought to their knees, but you will stand firm and be lifted up (Psalm 20:7–8).

*Father, thank You for providing a good life for me. I put my trust in You and I'm thankful that You hear and answer my prayers.*

# UNENDING BLESSINGS

*Surely you have granted him unending blessings and made him glad with the joy of your presence.*

**PSALM 21:6**

In Psalm 21, David declares how God has blessed the king, but I firmly believe we can take all these blessings for ourselves, so I will write this to you personally: God will grant you your heart's desire and not withhold the request of your lips. He will greet you with rich blessings and give you long life. He will bestow splendor and majesty on you and grant you unending blessings (Psalm 21:2–6). As you trust in the Lord, you will not be shaken. You will defeat all your enemies, for the Lord will swallow them up in His wrath, and He will consume them. People may plot evil against you and devise wicked plans, but they will not succeed (Psalm 21:7–11).

God has made you more than a conqueror through Christ (Romans 8:37), and to me this means we can be sure that we will be victorious even before the battle begins. You do not have to live in fear, because God is on your side. He is for you, so it doesn't matter who is against you, because you will win in the end (Romans 8:31–39). Remain strong in faith and be faithful to the Lord, and He will take care of anything that threatens you.

*Father, thank You that I can rest in Your love and that You care for me. You do hear and answer my prayers and give me the desires of my heart.*

# WHEN YOU'RE FEELING FORSAKEN BY GOD

*My God, my God, why have you forsaken me? Why are you so far from saving me, so far from my cries of anguish?*

**PSALM 22:1**

Have you ever felt forsaken by God? Jesus did. As He hung on the cross, suffering for our sin, He asked God why He had forsaken Him. Some theologians consider Psalm 22 to be a prophetic Psalm about Jesus' time on the cross, and it does correlate to much that Jesus said during the crucifixion. It can still be applied directly to our lives, because we sometimes feel forsaken, as Jesus did.

Psalm 22 also says that the psalmist still trusts in God and believes he will be delivered, despite feeling forsaken. In verse 19 he says, "But you, Lord, do not be far from me. You are my strength; come quickly to help me." This teaches us that we don't have to deny our feelings, but neither do we have to let them control us. Living according to feelings makes for a defeated and miserable life.

In the midst of suffering, David says, "*I will* declare your name to my people; in the assembly I will praise you" (Psalm 22:22, emphasis mine). I believe his saying "I will" is based not on his feelings but on his decision to praise God. Sadly, many Christians still behave according to the way they feel. They walk in the flesh (human nature without God), not in the Spirit, and they remain carnal. Feelings are fickle and ever changing, and although we will always have them, we must not trust them but instead put our trust in God's Word.

*Father, help me cling to the promises in Your Word instead of following my feelings. I may feel at times that You have forsaken me, but I know You have not. You have promised to never leave or forsake me. This is what I believe, no matter how I feel.*

# GOD DWELLS IN US

*Yet you are enthroned as the Holy One; you are the one Israel praises.*
**PSALM 22:3**

In the King James Version of the Bible, today's scripture says that God *inhabits* ("inhabitest") the praises of His people, and the Amplified Bible, Classic Edition says He *dwells* where praises "are offered." To me, this means that He is comfortable in the midst of our sweet praises and thanksgiving, but not in negative attitudes or complaining.

Not only does God dwell in our praises, He dwells in our hearts by the Holy Spirit (1 Corinthians 3:16; Ephesians 2:22). During Old Testament times, before Jesus came to earth, God's presence dwelled in a portable tabernacle (Exodus 25:8). His people, the children of Israel, were on a journey through a wilderness at that time, on their way to the good land He had promised them. Whenever they stopped, they could worship God and enjoy His presence because He dwelt in the tabernacle.

The tabernacle had an outer court and an inner court. Various activities took place in the outer court, but the inner court was a holy place, set aside for God. Today, God dwells in the innermost part of our being: the heart. This is why we should be careful about what happens in our hearts and keep them free from jealousy, lust, bitterness, unforgiveness, and all sorts of sin.

I encourage you today to examine your inner life and make sure that your heart is a comfortable place for God to dwell.

*Father, help me to live my inner life in such a way that You are at home there.*

# GOD WILL REFRESH YOUR SOUL

*He leads me beside quiet waters, he refreshes my soul. He guides me along the right paths for his name's sake.*

**PSALM 23:2-3**

Psalm 23 is one of the most encouraging psalms in the Bible. It gives us many promises, including the refreshing of our souls. The soul consists of the mind, will, and emotions, and just as our body needs rest and refreshing, so does our soul.

Is your mind tired and weary from worry, reasoning, and trying to figure out what you should do about your problems? Are your emotions frazzled and on edge due to being upset or angry about things other people have that you don't have? Is your will weak from trying to be determined to stay strong while feeling that you constantly fail? If so, I know how you feel, because we all experience feelings such as these at times.

According to Psalm 23, the Lord is your shepherd; you will lack nothing, and He will make you lie down in green pastures, lead you beside the quiet waters, and refresh your soul. You don't have to work all the time or worry about how to solve your problems; you can take time to be refreshed and nourished. If you don't, you will definitely become weary, and weariness almost always causes us to make bad decisions. Spend regular time with God in a quiet place, and let His presence refresh and restore you. Time with God is a valuable investment every day.

*Father, thank You that You will refresh my soul. Help me be wise enough to spend time with You regularly and give You an opportunity to bring refreshment to my life.*

# COMFORT FOR WHEN YOU ARE AFRAID

*Even though I walk through the darkest valley, I will fear no evil, for you are with me; your rod and your staff, they comfort me.*

**PSALM 23:4**

Even people who don't know much about the Bible often turn to Psalm 23 when they are afraid and need comfort. Fear torments, but there is an answer for it. We don't have to fear because God is with us. When we know how much God loves us, we will believe that He will take care of us and not let more difficulty come on us than we can bear (1 Corinthians 10:13).

Although we may feel fear, we don't have to let it rule our decisions. Courage is not the absence of fear, it is moving forward in the presence of fear. God has not given us fear (2 Timothy 1:7); He gives us courage. Fear is from the enemy, and he uses it to prevent us from making progress in life.

If you run from fear, it will chase you, but if you confront it, it will back down. Don't allow the enemy to steal your life through negative emotions such as fear, worry, guilt, or jealousy. The best advice I know to give you is that when one of these emotions shows up (and you never know when that might be), pray and then go ahead and do what you would do if the emotion weren't there. If you let the emotion control you, you feed it and it gets stronger. But if you don't let it control you, you starve it and it will become weaker and weaker until it has no power in your life.

*Father, I want to replace all fear with faith in You, and I need Your help in order to do that. Teach me in this area how to not allow negative emotions to control me.*

# EVERYTHING BELONGS TO GOD

*The earth is the Lord's, and everything in it, the world, and all who live in it.*

**PSALM 24:1**

One word children learn to say early in life is *mine*. They tightly cling to a toy or other item they like, especially if someone tries to take it from them, and they declare ownership of it. This feeling of ownership often grows stronger, not weaker, as we become adults. We feel we have worked hard for our possessions, and any thought of losing them provokes fear in us.

I had to learn that, as God's child and servant, I am a steward of what He trusts me with and an owner of nothing. If we don't learn this lesson, we will have difficulty being generous and giving to others, and we will hang on to things God wants us to release so we can move forward in life. We should be ready to let go of anything anytime God directs us to do so.

Has God ever asked you to give away a favorite item? Once He asked me to give away a favorite coat. The person He wanted me to give it to was someone who had hurt me, so naturally, I didn't want to give it to her. I admit I wasn't obedient immediately. It took a little while for me to be willing, and even then, I struggled to do it with joy.

Let's be wise about the "mine" attitude and always remember that we have nothing unless God gives it to us. We are His stewards, and He is trusting us to manage His resources until He returns to take us to our eternal home.

*Father, thank You for trusting me to manage what belongs to You. Help me hold all things loosely and always be ready and willing to let them go when You ask me to.*

# CLEAN HANDS
# AND A PURE HEART

*Who may ascend the mountain of the Lord? Who may stand in his holy place? The one who has clean hands and a pure heart, who does not trust in an idol or swear by a false god.*

**PSALM 24:3–4**

Do you know that it is possible to have clean hands, yet not have a pure heart? We may do many good works but with a wrong motive. Jesus instructs us not to give to help others or to pray hoping that people will see and admire us (Matthew 6:3–5). If affirmation or applause is our motive, we will lose our reward from God.

Jesus strongly rebuked the Pharisees who did all the right works according to the law but wouldn't lift a finger to help anyone (Matthew 23:1–32). Jesus also talked about people who will tell Him of all their good works, yet He will say, "I don't know you" (Luke 13:27). Why we do what we do (our motive) is more important to the Lord than what we do. We may do good works, but if our motive is selfish in any way, then our heart is not right.

I encourage you to take time regularly to examine your motives and be aware of why you do what you do. Second Corinthians 13:5 teaches us to examine ourselves to make sure that we are "in the faith." Everything we do should be done for God because we love Him and are in obedience to Him. Only then can we do it in faith. We should never examine ourselves and then become condemned if we recognize a wrong motive; we should simply repent and then do things God's way.

*Father, I want to have clean hands and a pure heart. Help me recognize any impure motives I might have that I am unaware of. Thank You.*

# UNWAVERING TRUST

*O my God, in You I [have unwavering] trust [and I rely on You with steadfast confidence], do not let me be ashamed or my hope in You be disappointed; do not let my enemies triumph over me.*

**PSALM 25:2 AMP**

If you are like many Christians, you know that trusting God is necessary to living a life of faith, but deep inside, you may find it challenging to truly trust Him at times. You may have days when your trust feels solid and other days when you aren't so sure whether you really trust Him or not. You may even have days of such frustration as you wait for God to move in your situation that you don't want to trust anymore, so you take matters into your own hands. (That doesn't usually work out very well.)

I think we all have had moments of saying, "I'm trusting God," when we were really worrying, speaking negatively, and trying to figure out everything on our own. We wanted to trust God and were trying to learn to trust Him, but we were not quite there yet. I did that for many years myself.

Today's scripture speaks of unwavering trust and steadfast confidence in the Lord. Such solid trust and confidence don't come quickly; they develop over a period of time. This is why it is so important to "hang in there" with God. Don't quit or give up, because you gain experience and spiritual strength as you stand firm in trust, resisting the temptation to grow weary or waver in your faith. Sooner or later, if you remain steadfast and don't give up, you will see God move.

*Lord, help me not to waver in trusting You, and help my confidence in You to be steadfast.*

# LEARNING THE WAYS OF GOD

*Show me your ways, Lord, teach me your paths. Guide me in your truth and teach me, for you are God my Savior, and my hope is in you all day long.*

**PSALM 25:4–5**

Knowing God's ways is more important than having Him do something for us. We usually ask God for things or for His help with our problems, and these requests are not wrong. But even more than wanting things or help, we should want to know God's ways. If we know and operate in His ways, we will also have everything else we need.

Jesus says that if we seek first God's Kingdom, all other things will be added to us (Matthew 6:33). Let's be sure we are focused more on pleasing God than we are on getting what we want. Paul writes that all things will work together for good if we want God's will and love Him (Romans 8:28).

Let me encourage you to develop a habit of seeking God's will and desiring to please Him in all things before asking Him to meet your needs. Pray as Jesus taught us to pray: "Your kingdom come, your will be done, on earth as it is in heaven" (Matthew 6:10).

*Father, I want to know Your ways and always do what is pleasing to You. Please teach me and help me to trust You to meet my needs. I will seek You above all, and You can add what You want me to have.*

# GOD'S FORGIVENESS

*For the sake of your name, Lord, forgive my iniquity, though it is great.*
**PSALM 25:11**

The gift of God's forgiveness, which is available to each of us, is truly amazing. It is God's nature to forgive. It is what He wants to do, and all we need to do is admit our sins, be willing to turn from them, and ask for and receive His gracious forgiveness. God's forgiveness is complete. He actually forgets our sins and removes them as far as the east is from the west (Hebrews 8:12; Psalm 103:12).

Today's scripture states that God forgives our sins for the sake of His name. What does this mean? God doesn't forgive us because of anything we have done to deserve it, but because He is love, and love must forgive. Actually, God has already forgiven us in Christ for all our sins, and He is ready and waiting for us to ask for and receive forgiveness.

The Lord wants a relationship with us, and for that to happen, our sins cannot be standing between Him and us. He wants to remove them so we can comfortably spend time with Him and enjoy His presence. It is amazing to think of how wonderful God's total and complete forgiveness is.

Confession is our way of acknowledging our sin and letting go of it. We breathe out our sin, guilt, and shame, and we breathe in God's forgiveness and mercy. And what's even better is that there is no limit on how much forgiveness we can have, because where sin increases, God's grace increases more (Romans 5:20).

*Father, I am sorry for all my sins, and I ask for and receive Your forgiveness now. Thank You for Your mercy and grace. I love You.*

# THE REVERENTIAL
# FEAR OF GOD

*Who, then, are those who fear the Lord? He will instruct them in the ways they should choose. They will spend their days in prosperity, and their descendants will inherit the land. The Lord confides in those who fear him; he makes his covenant known to them.*

**PSALM 25:12–14**

Today's scripture speaks of "those who fear the Lord." What does this mean? The fear of God is the reverential fear and awe of Him and of His power. When we have it, we realize that when He says something, He means it, and that His ways are the best ways to live. Sadly, many people don't understand the reverential fear of God, and it causes them to compromise their morals and do things they should not do. We don't have to be afraid of God harming us, because He is good, but when we have reverential fear of Him, we don't want to do anything to offend Him.

Our scripture for today says that if we have reverential fear of God, we will spend our days in prosperity, our descendants will be blessed, and the Lord will confide in us. I want Him to confide in me, don't you?

All of God's ways are right, and if we follow them, our lives will be blessed. This does not mean we will never experience difficulty, but God will always provide a way out of it, an escape to safety (1 Corinthians 10:13). I urge you to know that God is good and that everything He tells you to do or not to do is only for your benefit. Proverbs 9:10 teaches us that the fear of God is the beginning of wisdom. Have a healthy, reverential fear and awe of Him, and it will help you make good decisions throughout your life.

*Father, I want to know You more and to have a reverential fear and awe of You that will always urge me to follow Your ways.*

# MINDFUL OF GOD'S
# UNFAILING LOVE

*Test me, Lord, and try me, examine my heart and my mind; for I have always been mindful of your unfailing love and have lived in reliance on your faithfulness.*

PSALM 26:2-3

I think a person would need a high level of confidence in order to invite God to examine their heart and mind. I'm not talking about confidence in their own goodness, but confidence in God's love, mercy, long-suffering, and forgiveness. David had no fear of inviting God to examine him, because he knew that even if God found flaws in him, he could be forgiven. He wanted to know if there was anything in his life that was offensive to God. He wasn't afraid to face his weaknesses, and we should not be either.

Being honest about where we are is the only way to get to where we want to be. If we hide from our sins or make excuses for them, we can never be free of them. Anything we run from will chase us. But if we confront things, we can defeat them in God's strength.

The apostle James teaches us to confess our faults to one another so we can be healed (James 5:16). Things hidden in darkness always threaten us, but when they are brought into the open, they are exposed and no longer have control over us. Our secrets make us sick, but the truth makes us free (John 8:32). You can talk to God about anything—after all, He already knows all about it. God is not shocked or surprised by anything you tell Him. He loves you and knew all about you before you ever knew Him, so, like David, let's rely on His faithfulness and be mindful of His unfailing love.

*Father, I invite You to examine my heart and mind because I trust Your unfailing love and mercy. Thank You for Your amazing goodness.*

# AUTHENTICITY

*I do not sit with the deceitful, nor do I associate with hypocrites. I abhor the assembly of evildoers and refuse to sit with the wicked.*

**PSALM 26:4–5**

One of the best compliments anyone can give us is that we are the same in public as we are in private. An authentic person is one who is always the same. They don't pretend to be what they are not, nor do they do things just to impress certain people while perhaps mistreating others they deem less important.

We are to avoid people who are not genuine and instead associate with honest, sincere people who can be depended on and trusted. Jesus told the religious Pharisees of His day that they were hypocrites because their actions were done to be seen by people, and they loved places of honor at banquets and important seats in the synagogues (Luke 11:43). Jesus said to do what the Pharisees told them to do, but not to do what they did (Matthew 23:3). In other words, they gave lots of good advice but didn't follow it themselves, like actors in a play.

Jesus called them "whitewashed tombs" filled with dead people's bones (Matthew 23:27). They looked good on the outside, but their hearts were wicked. We may fool a lot of people through insincerity, but we can never fool God. He always sees the motives behind our actions. We should always do what we say we will do and be sincere with our words, remembering that God sees our heart.

*Father, help me to be a sincere, genuine person at all times, one who is the same in private as I am in public.*

# WHOM SHALL I FEAR?

*The Lord is my light and my salvation—whom shall I fear? The Lord is the stronghold of my life—of whom shall I be afraid?*

**PSALM 27:1**

I think that if we really understood how powerful God is and how much He loves us, we would have a lot less fear in our lives. The psalmist David writes often of fear and how to avoid it. Fear prevents us from going forward in life. It hinders us from doing the things God wants us to do. We can feel fear and still do what God wants us to do, remembering that He is our stronghold. A stronghold is a defensive structure, a refuge in times of trouble. It is a place we can run to and know that we will be safe.

When you have trouble, who do you run to? Some people run to their friends, their spouse, or their pastor, but we should always run to God first because He is our stronghold "in times of trouble" (Nahum 1:7). He wants us to trust Him and be courageous. Courage is not the absence of fear, but moving forward in the presence of fear.

Why can we do this? Because we know that God is always with us, and His strength "is made perfect" in our weakness (2 Corinthians 12:9). Don't live your life in fear; instead confront fear in faith, and it will run from you.

*Father, help me to do all that You want me to do and not ever to let fear stop me.*

# SEEKING THE PRESENCE OF GOD

*One thing I ask from the Lord, this only do I seek: that I may dwell in the house of the Lord all the days of my life, to gaze on the beauty of the Lord and to seek him in his temple.*

**PSALM 27:4**

What have you been asking God for? A time came in my life many years ago while reading Psalm 27 when I was faced with this same question. Was I asking God for the "one thing" that was the most important, or was I asking for all kinds of things that were much less important? I had to admit I was seeking what God could do for me more than I was seeking Him for Himself.

Realizing this was life-changing for me. I stopped asking God for so many *things* and started asking for more of *Him*. As I developed a more intimate relationship with Him, I realized that while I was seeking Him, He gave me everything I needed. There is nothing wrong with asking God for things we want and need, but if they are always first on the list of what we ask for in prayer, then our priorities are wrong and we need to make a change.

Seek God first—seek His will and His ways—and you won't lack any good thing. Sometimes my children call me and ask me to help them with something, but quite often they call, text, or visit just to tell me they love me. They do things for me as well as asking me to do things for them, and this keeps our relationships healthy.

Ask God what you can do for Him and who you might be able to help on a daily basis, and pray that His will would be done in your life.

*Father, I am sorry if I have sought things more than I have sought You. Forgive me and help me to always put You first in everything and in all my prayers.*

# THE BEST WAY TO OVERCOME REJECTION

*Though my father and mother forsake me, the Lord will receive me.*

**PSALM 27:10**

The psalmist writes of an extremely painful type of rejection—abandonment by a father and mother. Rejection of any kind, by any person, can cause a person to feel sad, hopeless, and even depressed.

To be rejected means to be cast aside, to be thrown away as having no value, or to be unwanted and ignored. Human beings are created for love and acceptance, not for rejection, and the emotional pain of rejection is one of the deepest wounds a person can suffer. The closer we are to the person who rejects us, the deeper the hurt.

Overcoming rejection is not easy. It does take time, but it is possible through the love of God. Receiving His love is the best way to break free from the pain inflicted when people reject you.

God never rejects us but accepts us completely and loves us unconditionally in Christ. The apostle Paul prays for believers in Ephesians 3:17–19 that we will be "rooted and established in love" and have the "power…to grasp how wide and long and high and deep is the love of Christ, and to know this love that surpasses knowledge."

Let me encourage you to be looking for all the ways God shows His love to you. He does this through various means, and if you ask Him to help you recognize His love, you will soon begin to see it all around you. The revelation and understanding of God's love for you will heal any rejection you have experienced.

*Father, thank You for loving and accepting me unconditionally. Heal me from the pain of any rejection I have experienced in the past, as I continue to walk with You.*

# YOU WILL SEE
# THE GOODNESS OF GOD

*I remain confident of this: I will see the goodness of the Lord in the land of the living. Wait for the Lord; be strong and take heart and wait for the Lord.*

**PSALM 27:13–14**

Are you confident that you will see the goodness of the Lord during your lifetime? Some people think everything will be great when they get to heaven, but they fail to expect good things while they are alive on earth. The Amplified Bible, Classic Edition renders verse 13 of today's scripture this way: "[What, what would have become of me] had I not believed that I would see the Lord's goodness in the land of the living!"

I think the psalmist was saying that without the hope of seeing God's goodness, he would have become discouraged and perhaps even depressed. Hope is powerful; it keeps us going forward when all our circumstances look hopeless. The Bible says that Abraham had no reason to hope, but he still hoped in faith that he would see God's promise come to pass (Romans 4:18). And he did.

Psalm 27:14 tells us to wait on God, which means we are to wait with the expectation that something good is going to happen at any moment. Expect God to do great things in your life, not necessarily because you deserve them, but because He is good. Be confident that you will see God's goodness.

*Father, I am excited to see all the good things You will do in my life. I wait on You with hope and expectation. Thank You.*

# YOU CAN HEAR FROM GOD

*To you, Lord, I call; you are my Rock, do not turn a deaf ear to me. For if you remain silent, I will be like those who go down to the pit.*

**PSALM 28:1**

One word from God can change our life forever. We have His written Word, but He also speaks to our heart. First Kings 19:12 refers to this as "a still, small voice" (AMPC). God speaks to His people in many ways, and we should expect Him to speak to us.

This morning, I asked the Lord if there was anything He wanted to say to me. As I waited quietly for His response, I heard the whisper of God in my heart. What I heard encouraged me greatly and left me excited about the future. The Bible is filled with stories of God speaking to His people, and we are no different. Most often He speaks to us through His Word, but He also speaks in other ways. I encourage you to listen for His voice and learn how to hear from Him.

David writes in today's scripture that if God were silent, he would feel as though he lived in a pit. How discouraging! Obviously, we need to hear from God to stay encouraged.

Don't be afraid of making mistakes as you grow in hearing God's voice. You probably will make some mistakes, as we all do, but you can learn from them. God loves you, and as long as your heart is right and you want to learn, He will work with you, teaching you to recognize His voice. Just remember that God never says anything to us that doesn't agree with His Word.

*Father, I want to hear Your voice, and I pray that I will not be deceived. I am ready to learn from You, and I ask You to teach me.*

# ASK FOR AND RECEIVE GOD'S MERCY

*Praise be to the Lord, for he has heard my cry for mercy.*

**PSALM 28:6**

The Bible is filled with scriptures about God's mercy, which is available to us. God is merciful; mercy is part of His character. Lamentations 3:22–23 says it is because of God's great mercy that "we are not consumed" and that His mercies are "new every morning" (NKJV). Mercy is available, but we must receive it in order for it to help us.

Receiving mercy is often difficult because we feel that we don't deserve it, but the whole point of mercy is that it cannot be deserved; it is a gift freely given. Not only does God give us mercy, He also urges us to be merciful to others, because mercy is much greater than judgment (James 2:13).

Perhaps you are suffering from a past sin and you need to receive God's mercy. It is available right now; all you need to do is ask for it and receive it by faith. Or perhaps you are angry with someone and you need to extend mercy to that person. If so, there is no better time than right now to do so. When you show someone mercy, you actually help yourself more than you help them. Mercy is beautiful, and it is something we all need to receive and to give.

*Father of mercies, thank You for giving me mercy and being gracious to me. Help me to always be willing to be merciful toward others.*

# OUR IMPENETRABLE SHIELD

*The Lord is my strength and my [impenetrable] shield; my heart trusts [with unwavering confidence] in Him, and I am helped; therefore my heart greatly rejoices, and with my song I shall thank Him and praise Him.*

**PSALM 28:7 AMP**

Obedience to God is a vital part of the Christian life, and as I have said many times, when we obey God, we are blessed, and when we don't obey, we should not expect to be blessed. The more we love God and the more we receive His love, the more we are able to obey Him promptly and reverently. Everything God instructs us to do is motivated by His love for us and is designed to bless us and benefit our lives. When God tells us to not do something, He is never trying to take something away from us. Instead, often He is protecting us as our "[impenetrable] shield" from something harmful. The idea that He is an impenetrable shield is powerful, meaning that He protects us so strongly and so completely that absolutely nothing can get to us unless He allows it.

Jesus says in John 14:15 that if we love Him, we will keep His commands, meaning that we will obey Him. If we love Him, we will trust Him and His direction in our lives. Next time you struggle to obey, especially if you really want to do something and know in your heart that you are not supposed to do it, remember that God's impenetrable shield is around you, and He may be protecting you from things you cannot imagine.

*Help me, Lord, to show my love for You by obeying You in every situation and trusting in Your love for me and Your protection over my life.*

# STRENGTH AND PEACE

*The Lord gives strength to his people; the Lord blesses his people with peace.*

**PSALM 29:11**

The first ten verses of Psalm 29 speak of how mighty and powerful God is, and the psalmist David praises Him for His mighty attributes. Worship and praise will add strength and the blessing of peace to our lives. Focusing on God's power helps us put our faith in Him when we have needs and want His help. It also increases our faith to praise and worship Him for what we know He does in creation, in our lives, and in the lives of others. We should frequently ponder all the amazing things that God does and has created.

Recently I have been thinking about the gifts, talents, and abilities that God has placed in people. Think of the great singers, artists, inventors, builders, and writers, and those with management abilities. It is good to appreciate them, but we should remember that God is the one who enables them to do what they do.

Jesus healed ten lepers, but only one of them returned to thank Him. He asked where the other nine were, and that is a sad question for Him to have to ask (Luke 17:11–19). I recently heard that the emotion of gratitude is the shortest lived. In most people's lives, petitions (requests) far outweigh praise, and if this is the case for us, we need to make an effort to correct it.

We all want strength and peace, and today's scripture promises both, but let's remember that worship and praise are the keys to experiencing them in our lives.

*Father, You are more powerful and amazing than I can imagine, and I praise and worship You for Your greatness. Thank You for blessing me with strength and peace.*

# ONLY FOR A MOMENT

*For his anger lasts only a moment, but his favor lasts a lifetime; weeping may stay for the night, but rejoicing comes in the morning.*

**PSALM 30:5**

Throughout the Bible, we see instances of God's righteous anger—anger toward sin and injustice. It is important for us to know that although He may become angry in certain situations, His nature and character are not those of an angry God.

Perhaps I can explain it this way: My father was an angry man, and he punished our family swiftly for even the slightest infraction of his many rules, which changed often. Being in his presence caused my mother, my brother, and me to feel fearful and tense. Around him, we felt guilty and condemned for something all the time. Although we tried desperately to please him, anger was so embedded in his nature that we lived in an atmosphere of constantly awaiting punishment.

In contrast, my husband, Dave, is not an angry man. He can become angry if I do something he really does not like, but his anger lasts only a short time. Dave knows that my personality is a bit feisty at times and that I am sorry when I behave badly, so he extends mercy to me and is always willing to forget my misdeeds and return to peace.

Dealing with an angry person is much different from dealing with someone who can become angry but does not have an angry nature. God's anger is only for a moment. His mercies are "new every morning" (Lamentations 3:23), and His favor lasts for a lifetime. Mercy, favor, love, and peace are parts of His nature and character, and we can experience them each day.

*Thank You, Father, that You are not an angry God. Your nature is merciful, kind, and loving. Thank You that Your favor lasts all my life.*

# THE BENEFITS OF JOY

*You have turned my mourning into dancing for me; You have taken off my sackcloth and clothed me with joy.*

**PSALM 30:11 AMP**

Are you a glad, happy person? Do you have joy most of the time? Would you consider yourself joyful in most circumstances?

At one point in my life, after being a Christian and a minister for many years, I had to answer these questions for myself, and I realized I was frustrated and sad more than I was glad. I also knew that had to change.

As I investigated the root of my lack of joy, one thing I discovered was that I did not truly understand the great benefits of joy. Joy is to our lives like gasoline is to an engine. Without gasoline, the engine will not run. Without joy, I don't believe human beings run well either. If we do not have joy, everything is "down"—negative, dreary, flat, and tasteless. Our thoughts are negative, our attitudes are negative, our emotions are depressed, and even our heads, shoulders, and arms hang down.

Jesus did not die to give us "down" lives. He is our glory and the lifter of our heads (Psalm 3:3). He is full of joy (John 17:13), and He wants us to be people of joy. Today's scripture tells us that the Lord turns our mourning into dancing and that He clothes us with joy. According to Nehemiah 8:10, the joy of the Lord is our strength. Joy can give us physical energy, and it provides the zeal and enthusiasm we need in our lives. Choose joy today.

*Father, thank You for being the source of my joy. Help me to be a joyful person and to bring joy to others.*

# DEALING WITH DISCOURAGEMENT

*Be gracious and compassionate to me, O Lord, for I am in trouble; my eye is clouded and weakened by grief, my soul and my body also. For my life is spent with sorrow and my years with sighing...I am forgotten like a dead man, out of mind; I am like a broken vessel.*

**PSALM 31:9–10, 12 AMP**

In today's scripture, the psalmist David is clearly discouraged, perhaps even depressed. Discouragement and depression destroy hope, so naturally the enemy works hard to discourage us. Without hope we give up, which is exactly what he wants us to do.

When discouragement tries to overtake you, the first thing to do is to follow David's example and cry out to the Lord, remembering that He is always gracious to us. When we call out to Him in our trouble, He hears us, and His heart is merciful toward us (Psalm 116:4–6).

The next thing to do is to examine your thought life. Remember, your thoughts are powerful, and you become what you think. If you think discouraging thoughts, you will become discouraged. But if you think encouraging thoughts that align with God's Word, you will be encouraged and strong.

Instead of filling your mind with negative thoughts, think more like this: *Well, things are going a little slowly, but, thank God, I am making some progress. I am sure glad I'm on the right path that will lead me to freedom. I had a rough day yesterday and chose wrong thinking all day long, so Father, forgive me, and help me to keep on keeping on.*

I hope you already sense the victory in this type of cheerful, positive, godly thinking and will choose to think these kinds of thoughts today.

*I choose to believe, God, that today will be a great day. Help me think thoughts that will keep me encouraged.*

# GOD'S TIMING

*But I trust in you, Lord; I say, "You are my God." My times are in your hands.*

**PSALM 31:14-15**

Most of us would like to know when God will do what we are waiting on Him to do. But He has His own timing for everything, and He doesn't seem to want to tell us when it will happen.

God wants us to trust that His timing will be perfect. While we wait for it, we are to keep loving Him, loving people, serving Him and others, being obedient to Him, being thankful, and walking in His ways. Although His Word doesn't tell us when He will do things, it does tell us that He will not be late. It may be later than we would like, but He sees and knows things we don't, and what seems late to us is right on time as far as God is concerned.

We can eliminate a lot of stress by trusting God not only to do what needs to be done, but also to do it at the perfect time. If certain blessings come too early, we may not be ready to handle them, so it is best to pray for God's timing instead of wanting Him to conform to our schedules.

I once told God I was sure I was ready to go to the next level in my ministry. He whispered in my heart that I was ready, but that some of the people I would need to help me were not, and I would have to wait for them. We never know with certainty why things take longer than we would like, but let's learn to enjoy life while we wait.

*Father, I am sorry for all the times I have been impatient. Help me learn to wait patiently and with a good attitude, trusting that Your timing in my life is perfect.*

# BE AN UNASHAMED CHRISTIAN

*Oh, how abundant is your goodness, which you have stored up for those who fear you and worked for those who take refuge in you, in the sight of the children of mankind!*

**PSALM 31:19 ESV**

Today's scripture teaches us that God stores up goodness for those who reverently fear Him. Notice also that this verse mentions the importance of trusting, or taking refuge in God "in the sight of the children of mankind." This phrase says to me that if I refuse to be what some might call a "closet Christian" and instead live my Christianity openly before all people, God will store up His goodness for me.

Some people today claim to be Christians, but they do not want to admit it or live the principles of their faith outside their Christian circles. I was once this way. I used to do all the "right" things in the right Christian circles, but I was not demonstrating vital faith elsewhere. In my neighborhood or at work, people could not tell the difference between my behavior and the behavior of an unsaved person. Perhaps there was some difference, but not enough for people to notice. I was not standing strong for God, as I should have been.

This is true for many believers. Because we are afraid of being rejected, isolated, or mocked, we shrink back from taking a stand for God. Yet there are many ways we can demonstrate our faith and our love for Him by refusing to live by the world's standards. We must care more about our reputation in heaven than our reputation among people on earth. Stand strong for God, and never be ashamed or embarrassed to live the Christian life openly and boldly before other people.

*Help me, Lord, to live for You everywhere I go, in every situation I face.*

# CONFIDENT EXPECTATION

*Be strong and let your hearts take courage, all you who wait for and confidently expect the Lord.*

**PSALM 31:24 AMP**

When the changes or successes we are believing God to bring in our lives do not come easily and we find ourselves frustrated and weary in our efforts, we have a choice to make. We can take matters into our own hands and try to change things through our natural abilities, or we can wait for the Lord. Waiting for the Lord, as David urges us to do in Psalm 31:24, simply means spending time with Him, being in His presence, meditating on His Word, worshipping Him, and keeping Him at the center of our lives. Waiting on God properly requires that we wait with an attitude of expectancy and confidence, believing that He will do what is best for us.

Are you waiting for God today? Or have you grown tired of seeing nothing change and now you feel tempted to try to do something about it on your own? Let me encourage you today to wait on God confidently, expecting Him to do something wonderful in your life. When you wait on Him, you draw everything you need from Him. He is your refuge, your enabler, your joy, your peace, your righteousness, and your hope. He gives you everything you need to live in victory over any circumstance. Stay close to Him and receive the strength you need every day. When He decides to move on your behalf, you will be so glad you chose to wait for what He does for you.

*God, I choose today to wait for You. Help me to stay confident and expectant as I watch for Your hand to move in my life.*

# GRACE INSTEAD OF GUILT

*Then I acknowledged my sin to you and did not cover up my iniquity. I said, "I will confess my transgressions to the Lord." And you forgave the guilt of my sin.*

**PSALM 32:5**

When Jesus died on the cross, He not only forgave all our sins, but He paid the price for our guilt as well. His sacrifice not only cleanses us from sin, but it also frees us from feelings of guilt and condemnation. When we follow the advice of today's scripture and acknowledge (admit or confess) our sin to God, telling Him everything and refusing to hide our sin, we are able to receive His gift of grace.

Confession is truly good for the soul; it allows us to release the heavy burdens of guilt we may feel over what we have done or failed to do. We should always remember and stand on the promise of 1 John 1:9: "If we confess our sins, he is faithful and just and will forgive us our sins and purify us from all unrighteousness."

When we admit our sin to God, lay our hearts open before Him, and repent, He forgives us immediately. However, feelings of guilt do not always go away instantly. But we can take God at His Word and say, "By God's grace, I am forgiven, and the guilt has been removed." Our feelings will eventually catch up with our decisions. We can live by the truth in God's Word, not according to the way we feel. His forgiveness and grace are always available to us.

*Father, thank You for Your promise to forgive my sin, release me from guilt, and give me grace when I acknowledge my sin and repent.*

# GOD, OUR HIDING PLACE AND DELIVERER

*You are my hiding place; you will protect me from trouble and surround me with songs of deliverance.*

**PSALM 32:7**

We can easily see that David must have been afraid when he wrote today's scripture. He refers to God as his "hiding place" and declares his confidence that God will protect him from trouble. Fear causes us to want to run from a person or a situation and hide in a safe place. David's way of dealing with fear was to run to God as his hiding place. We learn from Psalm 42, where David says his soul was "disturbed" or disquieted, that when faced with anxious or discouraging situations, he put his hope in God and waited expectantly for Him, praising Him as his Savior and his God (v. 5).

When David needed to settle his emotions and strengthen his faith, he often used songs and shouts of deliverance. David also talked to himself at times, encouraging and strengthening himself in the Lord (1 Samuel 30:6).

When we find ourselves fearful, we, like David, should run to the Lord as our hiding place. We also should wait expectantly for Him, praise Him who is our help and our refuge, and encourage and strengthen ourselves in Him. When we feel afraid, we can remember how God has delivered us in the past and expect Him to do it again.

We who are righteous—in right standing with God—by believing in Jesus Christ can take refuge in the Lord, put our trust in Him, sing, and shout for joy. The Lord is our protector and our defender.

*Thank You, God, for being a safe hiding place for me when I am afraid and for surrounding me with songs of deliverance.*

# GOD WILL SHOW YOU WHAT TO DO

*I will instruct you and teach you in the way you should go; I will counsel you with my loving eye on you.*

**PSALM 32:8**

Often in life, situations require us to take some kind of action, but we don't know what to do. However, we can trust God to show us what to do at exactly the right time. We need to be willing to obey Him, because what He leads us to do may not be what we would have done, or it may seem to our way of thinking that it won't work.

In Luke 5:4–7, Jesus tells Peter and some other disciples who had been fishing all night and caught nothing to go out into deeper water and cast their nets again. Peter indicated that he didn't think it would work and that they were tired, but he also said they would obey whatever He told them to do. As a result, they caught so many fish that their boats began to sink.

Let me encourage you to be sensitive to the leading of the Holy Spirit, because God has given Him to us to guide us (John 16:13). We can always be confident that He will do it, but we must be willing to follow His guidance.

One way the Holy Spirit guides us is through peace. I teach people to not do anything they don't have peace about doing or anything that doesn't agree with God's Word. God has promised to guide us even until the time we die (Psalm 48:14). Let this knowledge comfort you as you make decisions, and believe that you can and will be guided by the Holy Spirit in your decision making.

*Father, I trust You to guide me in all the decisions that I make. I want to do Your will, not mine.*

# THE BIT AND THE BRIDLE

*Do not be like the horse or the mule, which have no understanding but must be controlled by bit and bridle or they will not come to you.*

**PSALM 32:9**

If you have ever dealt with a horse or a mule, you know that the way to get the animal to go where you want it to go is to use a bridle, which includes a bit and reins. Horses and mules do not have the understanding needed to know where their masters want them to go. Instead, they have to be pulled in the right direction by the reins, which are attached to the bit in the animal's mouth. If the horse or mule resists the direction in which its master wants it to go, the bit causes pain.

The same principle that applies to horses and mules applies to you and me in our walk with God. He always knows where we need to go and what we need to do. His Holy Spirit is like the bit and the bridle. He can prompt us to go in a certain direction or to take a specific action, and if we resist, it can be painful. But as we allow Him to lead us, we end up in the situations we should be in and avoid the ones we shouldn't be in.

I hope you will choose today to respond to God's leading in your life without resisting Him, so you will go where He wants you to be.

*Lead me today, Lord, and help me to follow Your promptings without resistance.*

# PRAISE GOD
# THROUGHOUT THE DAY

*Rejoice in the Lord, O you righteous! For praise from the upright is beautiful.*

**PSALM 33:1 NKJV**

First Chronicles 16:1–36 tells us that when the ark of God, which represented His presence, was placed in the tabernacle, David led the people in praise and worship to God. Everyone stopped what they were doing and began to worship Him. Anytime anyone stops for even the briefest moment and turns their heart toward God, I believe it blesses Him greatly.

In Psalm 119:164, the psalmist says that he praised God seven times a day. The number seven can represent an ongoing action, meaning that he may have praised God many, many times throughout his day.

Can you imagine what would happen if, all over the world, each day, people stopped for just a moment to praise and thank God or simply to say, "I love You, Lord"? What if businesspeople, homemakers, teachers, medical professionals, bankers, police officers, and anyone doing anything just paused for a moment to honor God? This could be done without drawing attention to it or without any physical action, for God sees our hearts and knows when they are turned toward Him. It would only take a few seconds, but it would be powerful.

I encourage you, whatever you do today, to remember how good God is and to give Him praise throughout your day.

*God, right now, in this moment, I give You thanks and praise. Help me remember to stop what I am doing and praise You all day long.*

# GOD SEES ALL

*From heaven the Lord looks down and sees all mankind; from his dwelling place he watches all who live on earth—he who forms the hearts of all, who considers everything they do.*

**PSALM 33:13–15**

Just yesterday I was thinking about how differently we would live and behave if we kept in mind that God is watching us at all times. I like to refer to this as "living under the all-watchful eye." We cannot hide anything from God, and nothing surprises Him. He even knows what we are going to do before we do it, and if it is something wrong, I feel certain that He tries to deal with us about it, hoping to stop us from taking the wrong action.

There are surely many times when God's chastisement prevents us from doing what is wrong, and I am thankful for it. I know there are times when I am about to say something, and God lets me know that speaking it would be unwise. It is comforting to know that God is watching us all the time, but it can also produce reverential fear and awe, and that is a good thing.

We worry too much about the people who are watching us, and we are concerned about what they think when we should be remembering that God is watching us and be concerned about what He thinks. Our reputation with God is much more important than our reputation with people.

*Father, I am grateful that You are watching over me all the time, and I invite You to bring any correction to me that is needed. I want to do the right thing, the thing that pleases You. Thank You for helping me.*

# HOPE IN GOD'S LOVE

*But the eyes of the Lord are on those who fear him, on those whose hope is in his unfailing love.*

**PSALM 33:18**

People put their hope in all kinds of things—money, intellect, abilities, jobs, professional connections, possessions, human relationships, and many others. But these will eventually disappoint them. The only place we can put our hope and not be disappointed is in God. As today's scripture teaches us, we can hope and rest in His unfailing love.

Godly hope is not the same as what the world calls hope. People use the word *hope* frequently, making comments such as "I hope it doesn't rain today" or "I hope my team wins the ball game." This kind of hope is more like a vague type of worldly wishing instead of biblical hope. True biblical hope is solid and based on confidence in God's character. It is a springboard from which our faith can take off and stand on the promises of God.

We demonstrate our hope by having a constant positive attitude that, regardless of what is happening, God loves us and is able to change things for the better. As it says in Matthew 19:26, all things are possible with God. We also know from countless verses throughout the Bible that God loves us and is always working for our good. We can choose to believe these truths and use them as the foundation of our hope in every situation.

*Thank You, God, that I can have true hope—hope in who You are and hope in Your love for me.*

# AT ALL TIMES,
# IN EVERY SITUATION

*I will extol the Lord at all times; his praise will always be on my lips.*

**PSALM 34:1**

Notice that David says he will extol (meaning to bless or praise) the Lord *at all times*. He does not say, "I will bless the Lord when everything is going my way" or "I will bless the Lord when this big problem gets solved." He's determined to speak words of praise and exaltation to God *all* the time, in *every* situation.

We learn from today's scripture that David did not allow his circumstances or his emotions to affect his worship. In fact, throughout the Bible, we read stories of people who chose to praise God in difficult situations. God *always* brought them through those hard times and gave them victory. This is a powerful lesson, and one you can begin to apply to your life today.

If things in your life are *not* going as well as you would like—perhaps you are facing a stressful situation or dealing with fear, disappointment, or confusion—you may not feel like praising God. But you can *choose* to praise Him. He is much bigger than any circumstance, and you can praise Him for who He is, for what He has done in the past, for never forsaking you, and for working all things for your good, whether you can see it right now or not.

Emotions are fickle. Don't let them determine whether or not you praise God. Remember today that you do not have to speak according to how you feel. You may feel a certain way, but you can choose to speak God's Word in spite of it. *That* will bring you victory.

*Father, I declare that Your praise will always be on my lips. Help me to choose to praise You in every situation, no matter what I am going through.*

# SPEAK YOUR TRUST IN GOD

*I sought the Lord, and he answered me; he delivered me from all my fears.*

**PSALM 34:4**

The psalmist writes in today's scripture that God delivered him from all his fears. Fear is closely related to worry, dread, anxiety, and various other negative emotions. The enemy wages a spiritual war against us in our minds, and to win the battle of the mind, we must learn to handle fear and worry in a godly way.

Let me ask you: How often do you hear yourself saying, "I'm afraid…," "I'm concerned that…," or "I'm worried about…"? Many people use these phrases perhaps millions of times throughout their lives. But what's the purpose? These words don't help us in any way; they simply reinforce the fear or worry we feel. Anxiety and fear don't change our circumstances, but they do influence us in negative ways by moving our minds away from hope and faith, by stealing our peace, and by causing us to feel stressed.

Whenever you are tempted to say, "I'm worried about…" or "I'm afraid that…," say instead, "I trust God." Declaring that you trust God releases His power to work in your life. Next time you feel anxious or fearful, instead of talking about it, study God's Word and remember His faithfulness to you in the past. He will deliver you from all your fears, as Psalm 34:4 says, and you can do your part to help reach that breakthrough. Move in the right direction by eliminating "I'm worried" and "I'm afraid" from your vocabulary.

*Father, I trust You.*

# HOLD YOUR TONGUE

*Keep your tongue from evil and your lips from telling lies.*

**PSALM 34:13**

When I first started in ministry, I knew that God had given me the gift of communicating effectively and called me to use it in His service. But occasionally my gift has also been my greatest problem. I struggled for a long time with the right use of my tongue. Over the years, people, especially family, asked me questions such as, "Do you always speak first and think later?" and "Must you sound so harsh?"

I finally realized that for God to use me as He desired, I needed to obey Him concerning the proper use of my words—not only when I taught His Word, but all the time. I had a choice: I could continue to hurt people with my words, or I could submit my mouth to God. I wanted to surrender to God concerning my words, but taming my tongue was still a battle.

I learned to listen to my own words, which taught me a lot about myself. Some of the lessons I learned did not please me, but they helped me realize that my words were not pleasing to God, and I wanted them to be. Once I confessed my failure to God, victory came—not all at once and not perfectly, but God is patient, and He continues to work with us as long as we work with Him.

You may struggle, as I did, with your words. But God wants to change you. It may not be easy, but you can change, and you can use your words in ways that honor and glorify Him.

*Lord, help me not to sin against You with my tongue. Let the words of my mouth be pleasing to You.*

# GOD CARES ABOUT YOUR PAIN

*The righteous cry out, and the Lord hears them; he delivers them from all their troubles. The Lord is close to the brokenhearted and saves those who are crushed in spirit. The righteous person may have many troubles, but the Lord delivers him from them all.*

**PSALM 34:17–19**

It is comforting to know that even though we face troubles in life, we also have God's promise of deliverance. Satan arranges for us to encounter various trials, hoping they will divert our attention from God and steal our faith in Him, but when we cry out to God, He hears us and delivers us. We are never promised a trouble-free life, but we are promised God's help and deliverance.

If you have children, you know that when they are hurting, it hurts you, and that you would do anything you could do to alleviate their pain. God feels the same way about us. He is close to those who are lonely, abandoned, abused, and brokenhearted and will save them and bring justice into their lives. If you are hurting because you have been mistreated, or if you are weary from many troubles, you can count on God to lift you up as you put your trust in Him. Perhaps you are sick or in pain physically. If so, God cares about you, and He hurts when you hurt. You can allow His unconditional love to comfort you and give you hope for healing. Whatever your situation, trust God to deliver you.

Although the pain I have gone through in my life has been unpleasant, I have experienced God's deliverance and justice, and it is sweet. It makes up for the hard times. God is good, and He has something good planned for you.

*Father, thank You that You will not leave me alone in my pain and trouble, but You promise to deliver me. I look forward to Your justice, and while I wait, I am glad to know that You are close and that You love me.*

# GOD WILL FIGHT YOUR BATTLES

*Contend, Lord, with those who contend with me; fight against those who fight against me.*

**PSALM 35:1**

We can wear ourselves out trying to fight our own battles, or we can trust God to fight for us. The psalmist David prayed for God to fight his battles. Perhaps he was following the example of King Jehoshaphat. In the midst of a great battle, Jehoshaphat cried out to God for help and was told that he would not need to fight in the battle, but that he could take his position, "stand firm," and see the deliverance the Lord wanted to give him (2 Chronicles 20:17).

Jehoshaphat's position was one of prayer, praise, and worship, and as he took this posture in his heart, God caused his enemies to become so confused that they slaughtered one another (2 Chronicles 20:22–24). When Satan tries to upset us, but we remain calm and worship God instead, it confuses him, and he loses the battle.

You can surprise your enemies by doing what they would never expect you to do. Sing, praise, worship, and remain joyful. If your enemy is another human being, you can pray for them, forgive them, and bless them. This also will confuse them, and the fire of God's love will melt their hard hearts. God has given us a battle strategy that always makes us winners, but we must be willing to use it instead of doing what we feel like we want to do. We always overcome evil with good (Romans 12:21).

*Father, thank You for giving me Your battle strategy. Help me use it instead of trying to fight my battles in my own strength. Amen.*

# WHEN YOU ARE FALSELY ACCUSED

*They do not speak peaceably, but devise false accusations against those who live quietly in the land. They sneer at me and say, "Aha! Aha! With our own eyes we have seen it." Lord, you have seen this; do not be silent. Do not be far from me, Lord. Awake, and rise to my defense! Contend for me, my God and Lord.*

**PSALM 35:20-23**

I am sure you have experienced the pain and frustration of being falsely accused at some time in your life. I know I have, and it is an unpleasant experience. Our first response is usually to try to defend ourselves and convince the accusing party that we are not guilty. When David was falsely accused, he prayed and asked God to rise to his defense.

Jesus was accused of many things of which He was not guilty, but in most instances, He either said nothing or told His accusers to think what they wanted to. This kind of response can only come from someone who isn't concerned about what others think of them, and they know that God will show them to be in the right if that needs to happen.

When we argue with people who accuse us unjustly, it only tends to make us look guilty. But if we keep quiet, it gives God a chance to use the silence to bring conviction on the accuser. Offering an explanation in some instances isn't wrong, but if it does not help, then the best thing to do is pray and ask God to arise to your defense, as David did.

*Father, when I am falsely accused, I ask You to rise to my defense. Grant me the grace to not say anything that You don't want me to say. I trust You with my reputation.*

# GOD DELIGHTS
# IN YOUR WELL-BEING

*May those who delight in my vindication shout for joy and gladness; may they always say, "The Lord be exalted, who delights in the well-being of his servant."*

**PSALM 35:27**

When our lives are going well, we may easily praise and thank God. This is good. When things are not going so well and we are having problems, we sometimes wonder if we are being punished for something we have done wrong. We must understand that God does not operate this way—punishing us or disciplining us by orchestrating troubles in our lives. We encounter difficulties for various reasons, and one way that God redeems them is to teach us through them or strengthen us in the midst of them. We should learn and grow in every way we can during seasons of struggle, but we should not view them as punishment.

God is merciful and good, and He wants the very best for you. He desires for your every need to be met. He wants you to have a good job, a decent place to live, transportation to get you where you need to go, good friends, and a great spiritual life. God wants you to be blessed in every area of your life—spiritually, mentally, emotionally, physically, financially, and socially. In fact, when you are doing well, God is delighted.

When you face hardships or trials, remember that God loves you and is working for your good (Romans 8:28). He will be faithful to you in your struggle. Be patient and know that He will come through for you and delight once again in your well-being.

*Thank You, God, for being with me and loving me in my struggles. Help me to learn and grow through them and to trust You to restore me to a place of well-being, in which You will delight.*

# HOW TO PRAY FOR THOSE WHO DON'T KNOW GOD

*I have a message from God in my heart concerning the sinfulness of the wicked: There is no fear of God before their eyes. In their own eyes they flatter themselves too much to detect or hate their sin.*

**PSALM 36:1-2**

People who don't know God need others to pray for them because they don't know how to pray for themselves, nor do they even care that they are wicked. God can use you and me to bring many souls into His Kingdom by praying compassionately for the lost. In our verses for today, we see that the wicked have no fear of God and they lack humility; therefore, they continue blindly in sin, having no realization of their desperate and dangerous position.

I recommend that we pray specifically for these types of individuals to see how powerful God is and to realize that someday they will have to stand before Him and give an account of their life (Romans 14:12). Let's also pray that they will have reverential fear of continuing in a life of sin and the humility to admit they are sinners in need of a Savior.

We often pray merely that sinners will be saved, but being more specific in our prayers is better. I also pray quite often that God will soften the hard hearts of those who are against Him. I have seen Him answer those prayers and have seen reconciliation between them and the Lord. In addition, I have prayed that their sin will become disgusting to them and that they will become weary of their empty lifestyle. God will lead you as you pray, and I believe you will see results.

*Father, I want to pray for the lost, and I ask You to teach me how to specifically pray for people I know who need You. Thank You for leading me.*

# TRUST IN THE LORD AND DO GOOD

*Trust in the Lord and do good; dwell in the land and enjoy safe pasture.*
**PSALM 37:3**

Most of us know that when we have problems or needs, we need to trust God, but I love Psalm 37 because it teaches us not only to trust God while we wait for our deliverance, but also to do good. We can pray for others and help them in practical ways, such as giving financially to help those in need, encouraging them, and doing many other things that would be considered good.

When we are suffering, it is easy to withdraw and isolate while feeling sorry for ourselves, which can lead us to a place of discouragement and even depression. But retreating into aloneness and self-pity is the worst thing we can do. It is important to stay active and be a blessing to others while we are waiting for a blessing for ourselves. When people ask me what they should do when they are hurting, I tell them to do what they would do if they weren't hurting: Keep their commitments, be kind, walk in love, give, attend church, study the Bible, and do anything else they would normally do.

If you are sick and unable to do some of these things because of physical limitations, then do what you can do. When we trust God and do good, it doubles our resistance to evil and releases our breakthrough.

*Father, help me not to only trust You when I am suffering, but also to remember to do good to others. You are good all the time, and I want to be like You.*

# GOD WILL GIVE YOU
# THE DESIRES OF YOUR HEART

*Take delight in the Lord, and he will give you the desires of your heart.
Commit your way to the Lord; trust in him and he will do this.*

**PSALM 37:4-5**

Trying to get what we want in our own strength can become frustrating because we're often trying to do through human effort what only God can do. If God gives us something to do, then it is His work, and we can expect His grace as we do it. It may not always be easy, but we will have an inner knowing that He is with us in it, guiding us and leading us to a good outcome. Our ways usually are not His ways (Isaiah 55:8–9), and today's scripture tells us to commit our way unto Him.

Instead of occupying yourself with trying to get what you want, spend time with God, serve Him by helping others, and find delight in simply being with the Lord, knowing that He will give you what is best for you at the right time. I wasted many years trying to do in my own strength what I thought was best for me, and all it did was frustrate me.

I am thankful for today's scripture, which reminds me that my part is to love and be delighted in God, and He will give me the desires of my heart. Matthew 6:33 is a similar verse, which says, "Seek first the kingdom of God and His righteousness, and all these things shall be added to you" (NKJV). I recommend that you relax, enjoy God, and joyfully watch Him work in your life.

*Father, remind me anytime I try to use my own strength to get what
I think I want to simply delight myself in You instead and wait for
You to give me the desires of my heart. Thank You.*

# THE POWER OF GENEROSITY

*I was young and now I am old, yet I have never seen the righteous forsaken or their children begging bread. They are always generous and lend freely; their children will be a blessing.*

**PSALM 37:25-26**

Generosity not only ushers God's blessings into our own lives, but it affects our children and even our grandchildren. Thankfully, God taught Dave and me how to be generous givers, and all our children are the same way. I am proud of them because they know the importance of being a blessing to others instead of living self-ish, self-centered lives.

The psalmist David writes, "I was young and now I am old," and I can tell you that this progression happens to everyone. No matter what age you are now, someday you will be seventy, eighty, or ninety years old, depending on how many years God gives you on earth. If during those years you live righteously, you will never be forsaken nor will your children be in need. The blessings we receive as a result of godly decisions are inherited by the next generation.

At different times, our children have thanked Dave and me for teaching them to be generous and for setting an example they could follow. Live a godly life in front of your children, and it will teach them much more than mere words ever could.

*Father, I am excited to know that You will always meet my needs and those of my children. I pray that we would always be generous and obedient to You.*

# NEVER FORSAKEN

*Many have become my enemies without cause; those who hate me without reason are numerous.*

**PSALM 38:19**

Jesus said that people hated Him "without a cause" (John 15:25 AMPC), and I think this is one of the saddest scriptures in the Bible. Jesus came to earth of His own free will to do nothing but help us, yet people hated Him. We often experience a similar type of situation, and when we do, it is difficult to deal with. When we are trying to do good or help people, but they still find fault with us or even hate us, it is painful. Remembering that this happened to Jesus helps me during hard times.

In Psalm 38:21–22, David boldly prays for God not to forsake him but to stay close to him and to come quickly and help him. God promises us in His Word that He will never leave us or forsake us (Deuteronomy 31:8). Even when we don't feel God's presence or see any evidence that He is working in our lives, we know He is working because of His promise to never forsake us. It is impossible for God to lie, so we can always depend on His promises.

In Matthew 28:20, before Jesus ascends to the right hand of God, He promises, "I am with you always, even to the end of the age" (NKJV). If you are going through a difficulty right now, please believe that you are not forsaken or forgotten. God sees you, and He has planned your breakthrough; just wait patiently for it, and at the exact right time, it will come.

*Father, thank You that You will never forsake me. I am grateful that You see me and know all I am going through, and that Your plan for me is good.*

# WATCH YOUR MOUTH

*I said, "I will watch my ways and keep my tongue from sin; I will put a muzzle on my mouth while in the presence of the wicked."*

**PSALM 39:1**

Our witness (example) to unbelievers can impact whether or not they accept Jesus as their Savior. We are Christ's representatives on the earth, and He is "making His appeal" to the sinner "through us" (2 Corinthians 5:20 AMPC).

Our verse for today teaches us how important it is to speak wisely in the presence of those who do not know God. One example would be not to complain in front of them. It seems the whole world is complaining these days, and Christians need to be different. We are to shine like bright stars in the midst of wickedness around us. One way we can do this is to speak life and not death, meaning to be positive and not negative.

Philippians 2:14–15 says: "Do everything without grumbling or arguing, so that you may become blameless and pure, 'children of God without fault in a warped and crooked generation.'" If you don't complain even when there is something to complain about, people who do not know Jesus will notice it and may eventually ask you how you can be so positive in the midst of such negative situations. And then the door is wide open for you to share your faith in God.

*Father, help me speak only words that bring life at all times, and especially when I am in the presence of people who do not know You. I can't succeed in this area without Your help. Thank You.*

# LIFE IS SHORT

*Show me, Lord, my life's end and the number of my days; let me know how fleeting my life is. You have made my days a mere handbreadth; the span of my years is as nothing before you. Everyone is but a breath, even those who seem secure.*

**PSALM 39:4–5**

Even if we live to be one hundred years old, those long years are still nothing compared to eternity. It is good to think about this occasionally, because we should not waste any of the time God has given us on earth. David asked God how long he would live, but he didn't get an answer, and neither will we. There is a time appointed for each of us to leave this earth, and only God knows when it is.

We should live every day as though it is our last—make wise choices, walk in love, be obedient to God, and bear good fruit. You may have many more days left to live, but you might not, and it would be a shame to waste the last one you have.

One time I was angry with Dave and wasn't talking to him, and he said, "Wouldn't it be a shame if this was your last day on earth and you spent it like this?" He got my attention and made me think. Don't waste one more day being angry, jealous, or disobedient, or feeling anything else that steals time from you and does no good at all. Make your time count so you don't end up regretting wasted years.

*Father, thank You for the reminder that life is short. I ask You to help me not to waste one day of mine.*

# RESTORATION

*I waited patiently for the Lord; he turned to me and heard my cry. He lifted me out of the slimy pit, out of the mud and mire; he set my feet on a rock and gave me a firm place to stand.*

PSALM 40:1-2

God is a God of restoration. He can take old, worn-out things and make them brand-new. Have you ever known anyone who was good at restoring old furniture? It is amazing how they can take something that looks ready for the trash heap and make it beautiful again. This is what God does for us.

At the age of twenty-three, because of abuse, abandonment, and rejection, I was completely worn-out and living in the kind of slimy pit that David speaks of as a metaphor in today's scripture. I did finally cry out to God and surrendered my life to Him. Over the years He has restored me, and He will do the same for you.

Just as restoring a piece of furniture requires a variety of steps, so does our restoration. It doesn't happen overnight. It often seems to be a slow process, but eventually you will say, "It was well worth it." God has taught me how to think in ways that add joy and peace to my life; He has taught me to love, to have confidence in Him, and to know that I have value and am loved, and, very importantly, He has taught me how to help other people.

His Word is the solid foundation on which we learn to stand. Anyone who builds their life on the Word will withstand the storms of life and remain stable and solid. I urge you to keep pressing deeper and deeper into God. He is turning you into something beautiful that will amaze those who knew you when you were in the slimy pit.

*Father, I know that You are working in me, and I believe You are making something beautiful. Help me cooperate with You each step of the way. I am excited to see the finished product.*

# THE CAPACITY TO
# HEAR AND OBEY

*Sacrifice and meal offering You do not desire, nor do You delight in them; You have opened my ears and given me the capacity to hear [and obey Your word]; burnt offerings and sin offerings You do not require.*

**PSALM 40:6 AMP**

Some people say they don't know how to hear God's voice, and maybe you are one of them. But Psalm 40:6 says otherwise. As a believer, the Holy Spirit lives in your heart, and He quickens God's voice to you. God may speak to you through various means—through His Word, through prayer, through Bible teaching, through the conviction of the Holy Spirit, through the wise advice of a trusted godly friend, or in some other way. Whatever He says to you will always agree with His Word, and when He is speaking to you, you will sense His peace.

Today's scripture assures us that we have the capacity to both hear and obey God. It doesn't do any good for Him to speak to us if we don't obey Him, and He delights in our obedience. One of the primary lessons of the Bible is that when we are obedient, we are blessed, and when we are not obedient, we can't experience the blessings God wants to give us.

In my walk with God, hearing and obeying have been vital to all the blessings I have enjoyed. The blessings have come because I prayed, heard God's voice, and obeyed. My obedience hasn't always been popular with other people, but I have done my best to follow God's leading in my life. I continue to do that every day. I pray that you will also live your life by hearing and obeying God—and that you will enjoy the blessings that come from a life of obedience.

*Father, thank You for giving me the capacity to hear Your voice and obey. I pray that every decision I make would be based on hearing and obeying You as You lead me.*

# LORD, HELP ME QUICKLY

*For troubles without number surround me; my sins have overtaken me, and I cannot see. They are more than the hairs of my head, and my heart fails within me. Be pleased to save me, Lord; come quickly, Lord, to help me.*

**PSALM 40:12–13**

David certainly sinned, but he was quick to repent and always seemed to be confident that no matter what he had done, God would help him. He prayed bold prayers, and we should do the same. God wants to help us, but we must ask for help in order to get it. Sometimes we may not feel that we have a right to ask for help, but in Jesus' name, we do.

Asking God for help is a right and a privilege that Jesus purchased with His blood, and one we should take advantage of. Like David, we have all sinned and come short of the glory of God (Romans 3:23). But we can be justified through the blood of Christ (Romans 5:1–2), and because of His sacrifice on the cross for us, we can come boldly to Him with our needs (Hebrews 4:16).

In our scripture for today, David said that his sin and troubles were more than the hairs on his head. An adult human head has approximately 100,000 hairs, and blonds have about 150,000. These numbers are estimates and may change with age, but my point is that David must have thought that he had many troubles and sins, yet he prayed boldly for God to save him and to do it quickly.

You may be hurting right now, as you read this devotion, or you may be feeling guilty due to a sin you have committed. Regardless of how you feel, I urge you to pray boldly and even ask God to deliver you quickly.

*Father, thank You that You forgive my sins and deliver me from my troubles. Do it quickly, I ask, in Jesus' name.*

# WHEN YOU HAVE FINANCIAL NEEDS

*But as for me, I am poor and needy; may the Lord think of me. You are my help and my deliverer; you are my God, do not delay.*

**PSALM 40:17**

Most people have financial needs at some point in their lives. Perhaps you have such a need today. During times of need, the first thing to do is make sure that you are giving to God's work in the world. Give to your church, to missionaries, to the poor, and to anyone else God leads you to help in some way.

The Bible says we reap according to what we sow (Galatians 6:7–9). In other words, we receive according to what we give. God's Word also says that it is more blessed to give than to receive (Acts 20:35). I find great joy in giving, because seeing others blessed makes me happy.

Paul wrote to the Philippian believers that God would supply all their needs according to His riches in glory in Christ Jesus (Philippians 4:19). At times we are tested, and God stretches our faith by taking more time than we think He should take to meet our needs, but at the right moment, He always provides.

Stay full of hope that a blessing is coming at any minute, because hope always comforts us emotionally. Hope helps us wait peacefully, and although God may not give us everything we want, He will provide what we need.

*Lord Jesus, thank You for meeting my needs and blessing me above and beyond what I need. Help me to be mindful of all You've done and are doing for me, and show me each day what I can give to help others.*

# HELP THE WEAK

*Blessed are those who have regard for the weak; the Lord delivers them in times of trouble. The Lord protects and preserves them—they are counted among the blessed in the land—he does not give them over to the desire of their foes.*

**PSALM 41:1-2**

Today's scripture mentions those who are weak. People may be weak physically, spiritually, emotionally, mentally, or financially. They may be considered weak because they are unable to help themselves or unable to work; they may be weak in resisting sin in general or perhaps some specific sin. My mother was weak in that she allowed my father to abuse me sexually and to abuse her physically, verbally, and emotionally without doing anything about it. I grew up despising weakness and made an effort to be strong in all areas of life. In addition, I disrespected and critically judged anyone I viewed as weak.

God tells us to help the weak, encourage those who are weak, and be very patient with everyone (1 Thessalonians 5:14). My attitude was wrong, and thankfully God has helped me change it. His promises to those who help the weak are amazing. Our scripture for today makes this very clear. Helping the poor, the weak, the needy, the orphaned, and the widowed is something God speaks of often in His Word, and it is something each of us should do.

God helps us in our weaknesses, but He frequently works through people to help other people. Pray for those who are weak, and always be open to helping them in whatever way God may ask you to help them. If you are strong in an area, thank God for it, but don't fall into the trap of judging those who are weak where you are strong, as I did.

*Father, I repent for the times I have judged the weak instead of helping them. Grant me compassion for those who are weak or needy and show me how I can help them. Thank You.*

# COMFORT WHEN YOU ARE SICK

*Blessed are those who have regard for the weak; the Lord delivers them in times of trouble...The Lord sustains them on their sickbed and restores them from their bed of illness.*

**PSALM 41:1, 3**

Consider these prophetic words about Jesus: "But he was pierced for our transgressions, he was crushed for our iniquities; the punishment that brought us peace was on him, and by his wounds we are healed" (Isaiah 53:5).

Jesus is our Healer, and anytime we are sick or in pain, the first thing we should do is ask Him to heal us. Sometimes He heals us supernaturally, sometimes He does it through medical intervention, and several times I have experienced Him showing me something I am doing to cause a physical problem. One time I lacked energy. My workout trainer told me to drink a lot more water, and that was the answer. At other times, I have found that I felt bad because I wasn't eating enough protein.

I remember when God showed Dave that sugar and caffeine were causing him to feel shaky and nervous. Sugar and caffeine had never bothered him before, but since this change has happened, he has to consume them sparingly or avoid them altogether.

God will comfort you and minister to you when you are sick. If the sickness lasts for a long time, He will give you the faith and patience to keep you going and not give up. No one wants to feel bad. I really hate pain and having low energy, but I have found that doing what I am able to do keeps my mind off how I feel. God has healed me from many things over the years, and I encourage you to know that He will help you also.

*Jesus, I trust You for healing. Protect me from sickness and disease, and if I am doing something that is contributing to my sickness, please show me what it is.*

# BETRAYAL

*Even my close friend, someone I trusted, one who shared my bread, has turned against me.*

**PSALM 41:9**

The pain of betrayal is difficult, but we must not become bitter if and when it happens. Judas betrayed Jesus by revealing where He could be captured, and he did it for thirty pieces of silver (Matthew 26:14–16, 47–50). David's son, Absalom, betrayed him by conspiring to take the kingdom from him (2 Samuel 15:1–13). Joseph's brothers betrayed him by selling him to slave traders because of their jealousy of him (Genesis 37:17–36). Yet, in each of these cases, the offended person forgave the betrayer instead of being unforgiving or vengeful.

Many people experience betrayal at some point, and the way we respond to it is very important. Jesus, David, and Joseph were all great leaders, but they had to pass the "betrayal test." Being betrayed by someone you trust and love is one of the deepest pains we can endure. Getting over it completely may take a long time, but being resentful and bitter will only make it worse.

I was once betrayed by some ministry friends I thought would never do anything like what they did. I was hurt and shocked, and it took me about three years to totally recover from the incident. Ultimately, I realized that it was best for me to see the kind of people they really were before I became more deeply involved with them than I already was. If you have been betrayed, I pray you will find the grace to forgive and let it go, because if you don't, it will steal your strength and distract you from your true purpose.

*Father, help me never betray someone who trusts me, and help me forgive anyone who has ever betrayed me or may betray me in the future.*

# GOD'S PRESENCE IS WITH YOU

*As for me, You uphold me in my integrity, and You set me in Your presence forever.*

**PSALM 41:12 AMP**

God has promised that He will never leave you nor forsake you (Deuteronomy 31:8). When the psalmist David was in the midst of sickness and pain over the betrayal of a close friend, he said of the Lord, "You set me in Your presence forever." No matter what you are going through in life, you do not have to go through it alone. Every day with God will not be a perfect day without problems. But as I often say, your worst day with Jesus will still be better than your best day without Him. Whatever comes your way, you can handle it when you know that He is with you.

Let me encourage you to meditate on today's scripture and say throughout the day, "God is with me right now. Right now, God is with me." Know that He is with you when you wake in the morning, as you prepare for your day, as you go to work or school, or as you fulfill other responsibilities. He is with you in your car or on the train. He is with you while you buy groceries, clean house, or care for your family. He is with you on vacation and during times of rest and relaxation. I mention all these activities to emphasize that there is nothing you can do and nowhere you can go that God is not with you. He cares about everything you do.

*Thank You, Lord, for being with me always and for never leaving me nor forsaking me.*

# REMEMBERING THE GOODNESS OF GOD

*My soul is downcast within me; therefore I will remember you from the land of the Jordan, the heights of Hermon—from Mount Mizar.*

**PSALM 42:6**

The psalmist was depressed and discouraged (downcast), and his solution to the problem was to remember times when God had helped him and brought him through difficult situations in the past. The Bible frequently encourages us to remember the great things God has done, and this will keep our faith strong and make it easier to trust God to take care of current difficulties we face.

People spend too much time talking to one another about their problems and not enough time talking about the great things God has done in their life. God likes it when we talk about Him if we are saying what we should be saying. As a matter of fact, He likes it so much that He records it in a book of remembrance. Malachi 3:16 says, "Then those who feared the Lord talked with each other, and the Lord listened and heard. A scroll of remembrance was written in his presence concerning those who feared the Lord and honored his name."

I recommend that we all keep our own book of remembrance, so we can look back and be encouraged by remembering the good things God has done for us. I have kept one for many years, and it has been a big help to me on many occasions.

*Father, help me talk more about the good things You have done for me than about my problems. Help me remember Your goodness and grace, Your mercy and forgiveness, and Your deliverance. Thank You.*

# HOW TO HANDLE DISCOURAGEMENT

*Why, my soul, are you downcast? Why so disturbed within me? Put your hope in God, for I will yet praise him, my Savior and my God.*

**PSALM 42:11**

In Psalm 42:11, we see the psalmist feeling downcast and perhaps struggling with depression. The verses preceding today's scripture reveal the intensity of his pain: "I say to God my Rock, 'Why have you forgotten me? Why must I go about mourning, oppressed by the enemy?' My bones suffer mortal agony as my foes taunt me, saying to me all day long, 'Where is your God?'" (vv. 9–10).

Let's examine how the psalmist handled this situation, because it shows us what to do when we feel sad, discouraged, or depressed, as most people do at some time or another. Psalm 42:11 shows us three distinct ways the psalm writer responded to negative feelings. First, he puts a question to his own soul (mind, will, and emotions), asking, "Why, my soul, are you downcast?" Then he gives his soul an instruction: "Put your hope in God." Finally, he declares, "I will yet praise him, my Savior and my God." We might say the psalmist had a talk with himself.

This simple pattern of thought and action will be effective for you and me, as it was for the psalmist, and soon we will find ourselves encouraged and joyful again.

*Father, thank You for Your Word and for the way it teaches me to live. When my soul is downcast, may I remember what Psalm 42:11 teaches me to do.*

# GOD'S VINDICATION

*Vindicate me, my God, and plead my cause against an unfaithful nation. Rescue me from those who are deceitful and wicked.*

**PSALM 43:1**

Scholars differ about who wrote Psalm 43, but I believe David wrote it. If so, it seems there were not just a few people coming against him but an entire nation. He asks God to plead his cause against an unfaithful nation. I am sure there were times when the nation loved and favored him as king, and times when he had to make decisions they didn't agree with or like. During those times, they were probably against him.

I've certainly had individuals and even groups of people come against me, but never an entire nation, so I am sure David felt oppressed and rejected. He knew he could not vindicate himself and that only God could. When we are vindicated by God, we are shown to be in the right. He arranges circumstances in such a way that those who have falsely accused us must realize they were wrong. God's vindication feels good, but waiting for it is often difficult.

When we have been falsely accused or misunderstood, we want to defend ourselves and try to get people to see the truth about us. We want them to believe our actions were justified or at least that our motives were right in the decisions we made. Anytime we are responsible for making decisions that will affect a lot of people, it is almost impossible to make any decision that will make everyone happy. Therefore, we must follow our heart, do what we believe is right, and then trust God to vindicate us if people come against us.

*Father, thank You for being my Vindicator. When I am falsely accused, I ask You to defend me.*

# UPROOTING SHAME

*I live in disgrace all day long, and my face is covered with shame.*

**PSALM 44:15**

The psalmist writes in today's scripture about feeling "covered with shame." Many people are rooted in shame. Think of it this way: The root of a fruit tree ultimately produces fruit. Similarly, a root of shame produces fruit in the form of unhealthy thoughts and behaviors.

It's important to know that shame is different from guilt, and it affects many people more pervasively. We may feel guilty over something we have done wrong, but shame makes us feel bad about more than a specific action; it makes us feel bad about who we are. There is also a difference between normal shame and rooted shame.

When you and I make mistakes or commit sin, we feel bad for a while until we repent and are forgiven. Then we are able to put those mistakes behind us and go on. This is a normal response to shame.

But when people are rooted in shame, it impacts everything about their lives. Their negative attitudes toward themselves taint everything they try to accomplish.

Jesus bore our shame for us on the cross (Hebrews 12:2). He has paid the price for it and put it to death. Shame has been uprooted from our lives. When we live in Christ, we live with confidence and joy, and we do not have to live in shame anymore.

*Jesus, I pray that You would help me understand that on the cross, You took my shame, so I do not have to bear it any more. Heal me, so I can live free from shame. Thank You.*

# WHY DO THE
# RIGHTEOUS SUFFER?

*All this came upon us, though we had not forgotten you; we had not been false to your covenant.*

**PSALM 44:17**

In Psalm 44, the writer speaks of a time when, although the people had been faithful to God, they were suffering, and their enemies appeared to be winning the battle against them. Such times are difficult, but we all experience them. Verse 22 reads, "Yet for your sake we face death all day long; we are considered as sheep to be slaughtered." We find this text referenced in Romans 8:36, but in 8:37, Paul goes on to say, "In all these things we are more than conquerors through him who loved us."

God has never promised us a trouble-free life, but He has promised to deliver us: "Many are the afflictions of the righteous, but the Lord delivers him out of them all" (Psalm 34:19 NKJV). Even though these times are challenging, they are opportunities for us to trust God and grow in faith. They actually work out for our good, because as we stand firm, we are strengthened and we have less fear and worry the next time a difficulty arises.

There are situations that once caused me intense fear and worry that barely bother me at all now. Why? Because I have experienced the deliverance of God over and over, and my experience has strengthened my faith. I know that if God delivered me once, He will do it again. When you are suffering and it appears that God is not going to help you, look back and remember all those other times when you felt the same way, yet God did come through for you and bring you victory.

*Father, thank You for all the times You have helped me and delivered me from troubles that threatened to defeat me. When I am being attacked now, let me remember those times and be strengthened by them.*

# THE TABLET AND THE PEN

*My heart is stirred by a noble theme as I recite my verses for the king; my tongue is the pen of a skillful writer.*

**PSALM 45:1**

In today's scripture, the psalmist compares his tongue to "the pen of a skillful writer." And in the book of Proverbs, the human heart is compared to the kind of tablet on which people wrote by hand (3:1–3, 7:3). We see from these Old Testament scriptures that, metaphorically, the heart is the tablet and the tongue is the pen. We can use our words to write all kinds of things on the tablets of our hearts, but I believe what we most need to write is God's Word.

When you confess God's Word aloud with your tongue, you are effectively writing it on your heart. When you write it on your heart, it becomes more firmly established both in your heart and in the earth around you. God's Word is forever "settled in heaven [standing firm and unchangeable]" (Psalm 119:89 AMP), and we establish it in the earth each time we speak it.

When God's Word is written on your heart and it comes out in the words you speak, it empowers you to fulfill His will, and it is a mighty weapon against the enemy.

*Help me, Lord, to write Your words on the tablet of my heart.*

# GRACIOUS WORDS

*You are the most excellent of men and your lips have been anointed with grace, since God has blessed you forever.*

**PSALM 45:2**

Words are containers for power, and we decide what kind of power our words will carry. Will they be words of life or words of death? God created the whole earth with His Words. His Words were creative, and ours should be also, but if we are not careful, they can be destructive. They can build up or tear down. Our words should be gracious and "seasoned with salt" (Colossians 4:6). This means they should be good and filled with a flavor that will make them desirable. Salt was used as a preservative in Jesus' day and was even valuable enough to be used as currency. Our words should preserve the message of Christ and always represent Him and His character.

I love to be with people I can count on to be positive and encouraging, and I don't enjoy being with people who are negative, complaining, or discouraging. People's words affect me; they can add to my joy or detract from it, and I want all the joy I can get, don't you? I encourage you today and every day to be very careful about the words that you speak. Pray daily and ask God to help your words please Him. The psalmist David prayed that God would put a guard over his mouth so he wouldn't sin with his lips (Psalm 141:3). This is a good prayer for us to pray also.

*Father, I realize how important my words are, and I need Your help all the time in choosing to speak life and words that build up and edify. I can't do it without You.*

# ANOINTED WITH THE OIL OF JOY

*You love righteousness and hate wickedness; therefore God, your God, has set you above your companions by anointing you with the oil of joy.*
**PSALM 45:7**

God wants us to love what He loves and hate what He hates. He loves righteousness (doing right) and He hates evil (doing wrong). We should feel the same way God does and make decisions that will please Him. We are faced with choices all the time. Every day we must decide whether we will do the right thing or the wrong thing when situations arise. We decide if we will walk through the narrow gate that leads to life or through the broad gate that leads to destruction (Matthew 7:13–14). Each of us must decide for ourselves and be careful not to take wrong advice from the ungodly.

We will all stand before God eventually and give an account of our life (Romans 14:12), and the decisions we make now will impact how easy or difficult that day will be. All decisions have consequences. We can be forgiven for our wrong choices, but this doesn't mean that all the consequences of our actions disappear. A person may steal, lie, or even murder, and they can be forgiven for their sin, but they may still go to prison.

We should think carefully about our decisions, because wise people do now what they will be happy with later in life. A foolish person is one who does wrong things and hopes that they will avoid the consequences, but they don't. God promises to give favor and joy to the person who loves righteousness and hates wickedness, and I pray that you and I will fit this description.

*Father, please help me walk in righteousness and hate evil and wickedness. I want Your favor and the oil of joy.*

# GOD NEVER CHANGES

*Therefore we will not fear, though the earth give way and the mountains fall into the heart of the sea.*

**PSALM 46:2**

If there's anything in nature we view as solid and permanent, it's the mountains. For them to fall into the sea, as today's scripture describes, would represent change like we've never seen before. So the psalmist's point in Psalm 46:2 is that God is the only constant in our lives. Everything changes except God, and being fearful of change or letting it upset us won't keep it from happening. People change, circumstances change, priorities change, desires change, and our bodies change. There is one certainty in life: change!

During seasons of change, the first thing we need to deal with is our mind, because our thoughts directly affect our emotions and determine our behavior. When something in your life changes and you did not choose the change and do not feel ready for it, you will probably feel a variety of emotions about it. When change comes, if you will embrace the transition mentally and learn to adapt to it, you will be able to manage your emotions more easily and more effectively instead of allowing them to control you.

When change happens in your life, always look to the Word of God for guidance and ask the Holy Spirit to help you. By acting on God's Word and not merely *re*acting to your circumstances, you will be better able to handle the change, and it may turn out to be a great blessing.

*Thank You, God, that You never change and that You will help me and guide me through all the changes in my life.*

# SOMETIMES STILLNESS WINS THE BATTLE

*He says, "Be still, and know that I am God; I will be exalted among the nations, I will be exalted in the earth."*

**PSALM 46:10**

When we face challenges or find ourselves in some kind of battle against the enemy, God will give us the instructions we need in order to be victorious. Sometimes He will guide us to take specific steps, and sometimes He will lead us simply to be still.

When the people of Judah faced an intense conflict, God did not give them complicated battle plans or strict marching orders. He simply directed them to stand still. "You will not need to fight in this battle," He told them. "Position yourselves, *stand still* and see the salvation of the Lord, who is with you, O Judah and Jerusalem!" (2 Chronicles 20:17 NKJV, italics mine). At the end of this story, God gave them a mighty victory.

When we face difficulties, our natural tendency is to get busy trying to solve the problem. But God often has a different way of dealing with things. Today's scripture encourages us to "be still, and know" that He is God. He may lead us to do nothing at all for a period of time, except pray, worship, and wait on Him to work in our lives as we quietly place our confidence in Him.

The kind of stillness and waiting that God desires is not lazy or passive, but expectant and spiritually active. It is full of faith and aggressively hopeful, trusting Him to move at exactly the right time and being ready to respond in obedience when He does.

*Father, help me to understand that I do not always have to be busy or to try to solve my problems in my own strength, but that I can be still and wait on You. I trust You to handle every situation that concerns me.*

# SHOW GOD HOW YOU FEEL

*Clap your hands, all you nations; shout to God with cries of joy.*

**PSALM 47:1**

Among other things, the Book of Psalms teaches us how to worship God. It instructs us to dance, to play musical instruments, and to express our love and praise to God in various physical ways (Psalm 26:7, 150:3–5). Today's scripture encourages us to clap our hands and shout to God with joy. Many times, we need to worship God in tangible ways, not simply in our hearts. Showing Him how we feel brings a release in our lives, honors God, and aids in defeating the enemy.

Simply saying, "Well, God knows how I feel about Him; I do not have to make a big display of it" is not enough. I am convinced that God gave us emotions for more purposes than being enthusiastic at a ball game or about a new car. Surely He wants us to employ our emotions in balanced, appropriate ways to express our love and gratitude to Him.

I encourage you to be expressive in your praise and worship. If you feel excited about Him, give Him a shout or clap your hands. If you are sad and need His comfort, weep in His presence. He created every part of you, including your emotions and physical being, so use them to show Him how you feel.

*Help me, Lord, to express freely my love for You and my praise for all You are and everything You do for me.*

# PRAISE AND THE PRESENCE OF GOD

*God has ascended amid shouts of joy, the Lord amid the sounding of trumpets. Sing praises to God, sing praises; sing praises to our King, sing praises.*

**PSALM 47:5–6**

We know that Psalms is filled with praise for God, and as I mentioned in yesterday's devotion, it includes many instructions for us, as His people, to praise Him. God inhabits the praises of His people (Psalm 22:3), and when we praise Him, He comes and dwells in our praise.

Praise can be anything from simply saying "Thank You" to God for something He has done for us to telling others about His goodness. Praise can be musical or words without music, but it all glorifies God for the good things He has done, is doing, and will do in the future.

There is fullness of joy in God's presence (Psalm 16:11), so the more we praise Him, the greater our joy will be. Under the Old Covenant, people had to bring sacrifices of animals, grain, or other things as a means of covering their sin. But now under the New Covenant, Jesus has paid for all our sins, and God says the sacrifice we are to bring is one of praise (Hebrews 9:12, 13:15). This sacrifice of praise is the fruit of our lips (our words) glorifying God. We can see that praise is another great way to use our words and fill them with life.

*Lord, I praise You for who You are and all that You have done. You are amazing, awesome, and to be praised greatly at all times and in every situation. Help me to be mindful to praise You every day. I love You, Lord.*

# THE LOVE OF GOD

*Within your temple, O God, we meditate on your unfailing love.*

**PSALM 48:9**

We often hear that God loves us, but ask yourself if you truly believe it and if you're taking time to meditate on His love. The love of God is what casts out fear (1 John 4:18). If we know that God loves us, then we know He will take care of us and meet our needs.

Today's scripture speaks of meditating within His temple on His unfailing love. Remember you are the temple of God. First Corinthians 3:16 says, "Don't you know that you yourselves are God's temple and that God's Spirit dwells in your midst?"

We can and should think throughout each day about how much God loves us. Some people might view that as prideful, but God's Word tells us to do it. The Bible says that we know and rely on the love God has for us: "And we know (understand, recognize, are conscious of, by observation and by experience) and believe (adhere to and put faith in and rely on) the love God cherishes for us. God is love, and he who dwells and continues in love dwells and continues in God, and God dwells and continues in him" (1 John 4:16 AMPC).

We cannot dwell in God's love without also thinking about it. He doesn't love us because we deserve it, but because He is good, and He *is* love (Psalm 107:1; 1 John 4:8). As your revelation of God's love for you deepens, the less fear and worry you will have—and the bolder and more confident you will become and the more valued you will feel.

*Father, thank You for loving me. Help me think about Your love for me often.*

# GOD WILL BE WITH YOU TO THE END

*For this God is our God for ever and ever; he will be our guide even to the end.*

**PSALM 48:14**

Some translations of today's verse say that God will be with us even "unto death" or "until death" (KJV, AMP, NASB), and this is the way I like to think about it. This is comforting to me to know, and I hope it also comforts you. As we age, we often begin to think about what will happen to us and what death is like, but understanding this scripture removes all concern or fear about our latter years. God will be with us until we draw our last breath, and then He will take us home with Him.

Today's scripture also says that "This God is our God," and I think this is important to think about. He isn't just *a* god, but He is *your* God. He cares about you personally and watches over every move you make. He knows your thoughts and is aware of everything you do before you do it. Nothing you do surprises God, so even when you make mistakes or sin, He is not shocked, because He already knew about it.

There is never a moment in your life when you are not loved by God, and there is never a moment in your life when He is not with you. The more you realize this, the more relaxed and comfortable you will be. You don't always have to know what to do next, because the One who knows all things is with you and will reveal what you need to know when the time comes.

*Father, it is comforting to know that You will be with me until the very end. Help me remember this anytime I get concerned about the future and what it will hold. Thank You.*

# YOU CAN'T TAKE IT WITH YOU

*Do not be overawed when others grow rich, when the splendor of their houses increases; for they will take nothing with them when they die, their splendor will not descend with them.*

**PSALM 49:16–17**

Psalm 49 contains several references to wealth, all indicating that we will leave it on earth, for we cannot take it with us to heaven. We can easily fall into the trap of wanting more and more while ignoring what should be top priorities in our lives. For example, relationships are much more important than money, but many people prioritize gaining wealth over relationships and then wonder why they have no friends or why their family doesn't care for them when they get older.

We all need finances, and we all want to have enough provision to live comfortably. There is nothing wrong with this desire. God says plainly in His Word that He wants us to prosper in all we do (3 John 2). However, He never tells us to make wealth our number one pursuit. In fact, He says to seek Him and His Kingdom and that He will add the things we need (Matthew 6:33). This doesn't mean that we can stay home and pray all day and God will miraculously provide money for us, but it does mean that we don't need to make the pursuit of wealth our top priority.

We brought nothing into the world, and we will take nothing out of it (1 Timothy 6:7). It is sobering to think that everything we work for and accumulate here on earth will someday belong to someone else. Let's live for what matters most and be content with what God gives without becoming greedy for more and more.

*Father, I appreciate everything You have given to me, and I want to use it to live on and be a blessing to others. Help me keep my priorities in proper order and never put making money ahead of my relationship with You, my family, or my friends.*

# THE GREATNESS OF GOD

*The Mighty One, God, the Lord, speaks and summons the earth from the rising of the sun to where it sets.*

**PSALM 50:1**

It is important for us not to take for granted the mighty works God does, and it is good to stop and think about the world, realizing that there is no way it could run so perfectly without His continually keeping it in balance. God sustains and maintains everything by His Word (Hebrews 1:3). The sun rises every morning and sets every night, as today's scripture indicates. The stars, sun, moon, and all the planets stay in the sky, and grains of sand on a beach stop the waves of the mighty oceans.

God asked Job many questions that are good for all of us to think about. For example, God asked: "Where were you when I laid the earth's foundation?" (Job 38:4); "Have you ever given orders to the morning?" (Job 38:12); "Do you give the horse its strength?" (Job 39:19); "Does the eagle soar at your command?" (Job 39:27). God also asked Job if he knew where He keeps the snow, the hail, and the lightning, or where He stores the light and darkness (Job 37:3; 38:19, 22). God interacts with Job in this way in Job 38–41, and I suggest you read these chapters because of the ways they remind us of God's majesty.

Remembering God's greatness and involvement in the many details of the natural world helps us realize that no problem we have is too big for God and helps us not take for granted the things that He does. Our God truly is an awesome God.

*Father, help me to never forget how mighty and powerful You are, and help me to remember that nothing is impossible for You.*

# EVERYTHING BELONGS TO GOD

*For every animal of the forest is mine, and the cattle on a thousand hills. I know every bird in the mountains, and the insects in the fields are mine.*

**PSALM 50:10–11**

A word that children learn to say early is *mine*. They don't realize their parents provide whatever they think they own, and I think we do this with God. We are stewards, not owners of His gifts, but we quickly forget this. Today's scripture reminds us that everything is His—including you and me. We need to think in these terms rather than thinking like babies and saying, "Mine."

God takes care of what is His. Although He created us and, as such, we are His, He gives us free will and wants us to choose to give back to Him ourselves and the life He has given us. Have you given yourself and everything you have to Him?

Romans 12:1 (AMPC) says: "I appeal to you therefore, brethren, and beg of you in view of [all] the mercies of God, to make a decisive dedication of your bodies [presenting all your members and faculties] as a living sacrifice, holy (devoted, consecrated) and well pleasing to God, which is your reasonable (rational, intelligent) service and spiritual worship."

This means to present to God our bodies—eyes, arms, hands, feet, mouths, and minds. I believe we should include our finances, entertainment, choice of friends, career, desires, and anything else we think belongs to us. If you haven't yet done so, give up trying to run your own life and let God take control. You will like where you end up much better and have more joy along the way.

*Father, thank You for reminding me that everything belongs to You, including me. I give all that I am and all that I have to You for Your use and glory.*

# DEALING WITH A DAY OF TROUBLE

*Call on me in the day of trouble; I will deliver you, and you will honor me.*
**PSALM 50:15**

We all face problems or a "day of trouble" at times. Sometimes the trouble is minor, and sometimes it is serious. When a day of trouble comes, stress comes with it. One reason our troubles are so upsetting has to do with the circumstances themselves, and another reason is that troubles cause emotional, mental, relational, financial, or physical pressure.

The first key to dealing with stress effectively is to recognize or admit we have it. The second key is to identify and learn to respond properly to the stressors that affect us most and pray about them right away. Another important key to relieving stress is being willing to do anything God leads us to do.

There is a big difference between being under stress and being on top of a situation, and we can live on top of our stress, not underneath it. Even though we will experience stressful times, they won't last forever, and if we are obedient to God's Word and to His promptings, we can overcome them.

We all have days that seem filled with trouble, but with God's help, we can go through them in peace. The Holy Spirit leads us and often prompts us to think or do things that will relieve stress quickly.

God is guiding you into a place of victory, not defeat. When you feel stressed, listen to what God is saying to you and follow the Holy Spirit's promptings, and you'll soon find yourself in a place of peace, strength, and triumph.

*Thank You, God, for being with me in days of trouble and for helping me handle and gain victory over the stress that comes with them.*

# FORGIVE ALL MY SIN

*Have mercy on me, O God, according to your unfailing love; according to your great compassion blot out my transgressions. Wash away all my iniquity and cleanse me from my sin.*

**PSALM 51:1–2**

Today's scriptures come from the prayer David prayed after he committed adultery with Bathsheba. Later in this Psalm, David tells God that his joy would return if He would cleanse him (51:7–12). I have heard it said that our secrets make us sick, and certainly hidden and unconfessed sin and the guilt it brings makes people miserable.

Confession of our sin is a great privilege and a benefit to us, especially since we know that God will forgive us and make us new. You and I can talk to Him about anything; after all, He knows all things anyway. Confess your sin and repent, which means to turn away from it and turn toward God.

Don't worry that you have asked for forgiveness many times already and fear that God won't forgive you. Where sin increases, grace increases even more (Romans 5:20).

Thank God for His great mercy and compassion and for the forgiveness of sin. David's sin was instantly forgiven the moment he confessed, and ours will be also.

*Father, I am grateful for Your forgiveness, mercy, and compassion. I am sorry for my sin, and I confess it, turn away from it, and desire to serve You with all my heart.*

# JESUS HAS ALREADY PAID FOR OUR SIN

*For I know my transgressions, and my sin is always before me.*

**PSALM 51:3**

Guilt is a miserable companion. It eats away at your peace until you have none left. When you sin, as we all do, admit it, repent, and receive God's forgiveness. If you have hurt someone else, it is good to admit your sin, apologize to them, and ask them to forgive you also.

Once you have confessed, apologized, and asked forgiveness, if guilty feelings persist, tell them they have no legal right to take up residence in your life because of what Jesus has done for you. Romans 8:1 says that there is no condemnation (guilt) for those who are in Christ Jesus. Don't believe your feelings more than you believe God's Word.

In Isaiah 53:11, God says this about Jesus: "He shall see the labor of His soul, and be satisfied. By His knowledge My righteous Servant shall justify many, for He shall bear their iniquities" (NKJV). When God forgives us, according to Psalm 103:12, He removes our sins as far as the east is from the west, which is an immeasurable distance. And, according to Hebrews 8:12, He remembers them no more.

If God, who is perfect, can forget our sins, we should be able to forget them too. Guilt is often our human way of trying to pay for our sin, but Jesus has already paid for it in full, and He needs no help from us.

*Father, when the enemy piles guilt on me even after I have repented of my sin, help me realize that he is merely trying to control me and steal my peace. I declare that I am forgiven, and I will live free from guilt. Amen.*

# TRUTH IN THE INNERMOST BEING

*Behold, You desire truth in the innermost being, and in secret You will make wisdom known to me.*

**PSALM 51:6 NASB**

As I mentioned in yesterday's devotion, David wrote Psalm 51 after he sinned with Bathsheba, and we can sense his deep remorse and repentance in its words. In today's scripture, David acknowledges that God desires truth in "the innermost being." The innermost being is the core of ourselves, the real person we are down deep inside. An important aspect of living with truth in the innermost being is paying attention to our thought life, because our words, our emotions, our attitudes, and our motives come from our thoughts. We can even use our thoughts to deceive ourselves, but God has called us to be totally, completely, and scrupulously honest in our inner being.

We all fail at times, and when you fail, remember Psalm 51 and remind yourself that David, the greatest king of Israel, cried out to God, saying, "My sin is always before me" (v. 3). Our sins, failures, and shortcomings will always be before us, and we will think about them until we admit them and confess them to the Lord.

Let me encourage you to do your best to live with truth in your innermost being. You and God are the only ones who know what's in your heart. Only when you are honest with yourself and with God can you sincerely repent, as David did, and know the joy of God's complete forgiveness and freedom.

*Lord, help me to desire truth in my inner being and to pay attention to my thoughts. I desire truth in my innermost being so I will not be deceived or try to deceive You or other people.*

# A CLEAN HEART

*Create in me a clean heart, O God, and renew a right and steadfast spirit within me.*

**PSALM 51:10 AMP**

When we love God, we want to have clean, pure hearts before Him. But purity and cleanness of heart do not come naturally to us; the Holy Spirit works them into us. Notice that David asks God to create a clean heart in him. He knows he cannot do it for himself. When we cry out to God sincerely, asking Him to cleanse and purify our hearts, He lovingly does it.

Hebrews 10:22 speaks of the necessity of a clean heart drawing near to God, saying: "Let us approach [God] with a true and sincere heart in unqualified assurance of faith, having had our hearts sprinkled clean from an evil conscience and our bodies washed with pure water" (AMP).

There is a price to pay for a pure and clean heart, and that price is being willing to follow the leadership of the Holy Spirit. But there is also a reward for a pure, clean heart: We will be blessed; we will see God, meaning that we will hear from Him and recognize Him at work in our lives (Matthew 5:8). We don't have to be afraid to commit to allow God to do in us the deep work that cleanses and purifies our hearts. We may not always feel comfortable about the truths He will bring to us, but if we will take care of our part—holding to purity, integrity, moral courage, and godly character—God will make sure we are blessed. He is an expert at removing worthless things from our hearts and lives while retaining the things that are valuable.

*Father, I ask You to cleanse and purify my heart. I want to see You.*

# THE DAY OF RECKONING WILL COME

*Why do you boast of evil, you mighty hero? Why do you boast all day long, you who are a disgrace in the eyes of God?*

**PSALM 52:1**

The heading for Psalm 52 tells us that Doeg the Edomite had gone to Saul and told him where to find David so he could capture and kill him. But David knew that Doeg's boasting was a disgrace in the eyes of God and that a day of reckoning would come for those who do evil.

We have similar situations in our society today. Many people think they are heroes as they do evil things that are against God and His principles, but a day is coming when they will have to face God and give an account of their actions.

Don't allow those who do evil to upset you or cause you anxiety, but instead pray for them; pray that they will repent and turn to God before it is too late for them to do so. Stand firm in this evil hour in which we live, and let your light shine brightly for God and His principles.

God tells us in His Word that in the last days there will be great deception, and we are living in those days—days when some people call evil good and good evil (Isaiah 5:20; 1 Timothy 4:1; 2 Timothy 3:13). Let us all pray that we are not deceived during these dangerous times.

*Father, I ask You to keep me safe from deception, and I pray for all who are deceived, that they might see the truth and that the truth would make them free.*

# RELAX WHILE GOD WORKS

*But I am like an olive tree flourishing in the house of God; I trust in God's unfailing love for ever and ever.*

**PSALM 52:8**

How do you respond to a problem that seems too big or too complicated for you, a problem you know you cannot fix? Do you keep looking for new ways to solve it, or do you keep trying harder to take care of it? In such a situation, why not relax while God works on it? This is what it means to "trust in God's unfailing love," as today's scripture mentions. This may sound easy, but it took many years for me to be able to do it. I know from experience that the ability to relax and accept whatever happens in life depends on our willingness to trust God completely and to stop trying to control things or figure things out on our own.

When situations don't go your way, instead of getting upset, start believing that your way was not what you needed and that God has something better in mind for you. His love is unfailing, and He will give you what is best for you, even if it isn't what you think you want. The minute you recognize that He is in control and put your trust in Him, your soul and body relax, and you will be able to enjoy life. As Psalm 37:5 says, "Commit your way to the Lord, trust also in Him, and He will do it" (NASB).

*Help me, Lord, to trust confidently in You and relax while You work everything out for my good.*

# GOD IS WATCHING

*God looks down from heaven on all mankind to see if there are any who understand, any who seek God.*

**PSALM 53:2**

God is watching everything that goes on in the world, and He has a plan to deliver the righteous and all those who diligently seek Him. Hebrews 11:6 says that we should believe that God is "a rewarder of those who diligently seek Him" (NKJV), and I believe He is.

When we are going through difficult times and doing our best to remain steady, it is helpful to think about the day our reward will come. Those who are evil will be rewarded also, but their reward will not be pleasant. I encourage you not to become weary in doing what is right, for in due time you will reap a reward (Galatians 6:9).

If you are a person who seeks God on a regular basis, know that God sees you and that He is pleased. You may not always feel that God is with you, but He is, and your faithfulness puts a smile on His face. Be faithful even in little things, and God will reward you with greater things.

*Father, I believe that You are watching over everything. You are faithful, and You will reward those who are diligent. Help me remain faithful in seeking You and obeying You. Thank You.*

# GOD HEARS YOUR PRAYERS

*Save me, O God, by your name; vindicate me by your might. Hear my prayer, O God; listen to the words of my mouth.*

**PSALM 54:1–2**

Some prayers are answered right away, and others seem to take a long time. We don't know why this happens, but it should not discourage us or make us think that God doesn't hear our prayers. He has a perfect timing for all things. He promises to hear and answer prayers that are prayed according to His will.

First John 5:14–15 says, "This is the confidence we have in approaching God: that if we ask anything according to his will, he hears us. And if we know that he hears us—whatever we ask—we know that we have what we asked of him."

I believe that prayer is the greatest privilege we have and one of the most powerful things we can do, so I encourage you to never stop praying. Pray your way through the day, pray about everything and anything. Pray with all manner of prayer: thanksgiving, petition, intercession, praise, worship, and commitment.

"Ask and keep on asking and it will be given to you" (Matthew 7:7 AMP). After you pray, keep believing while you wait for your answer to come. Each time you think of your request, you can simply thank God that He is working and tell Him you are expecting an answer very soon. Don't ever give up.

*Father, thank You that You hear and answer my prayers. I wait on You and am thankful that You are working on my behalf.*

# GOD WILL KEEP YOU STRONG

*Surely God is my help; the Lord is the one who sustains me.*

**PSALM 54:4**

We should always depend on God for strength. He is our strength. He sustains and maintains us. He upholds us, guides us, and never gives us more to handle than we can bear. He is "our refuge and strength, an ever-present help in trouble" (Psalm 46:1). Isaiah 41:10 teaches us not to fear because He will strengthen, help, and uphold us in times of trouble.

The joy of the Lord is our strength (Nehemiah 8:10). I encourage you to avoid discouragement, depression, sadness, and despair as much as possible, because these negative conditions will weaken you and zap your strength. We all have times when things happen and discourage us or make us sad, but those are exactly the times when we need to pray for strength to stay strong in the Lord and to resist the temptation to sink into despair. If you are experiencing any of these difficult negative emotions right now, think about some prayers God has answered for you in the past, and know that He will do it again.

The apostle Paul urges us: "Be strong in the Lord and in the power of His might" (Ephesians 6:10 NKJV). You are created to do great things, but know that Satan will try to stop you through his lies and deception. Believe God's Word more than you believe how you feel or what things look like. Rejoice, for God is about to show Himself strong in your life.

*Father, I am expecting You to do great things. You are my strength, and I need strength right now to be steadfast and wait patiently on You. Thank You.*

# DON'T RUN FROM DIFFICULTY

*I said, "Oh, that I had the wings of a dove! I would fly away and be at rest. I would flee far away and stay in the desert; I would hurry to my place of shelter, far from the tempest and storm."*

**PSALM 55:6–8**

*To fear* means to take flight or to run away from. When God tells us not to fear, He is actually telling us not to run from what we need to face and deal with. I have done quite a bit of study on running from things, and I have discovered that when we run from them, God usually takes us back to them and teaches us to confront them before we can move on to new and better experiences.

Hagar ran from Sarah when she was being mistreated, and God found her in the wilderness and told her to go back to her mistress and submit to her (Genesis 16:9). I don't imagine that was easy to do. Moses ran away from Egypt when he was caught killing an Egyptian, but forty years later God sent him back to Egypt (Exodus 2:11–15, 3:10). Elijah ran from Jezebel and from the call on his life, but God told him to get back to work and do what he was asked to do (1 Kings 19:1–18). Elijah had to confront his fears, and we also have to confront our problems instead of running from them.

My mother ran from the fact that my father was sexually abusing me. She refused to deal with it because of fear, and that stole her life and eventually her sanity. God hasn't created us to run away in fear; we are to trust in Him and not fear.

*Father, help me to stand and face my difficulties and believe that through You, I can do anything I need to do.*

# CAST YOUR CARES

*Cast your cares on the Lord and he will sustain you; he will never let the righteous be shaken.*

**PSALM 55:22**

Do you feel burdened or weighted down by the cares of life? Do the situations that concern you distract you during the day or keep you awake at night as you try to figure out what to do about them? Life does have a way of becoming heavy when we try to carry its load—marriage and family matters, work, household responsibilities, busy schedules, health issues, caring for aging parents, financial issues, and other situations—in our own strength.

Sometimes, in the midst of our problems, we begin to wonder if God really cares about us. Today's scripture teaches us exactly what to do when we feel overwhelmed with cares and concerns. We are to cast them on the Lord, or to give them to Him completely, allowing Him to handle them while we rest in His love for us.

First Peter 5:7 is similar to today's verse. It speaks of humbling ourselves before God and "casting all your care upon Him, for He cares for you" (NKJV). This is good news! You do not have to handle your cares by yourself. God will do the caring for you.

Whatever cares or worries are burdening you today, let God have them, because He cares for you and He will sustain you.

*Lord, I choose today to cast all my cares on You, trusting that You will sustain me. Thank You.*

# "WHEN I AM AFRAID..."

*When I am afraid, I put my trust in you. In God, whose word I praise—in God I trust and am not afraid. What of mere mortals do to me?*

**PSALM 56:3–4**

Psalm 56 begins with David crying out to God because his enemies are "in hot pursuit" of him and "all day long they press their attack" (v. 1). In the midst of such pressure, David declares to God: "When I am afraid, I put my trust in you." Notice that he says "*when* I am afraid," not "*if* I am afraid." This tells me that David accepts the fact that fear is a human emotion; we all experience fear to some degree at some time. But he adds, "I put my trust in you." He did not trust himself or other people; he trusted God alone. David lived boldly and courageously because he knew God was always with him. We can live this same way. We can choose not to live according to the fear we feel, but according to God's Word.

Years ago, God taught me to use what I call the "power twins" to help me defeat fear in my life. They are "I pray" and "I say." When I feel fear, I begin to *pray* and ask for God's help; then I *say*, "I will not fear!" I encourage you to also use these power twins as soon as you feel fear about anything. This will help you manage the emotion of fear instead of allowing it to control you.

*When I am afraid, Lord, I will trust in You. I will pray for Your help and declare, "I will not fear!"*

# THE FEAR OF MAN

*In God I trust and am not afraid. What can man do to me?*

**PSALM 56:11**

The fear of man—meaning the fear of what other people will think of us, say about us, or do to us—is probably one of the most common fears that people deal with. These fears are rooted in our insecurities and the fear of being rejected. Once we know how much God loves us and that we can trust Him to take care of us, the fear of what others will think, say, or do can become a thing of the past.

The apostle Paul said that had he tried to be popular with people, he would have never been an apostle of Jesus Christ (Galatians 1:10). The fear of man can keep us from God's will. We must be God-pleasers, not people-pleasers, and we must obey God, not other human beings (Acts 5:29).

We do like for people to be pleased with us. God's Word encourages us to live for others, and sometimes we even sacrifice in order to show people how much we love them, but we are to do this out of love, not because we feel intimidated or because we think we can earn their favor. If we please people because of fear instead of pleasing God, it will keep us from living the life we desire to live.

Let this be a time to examine your actions and make sure they are done to please God and not because of the fear of man.

*Father, I ask You to show me any area in my life where I might be letting the fear of what other people will think, say, or do control me. I want to please You in all I do, even if that means people reject me.*

# GOD DEALS WITH OUR ENEMIES

*I cry out to God Most High, to God, who vindicates me. He sends from heaven and saves me, rebuking those who hotly pursue me—God sends forth his love and his faithfulness.*

**PSALM 57:2–3**

In order to enjoy our lives, we must trust God to deal with our enemies and those who treat us unjustly. Otherwise, we will waste our energy trying to do what only He can do. God is a God of justice, and He will make wrong things right if we wait on Him to do so. God doesn't always move as quickly as we would like Him to, but His timing is perfect.

A group of people once hurt me very badly and accused me of things I was not guilty of. They rejected me and spread rumors that hurt my reputation—and ten years passed before they apologized and told me that God had shown them that they were wrong. Ten years is a long time to wait, but during the wait, I grew in faith and learned to depend on God more than on people.

Pray for those who have hurt you. Bless them, do not curse them, and forgive them.

In these ways, you turn them over to God, and He will vindicate you and even reward you for the pain you've endured.

*Father, thank You for being my Vindicator. Grant me the grace and patience to wait on You to deal with those who hurt me while I pray for them.*

# A STEADFAST, CONFIDENT HEART

*My heart is steadfast, O God, my heart is steadfast and confident! I will sing, yes, I will sing praises [to You]!*

**PSALM 57:7 AMP**

David says that his heart is steadfast and confident, and this was a reason for him to sing and praise God. I totally agree with this. When our hearts are anxious, filled with shame, or feel hopeless, we tend to struggle in every area of our lives. But when our hearts are steadfast and confident in God, we are positioned for victory. We are filled with faith and praise, believing that God will do everything He has promised.

God wants you to be steadfast and confident, but the enemy wants you to be fearful, hopeless, and wavering in your faith. If he can cause your emotions to be up one minute and down the next instead of being steady, he can manipulate you in many ways. If he can steal your confidence by filling your mind with doubt about God and about yourself, he can keep you from growing in God and moving forward in His wonderful plans for your life.

Confidence will make you strong, and the best way to develop it is to believe and speak God's Word. Let me encourage you today to confess the Scripture-based statements below. They will help your heart grow in confidence and become increasingly steadfast.

- I can do all things through Christ who strengthens me (Philippians 4:13).
- I am more than a conqueror through Christ (Romans 8:37).
- Nothing can separate me from the love of God (Romans 8:38–39).
- In Christ, God always causes me to triumph (2 Corinthians 2:14 AMP).

*Father, help me to find my confidence in You and in Your Word so I can live each day in victory, with a steadfast heart.*

# DELIVERANCE WILL COME

*Do you rulers indeed speak justly? Do you judge people with equity? No, in your heart you devise injustice, and your hands mete out violence on the earth.*

**PSALM 58:1-2**

In reading Psalms, we frequently see David dealing with people who were wicked and unjust. But he always trusted God to deliver him and, ultimately, reward him. Psalm 58 includes eleven verses; in ten of them David describes the injustices of his enemies and asks God to deal with them, but in the last verse, verse 11, he offers hope that the righteous will be rewarded because God judges fairly.

Perhaps you have been waiting a long time for God to deal with your enemies and you are growing weary. If so, I want to encourage you today that God will judge and deal with anyone who has treated or is treating you unfairly. Just be patient and keep doing what you know to be right. It is important that we remain obedient to God no matter what other people are doing. Revenge is not ours to take. Our part is to forgive and pray for our enemies and let God bring justice and reward.

Waiting is hard, but the day of reward is sweet. God has rewarded me for the abuse in my childhood and for other situations in which I have been mistreated, and He will do the same for you. Just remain steadfast and keep your trust in Him. Your deliverance could come today.

*Father, waiting for deliverance is hard, but I ask for Your grace and strength to help me hold steady and not give up. Thank You.*

# DO YOU FEEL UNAPPRECIATED?

*Then people will say, "Surely the righteous still are rewarded; surely there is a God who judges the earth."*

**PSALM 58:11**

We all want and need appreciation for the work we do, but we don't always get it when we want it or from the people we hope will give it to us. You may do a great job at work, yet your boss never seems to notice it, or you may feel that your family doesn't appreciate you or even notice all you do for them. Perhaps you have worked in the nursery at church for years and you rarely even hear a thank-you.

I have found that when I am not getting what I need from people in a specific situation, I should go to God and ask Him to give it to me. He always does, but it may come in a different way than I expect.

When we do things for people, we should do them as unto the Lord, because our true reward comes from Him (Colossians 3:23–24). God will never forget the work you do for Him (Hebrews 6:10), and He always sees your faithfulness. Be encouraged today in the truth that God always appreciates you even if no one else does, and that He will reward you in due time. He knows exactly what you need and what would bless you, and His reward is always better than any reward this earth can offer.

*Father, I want to trust You always to meet all my needs, including giving me the appreciation I need. When I don't receive from people what I think I should, instead of getting angry with them, help me turn to You and trust You to always give me what is best for me.*

# GOD LAUGHS AT THE WICKED

*But you laugh at them, Lord; you scoff at those nations.*

**PSALM 59:8**

God laughs at the nations that don't believe in Him and think they can defeat His people. He laughs because He already knows what their end will be unless they repent. It is ridiculous for anyone to think they can defeat God.

We, too, can keep laughing and enjoying our life even in the midst of our trouble because we know that God will not leave us forsaken. Satan wants to make us sad, discouraged, depressed, and miserable, but our laugh of faith can defeat him.

It is God's will for us to enjoy our lives at all times. John 10:10 says, "The thief comes only in order to steal and kill and destroy. I came that they may have and enjoy life, and have it in abundance [to the full, till it overflows]" (AMP). And Jesus says in John 15:11, "I have told you this so that my joy may be in you and that your joy may be complete."

Joy and enjoyment are gifts from God, and powerful weapons against the enemy. The joy of the Lord is our strength (Nehemiah 8:10). When we focus on our problems, it is hard to enjoy life, but when we focus on the promises of God, our joy will be abundant.

*Father, help me enjoy my life and continue to laugh even in the midst of life's challenges. Thank You for the gift of joy and laughter.*

# THE LORD, YOUR STRENGTH

*You are my strength, I watch for you; you, God, are my fortress.*
**PSALM 59:9**

Today's scripture reminds us that God is our strength, a truth we are wise to remember in every situation, especially when we feel weak or overwhelmed. We all feel weak or tired at times, and we need the strength that only comes from God. Sometimes we need His strength to get through a season of prolonged sadness or stress, and sometimes we need it simply to get through the demands and pressures of each day.

Many people mentioned in the Bible knew and relied on God's strength. The psalmist David certainly knew that God was his strength and wrote about it several times (2 Samuel 22:33; Psalm 18:1; Psalm 28:7). The prophets Isaiah and Jeremiah referred to God as their strength (Isaiah 12:2; Jeremiah 16:19). The apostle Paul found God's strength so amazing that he gloried in his weaknesses so that "the strength and power of Christ (the Messiah) may rest (yes, may pitch a tent over and dwell) upon me!" (2 Corinthians 12:9 AMPC).

Whatever you are facing today, trust that God is your strength and that He will give you the strength you need.

*I praise You today, Lord, for You are my strength.*

# GOD'S ANGER DOESN'T LAST FOREVER

*You have rejected us, God, and burst upon us; you have been angry—now restore us!*

**PSALM 60:1**

God can become angry, but He is not an angry God. God is love, and although our sin can anger Him, He never stops loving us and always plans to restore us. Isaiah 12:1 says, "I will give thanks to You, O Lord; for though You were angry with me, Your anger has turned away, and You comfort me" (AMP).

There are times when things our children do cause us to become angry, but we always love them, and our anger does not last forever. Surely, we can believe God is the same way. Don't live your life thinking God is always angry with you because of your weaknesses and sins. Be quick to repent, and you'll find that He is quick to forgive.

Don't hesitate to pray for God's restoration or for His help and comfort. You may think you don't deserve these blessings, but that is what makes them so good. In God's great mercy, He restores, heals, and comforts us if we ask Him to, no matter what we have done.

*Father, Your mercy is amazing. Thank You that You don't stay angry, but You restore and heal me even when I don't deserve it.*

# HUMAN HELP IS WORTHLESS

*Give us aid against the enemy, for human help is worthless. With God we will gain the victory, and he will trample down our enemies.*

**PSALM 60:11–12**

When we are in trouble, we often go to our friends to ask for advice or help, but God's Word tells us in today's scripture that we should go to Him because "human help is worthless." The only way a human can truly help us is if God is working through them, and we are not to put our hope in what God calls the "arm of the flesh." King Hezekiah used this term when Israel faced a huge battle with a formidable enemy, and he told his military captains: "With him is only *the arm of flesh*, but with us is the Lord our God to help us and to fight our battles" (2 Chronicles 32:8, emphasis mine).

I often ask, "When you have a problem, do you run to the phone or to the throne?" Let's remember to go to God first—to His throne of grace (Hebrews 4:16). And if He chooses to use a person to speak to us, it will still be Him working through them.

We are frequently disappointed and disillusioned by trusting too much in people, because they let us down and disappoint us. Jesus said that He did not entrust Himself to people, because He knew the nature of human beings (John 2:24). This doesn't mean we cannot trust anyone; it does mean we should not give them the trust that belongs only to God. The arm of the flesh cannot help us, but the arm of the Lord always brings victory.

*Father, forgive me for putting too much trust in people when I should be trusting You. Help me remember to always go to You first when I need help.*

# LIVE BY FAITH IN GOD'S STRENGTH

*From the ends of the earth I call to you, I call as my heart grows faint; lead me to the rock that is higher than I. For you have been my refuge, a strong tower against the foe.*

**PSALM 61:2-3**

Notice in today's scriptures that David calls out to God because his "heart grows faint." Some translations refer to this faintness of heart as being overwhelmed (KJV, NKJV), or overwhelmed and weak (AMP). I think we can all relate, for at times everyone feels overwhelmed or that they just don't have the strength to keep going in life.

God's will is for us to live by faith in Him, not by our own strength. You may be thinking of how far you have to go in order to be all that God wants you to be, and that makes you feel overwhelmed. Your mind wants to think, *This is just too much; I will never be able to do all that He asks me to do.*

This is where faith comes in. When David's heart was overwhelmed, he cried out to God for help. In the Amplified Bible, Psalm 61:2 reads: "Lead me to the rock that is higher than I [*a rock that is too high to reach without Your help*]" (emphasis mine). You can think, *I don't know how I am going to do it, but I am expecting God's help. With God, all things are possible!*

If your heart feels faint today, decide now that you will simply take the next step. Then keep going day after day. Refuse to be discouraged by how far you think you still have to go. God is pleased that you are determined to reach your goal and are making progress each day.

*When I am overwhelmed, help me to call out to You, full of faith that You will answer and give me strength to go on.*

# GOD'S PRESENCE

*I long to dwell in your tent forever and take refuge in the shelter of your wings.*

PSALM 61:4

The psalmist David knew the importance of keeping God first in his life. He knew that God was his shelter from the storms of life. He had many enemies, but he never tried to fight them without first going to God for help.

Are you trying to fight with something in your life, in yourself, or in another person, right now? Are you frustrated because no matter what you do, nothing changes? If so, I know how you feel. I wasted many years trying to fight my own battles, and I never got any results either. If we seek God, He will fight our battles for us or show us what to do, and when He does, it will be something that will work.

The Bible says that if we draw close to God, He will come close to us (James 4:8). Jesus realized how much He needed to be close to the Father and be in His presence. He frequently went to a quiet place by Himself to pray. He even walked away from crowds of people who needed His help so He could pray (Matthew 14:23; Mark 14:32–38). He knew He had to stay full of God's presence and be strong in Him.

Be sure to take plenty of time to seek God and tell Him you need Him. If Jesus needed time in God's presence, surely we do too.

*Father, help me to never forget that You are my refuge from every storm. Forgive me for trying to solve my own problems without seeking You first.*

# REST FOR YOUR SOUL

*Truly my soul finds rest in God; my salvation comes from him.*

**PSALM 62:1**

Sometimes in the midst of our busy lives, we simply need to take a rest. In today's scripture, David says, "Truly my soul finds rest in God." No one can give rest to our souls (mind, will, and emotions) like God can. In fact, Hebrews 4:3 tells us that there is such a thing as God's rest and that, as believers, we can enter into it by faith.

I like to define rest for the soul as freedom from excessive reasoning, struggle, fear, inner turmoil, worry, frustration, and other things that upset us, even in the midst of trouble. To enter into God's rest is to cease trying to control people or circumstances, trusting God to handle them in His way, according to His timing. We try to control people or situations when we endeavor to do what only God can do instead of trusting Him to do it. God's kind of rest is not resting from physical activity, but resting while doing what we need to do, resting on the inside despite everything going on around us. Our bodies may be moving, but our minds, wills, and emotions are at peace.

If you are tired in your soul, God's rest is available to you. Ask Him to quiet your mind, will, and emotions and help you to trust Him in every situation.

*Father, I pray that You would give me rest in my soul today.*

# HOPE COMES FROM GOD

*Yes, my soul, find rest in God; my hope comes from him.*

**PSALM 62:5**

In today's scripture, the psalmist David makes a declaration that you and I would be wise to make as well. He says, "My hope comes from him," meaning God.

I believe hope is the happy and confident anticipation of something good. For a Christian, hope is the positive expectation that good is going to happen because of God's greatness. I believe that hope precedes and is connected to faith. A person of faith believes God exists, but more than that, a person of faith also believes that God is good, and that He rewards those who diligently seek Him (Hebrews 11:6). They expect and wait for His goodness, simply because He has promised to give it and they trust Him.

Let me ask you today: Where is your hope? Is it firmly in the Lord? If your hope is in a person, a job, a paycheck, a retirement fund, or a dream you are trying to make come true, it's in an unreliable source. You may be disappointed.

Hope is only as strong as its source, so put your hope in God today, trusting Him completely. He will never let you down!

*God, I declare today that my hope is in You and You alone.*

# AT ALL TIMES

*Trust in him at all times, you people; pour out your hearts to him, for God is our refuge.*

**PSALM 62:8**

Today's scripture teaches us that we are not to have faith in God just once in a while, but at all times, trusting Him when everything is going well for us and when nothing seems to go right.

Trusting God is easy when things are going well. But when life becomes difficult and we continue to trust Him anyway, that's when we develop character. And the more character we develop, the more our abilities—our God-given strengths and the ways in which He has gifted us and wants to use us—can be released. This is why I say that *stability releases ability*. The more stable we become, the more our ability will be released, because God will know that He can trust us.

Many people have gifts that can take them to places where their character cannot keep them. Gifts are *given*, but character is *developed*. As God helps us develop our character, we become stable enough to remain peaceful, no matter what our circumstances may be. I encourage you to desire and pursue stability in every area of your life so that all the ability in you can be released.

*Help me, God, to develop character and stability so the gifts You have given me can be released.*

# CHECK YOUR MOTIVES

*One thing God has spoken, two things I have heard: "Power belongs to you, God, and with you, Lord, is unfailing love"; and, "You reward everyone according to what they have done."*

**PSALM 62:11-12**

God rewards us according to what we have done, but the only works that receive a reward are pure ones. Someday, all our works will pass before God, and He will test the quality of each one. Only those done with pure motives will remain and be rewarded (1 Corinthians 3:10–15). We should always ask ourselves why we do what we do. Is it in obedience to God? Are we desiring to help another person? There are many good motives, but there are also some bad ones.

Doing good works to be noticed or admired does not represent a good motive (Matthew 6:1). We are encouraged to do our good works in secret when possible, because God who sees in secret will reward us in the open (Matthew 6:4).

I look forward to seeing what God's rewards are, don't you? I believe some of them come to us while we are here on earth, and others are reserved for us to receive when we get to heaven.

Be encouraged today that God's love for you is unfailing and that He has the power to do anything that needs to be done in your life. God loves you very much and has a good plan for your life. Let go of the past and get excited about the future—and remember to look for those rewards along the way.

*Father, I am so grateful that You love me and that I can count on Your love, which never fails. Help me be and do everything You want me to be and do. I look forward to what You have in store for me in the future.*

# MAKE A DECISION

*I will be fully satisfied as with the richest of foods; with singing lips my mouth will praise you.*

**PSALM 63:5**

I believe today's scripture represents an important decision David, the psalmist, made. When he wrote Psalm 63, life was not easy for him. In fact, he faced many difficulties in the wilderness of Judah. But instead of focusing on his problems, he made a decision, which reads like this in the Amplified Bible: "My soul [my life, my very self] is satisfied as with marrow and fatness, and my mouth offers praises [to You] with joyful lips."

Our lives are full of ordinary activities that are not always exciting—getting dressed, driving to work, going to the grocery store, running errands, cleaning house, paying bills, and many other activities. These things may be commonplace, but they are the things that make up our lives, and we can decide to be satisfied and praise God in the midst of them. At times, as was the case for David when he wrote Psalm 63, we may feel surrounded with challenges and hardships, but we can follow his example and declare that we are satisfied in God and that we will praise Him even through our struggles.

No matter what any given day holds for you, it is a gift from God. You can choose to appreciate it, have a good attitude about it, enjoy it, and praise God for it.

*Lord, thank You for the gift of this day. Today I choose to be satisfied with my life, and I give You praise.*

# THINK OF GOD OFTEN

*On my bed I remember you; I think of you through the watches of the night.*

PSALM 63:6

What do you think about while you're waiting to fall asleep or when you wake during the night? Do you worry about your problems or try to figure out what to do in certain situations? The psalmist remembered God on his bed and thought about Him through the night. We can do this too. We can meditate on the Word of God.

To meditate means to think deeply about or to focus your mind on a scripture for a period of time. It also means to mutter or speak quietly. Meditating on Scripture helps us remember it and releases its power to minister to us. God's Word has inherent power in it (Hebrews 4:12), and meditating on it is like chewing food to get the vitamins and nutrients out of it. To say power is *inherent* in the Word means that it is a characteristic of or an attribute of the Word; it is permanent and essential.

One of the fastest ways to go to sleep or get back to sleep if you wake during the night is to meditate on God's Word. If you are worried about something, meditate on scriptures that tell us not to worry, or if you are afraid, then meditate on scriptures that tell us not to fear. You can also meditate on the good things God has done in your life and thank God for them. Meditation will establish the Word in your heart and make it part of you.

*Father, help me remember to make meditation of Your Word part of my everyday life. Remind me to do it as I am going to sleep and even if I wake during the night. I believe it is a holy habit that will help me tremendously. Thank You.*

# FOLLOW THE LEADER

*My whole being follows hard after You and clings closely to You; Your right hand upholds me.*

**PSALM 63:8 AMPC**

The psalmist David says in today's scripture that his "whole being follows hard after" God and "clings closely" to Him. We can sense the intensity of David's heart as he follows God, the only worthy leader we could have.

You may remember, as I do, playing a childhood game called Follow the Leader. If the leader was creative and fun and kept everyone moving at a good pace, the game was enjoyable. If the leader was bossy, moved too fast, or was inclined to lead other children to do things that were too hard or dangerous, the game fell apart quickly. As we go through life, we get to choose which leader we will follow. We all reach a point where we must decide whether we will follow God or trust ourselves to lead our lives.

People who go through life with their own agendas—trying to set their own course, making their own plans, and running their own lives—often end up frustrated and unhappy. It's not that their plans aren't good; it's that God's plans are so much better.

When we follow God, we have a leader who moves at exactly the right pace and keeps life interesting for us. He also makes sure we miraculously end up just where we're supposed to be, when we're supposed to be there. Following God is a great adventure, and I hope you will embrace it today.

*God, I choose You as the leader of my life. Help me to follow hard after You with my whole being.*

# TELL GOD YOUR COMPLAINTS

*Hear me, my God, as I voice my complaint; protect my life from the threat of the enemy.*

**PSALM 64:1**

The Bible teaches us not to complain, but if we do, it is best to vent to God instead of to people. David complained to God a few times in Psalms (Psalm 55:2, 142:2), as did Habakkuk, Job, and Jonah (Habakkuk 1:1–4; Job 23:2; Jonah 4:1–11). The fact that people mentioned in the Bible complained doesn't mean complaining is good; it simply shows us that we can be honest with God about how we feel and what we think.

David's complaints were usually about his enemies. After he complained, he always praised God and declared his confidence that God would deliver him.

When Habakkuk complained, God told him to get a vision and write it down (Habakkuk 2:2). I often tell people, "Don't complain unless you have a vision to fix what you're unhappy about."

Had I been Job or Jonah, I think I might have complained too, but it didn't do either of them any good. As long as Jonah complained, he remained in the belly of the big fish, but when he shouted with grateful praise, the Lord commanded the creature to vomit Jonah onto dry ground (Jonah 2:9–10). Job's complaints never helped him either, but eventually God answered them. When He did, it humbled Job, and God eventually gave him twice as much as he had lost (Job 42:1–6, 10).

Complain to God if you must, but always end on a note of praise, because God is the only One who can help you.

*Father, I am sorry for the many times I have complained. I am glad I can talk to You honestly and tell You how I feel, but after my complaints, help me to always remember Your goodness and give You the praise You deserve.*

# KEEPING YOUR WORD

*Praise awaits you, our God, in Zion; to you our vows will be fulfilled.*
**PSALM 65:1**

David mentions to God that he will keep the vows he has made to Him. Vows are solemn promises. We make a vow when we tell someone we will do a certain thing. When we make a vow or promise God that we will do something, we should definitely follow through and do it. But it is also important to keep our word to people.

Numbers 30:1–2 reveals how serious vows are: "This is the thing which the Lord has commanded: If a man vows a vow to the Lord or swears an oath to bind himself by a pledge, he shall not break and profane his word; he shall do according to all that proceeds out of his mouth" (AMPC).

God always keeps His Word, and we can depend on that. In the same way, people should be able to depend on us. If an emergency comes up or something happens that prevents you from doing what you said you would do, then at least call and explain why you cannot do what you said you would do.

We want people to keep their word when they tell us they will do something, and we should always treat others as we want to be treated. I suggest you think about this, and if there are areas where you have not kept your word, either do what you promised or apologize for not doing it.

*Father, I am so grateful that You keep Your Word, and I also want to keep mine. Forgive me for the times I haven't, and help me in the future to not say I will do something unless I fully intend to do it.*

# ANSWERED PRAYER

*You who answer prayer, to you all people will come. When we were overwhelmed by sins, you forgave our transgressions.*

**PSALM 65:2–3**

It is so good to remember that God answers prayer. We are always encouraged to pray, but remembering that God answers prayer energizes us to pray even more. He may not always answer the way we think He should or at the time we would like, but He does answer.

James 4:2 says, "You do not have because you do not ask God." I encourage people to be bold in their prayers according to the Word of God, based on this verse. You cannot ask God for too much. He wants to do exceedingly, abundantly above and beyond all we could dare to hope, ask, or think (Ephesians 3:20 NKJV).

The scripture for today also reminds us that we don't have to let our sins overwhelm us, nor do we need to carry the guilt of them. God generously forgives them, and that is so amazing.

Just imagine how many people carry the burden of their sin and feel condemned and guilty because they don't know Jesus. But we know that we can be forgiven and that God answers prayer. This is the good news of the gospel.

*Father, thank You that You answer my prayers, and that You forgive my sins. You are so good.*

# GOD TESTS THOSE HE LOVES

*For you, God, tested us; you refined us like silver.*

PSALM 66:10

I don't know anyone who particularly enjoys being tested, but going through times of testing is part of the process of spiritual maturity.

Dictionary.com says a test is "the means by which the presence, quality, or genuineness of anything is determined." When we face tests, God is looking to see if we are genuine and if we truly love and trust Him. Tests and trials bring out what is inside of us, just as the refining process brings out pure silver.

Not only does God see what is within us as we deal with tests, we see it too. We become acquainted with ourselves when we are under duress in ways we never do when life rolls along without challenges. Consider the apostle Peter. He was convinced he would never deny Jesus, but when put to the test, he did deny his Lord (Matthew 26:31–35, 69–75).

When we are tested, we should always remember that God's goal is for us to pass the test, because He has something good for us on the other side of it. With Him, we never fail; we simply get to take the test again until He sees we are ready for Him to move us forward.

*Lord, during times of testing, help me learn every lesson You want me to learn and develop the strength You want for me so I will be ready for the blessings You have in store for me.*

# PASS YOUR TESTS

*For you, God, tested us; you refined us like silver. You brought us into prison and laid burdens on our backs. You let people ride over our heads; we went through fire and water, but you brought us to a place of abundance.*

**PSALM 66:10–12**

In yesterday's devotion, I wrote about the tests we face, and I want to look at them from a different perspective today. Sometimes we go through very difficult situations and don't understand why. We look for reasons, such as "Did I do something wrong? Is God angry with me?" But more often than not, our faith is simply being tested.

First Peter 4:12 says, "Dear friends, do not be surprised at the fiery ordeal that has come on you to test you, as though something strange were happening to you."

Focusing on passing our tests is much better than trying to figure out our difficulties. The psalmist described how he felt during a test that appears to have been painful, but let's not forget the end of the story: "But you brought us to a place of abundance."

God often tests us in order to promote us. Schoolchildren don't move to the next grade without passing exams to ensure that they have learned what they were supposed to learn in their current grade. Students sometimes fail, but with God we never fail. We simply get to keep taking the test over and over until we pass it.

For example, God may be trying to teach us not to be easily offended, and people keep offending us. We pray for them to stop, but God would rather teach us to become strong enough in our faith not to take the offense and to forgive quickly.

Trust God during times of testing, knowing that He will bring you into a place of abundance.

*Father, help me pass my tests so I can grow and become stronger in my faith. I trust that You will always bless me in the end.*

# A KEY TO ANSWERED PRAYER

*If I had cherished sin in my heart, the Lord would not have listened.*

**PSALM 66:18**

We know that God answers prayer, but sometimes our prayers seem to go unanswered and we do not understand why. This can happen when there is hidden sin in our lives, which is what the psalmist is talking about when he says, "If I had cherished sin in my heart." To explain this verse, let me simply say that the Lord will not hear us when we pray if we come before Him in prayer with sin hidden in our hearts.

If there is sin in our lives, we will not be able to pray boldly or with confidence. When we pray, if we sense that we are not comfortable, we need to stop and ask God why. We also need to ask Him to reveal anything hidden. If He convicts us of something that is sinful, we should call it what it is: sin. According to Romans 3:23, everyone sins, and when we do, God wants us to confess our sin so He may cleanse us and restore a clean conscience in our hearts (1 John 1:9). There is power in truth and honesty when we come clean before the Lord and receive His forgiveness. This enables us to pray effectively.

Make sure your heart is pure before Him so your prayers are offered confidently and in active faith. God answers our prayers when we approach Him with boldness and with clean, pure hearts.

*Lord, reveal any hidden sin in my life so my relationship with You may be restored and my prayers will be effective.*

# GOD IS GRACIOUS

*May God be gracious to us and bless us and make his face shine on us.*
**PSALM 67:1**

The psalmist was not shy about asking God to bless him. In some churches, services conclude with what is called a benediction, and today's scripture is part of some of the early benedictions.

To be *gracious* means to give grace, and grace is God's undeserved favor. Grace also refers to the power of the Holy Spirit helping us do what we need to do with ease.

When we ask God to make His face shine upon us, we are asking Him to bless us with His presence, and being in His presence is one of the greatest blessings we can have. David said that the one thing he would seek would be to dwell in the presence of God (Psalm 27:4).

Perhaps you haven't been taught to boldly ask for God's blessings, or you don't think you deserve them. Remember that grace, or God's graciousness, is *undeserved* favor. That is what makes it so wonderful. Not one of us can be good enough to deserve anything from God, but in Jesus' name, we can ask boldly and receive what we ask for.

*Father, I ask You to bless me and those I love, to be gracious to us, and to make Your face shine on us. Thank You.*

# GOD, OUR GOD, BLESSES US

*The land yields its harvest; God, our God, blesses us. May God bless us still, so that all the ends of the earth will fear him.*

**PSALM 67:6-7**

It is important for the unbelievers in the world to see God's blessings in the lives of His people, because it lets them know that He is good and that He blesses those who belong to Him. Seeing His blessings will cause those who do not know Him to have a reverential fear and awe of Him and may lead them to surrender their lives to Him.

This doesn't mean that believers in Jesus don't have problems, because we do. Unbelievers see our struggles and notice how we handle those problems, and this is important. We should remain steady, be at peace, and be joyful through hard times. Our confession should remain consistent, and when people ask why we are having troubles, we can tell them that although we do have difficulties in life, God delivers us out of them all.

People who try to live without God are fools, according to Psalm 14:1. They can have nothing but misery. They have no help except human help when they suffer, and human help rarely, if ever, does much good.

Let your life be a witness to others that God is good and say with the psalmist, "God blesses us, may God bless us still."

*Father, I want my life to be a witness to the lost. Let Your blessings be on me, and when I do have trouble, deliver me speedily and grant me grace to behave in a godly way while I am going through it.*

# LET MY ENEMIES
# BE SCATTERED

*May God arise, may his enemies be scattered; may his foes flee before him. May you blow them away like smoke—as wax melts before the fire, may the wicked perish before God. But may the righteous be glad and rejoice before God; may they be happy and joyful.*

**PSALM 68:1–3**

God is patient and long-suffering even with our enemies some-times because He is trying to deal with them and bring them to repentance. This is why He teaches us to forgive them and pray for them. But there does come a time when He arises and says, "That's enough," and He scatters our enemies.

The psalmist David had a strong faith that God would deliver him from his enemies, and he wasn't shy about asking God to deal harshly with them. We must remember that under the Old Covenant, the norm was an eye-for-an-eye mentality (Leviticus 24:20), and David prayed what could be considered harsh prayers about God dealing with his enemies, prayers that are not sug-gested or proper under the New Covenant (Matthew 5:38–42).

David prayed that God would blow his enemies away like smoke and let them perish. But Jesus teaches us to love our ene-mies and pray for them (Matthew 5:44). When we do, God still deals with them if they won't listen to Him, but our prayers give Him an opportunity to work in their life, hopefully bringing them to see the truth and surrender their lives to Him.

The important point to remember is that God will always deliver us from our enemies at the proper time. Our job, mean-while, is to keep doing what He asks us to do.

*Father, I know that You will arise and scatter my enemies if they will not listen to You, but I pray that they will come to know the truth and surrender their lives to You.*

# GOD HELPS THE LONELY

*A father to the fatherless, a defender of widows, is God in his holy dwelling. God sets the lonely in families, he leads out the prisoners with singing; but the rebellious live in a sun-scorched land.*

**PSALM 68:5-6**

Most of us have felt lonely at some time in our lives. A person can be lonely and not be alone. You might feel rejected or misunderstood; you could even feel invisible and think no one notices your talents and abilities. I believe Jesus felt lonely in the Garden of Gethsemane when He asked His disciples to pray with Him for only one hour and they all fell asleep (Matthew 26:36–46).

God has a special place in His heart for the lonely. Frequently in the Bible, we see the instruction to help the fatherless, orphans, and widows. In Exodus 22:22, God says, "Do not take advantage of the widow or the fatherless." God also instructs us to reach out to and not mistreat strangers (Exodus 22:21). We have all been in new places where we didn't know anyone, and these are lonely times in life.

I encourage you to look for the people in your church, neighborhood, or workplace who are lonely. Look for the single woman who has never been married and has no family. Look for the widow or widower; look for the children or youth who have no fathers. Reach out to these people. Invite them to your home on holidays. Take one of them out to eat with your family, or take the young man who has no relationship with his father to a ball game. You can ease someone's loneliness simply by including them.

*Father, help me notice people who are lonely and reach out to them in friendship. Show me ways I can help ease their loneliness.*

# HELP FOR THE WEARY

*I am worn out calling for help; my throat is parched. My eyes fail, looking for my God. Those who hate me without reason outnumber the hairs of my head; many are my enemies without cause, those who seek to destroy me.*

**PSALM 69:3-4**

Clearly, David the psalmist was weary when he penned the words of today's scripture. He actually says, "I am worn out." All kinds of situations can drain our physical and emotional resources, and too much stress over a long period of time definitely causes weariness.

When we are weary, we need our strength restored, and the Bible says that God will help us: "But those who hope in the Lord will renew their strength. They will soar on wings like eagles; they will run and not grow weary, they will walk and not be faint" (Isaiah 40:31).

I believe we can make ourselves weary through the way we think and talk about the situations we face in life. No doubt, some of them are draining because of all they demand from us, but we can make them better or worse with our thoughts and words.

The Holy Spirit is available to help, strengthen, and restore us. He will not help us complain or be negative about the pressures we face, but He will help us think and speak about them according to God's Word. He will give us wisdom to deal with our problems effectively. He will give us grace and make things easier than they would otherwise be. He will strengthen us in faith, and He will help us hope in the Lord, which, according to Isaiah 40:31, is where we will renew our strength.

*Lord, when I am weary, give me the grace to hope in You, trusting You to renew my strength.*

# BREAK THE POWER
# OF CONFUSION

*Because for Your sake I have borne reproach; confusion and dishonor
have covered my face.*

**PSALM 69:7 AMP**

In today's scripture, David mentions confusion, and I think many
people can relate to this. One way the enemy likes to prevent
us from moving forward in all that God has for us is to keep us
confused. He knows that if we don't know what to do, we may
not do anything.

One way to describe confusion is being double-minded,
meaning that we think one thing, and then we think something
else. Double-minded people simply cannot make up their mind,
and they second-guess themselves, so they stay stuck in indecision
and confusion.

One way to stop being confused is to weigh all your options,
identify the potential positives and negatives about each one, and
make the best decision you can make. Make sure the decision
agrees with God's Word, and check to see if you have peace in
your heart about it, because God does lead us through peace. As
you move forward, you will know whether your decision was a
good one or not. If not, make a change and keep moving ahead.

*Lord, I pray that confusion will not keep me from moving ahead
in Your plans for my life. Help me not to be double-minded or
indecisive, but to seek You and trust You to guide me in every
situation.*

# THE CONFIDENCE TO ASK FOR A QUICK ANSWER

*Answer me, Lord, out of the goodness of your love; in your great mercy turn to me. Do not hide your face from your servant; answer me quickly, for I am in trouble.*

**PSALM 69:16–17**

We want our answers and breakthroughs to come quickly, but the psalmist David had enough confidence to do more than wish for a speedy reply; he actually asked God to answer him quickly, saying, "Answer me quickly, for I am in trouble." Most of us could speak these words often, and we probably should. The Amplified Bible translation of Philippians 4:6 says that instead of worrying and being anxious, we should pray "specific requests." Perhaps sometimes we are not specific enough about what we want.

I am not suggesting that we can make God hurry, but I do find David's prayer interesting, and I, for one, am going to give it a try in the future. God's timing will still be perfect, but since we have not because we ask not (James 4:2), why not ask boldly? God answers us because of His goodness, love, and great mercy.

We should never say, "Well, I guess there's nothing left to do but pray," because prayer should always be the first thing we do. It is not a last resort but our first line of defense. David was a man of prayer, and we should be people of prayer also. God can do more in one moment than we can do in a lifetime.

*Father, help me quickly, for I am in trouble. I need You all the time, and I ask for Your presence in my life. Answer my prayers when I call on You. Thank You.*

# HELP FOR THE POOR AND NEEDY

*The poor will see and be glad—you who seek God, may your hearts live! The Lord hears the needy and does not despise his captive people.*
**PSALM 69:32–33**

Today's verses are good news for anyone who is dealing with lack. We can be poor and needy in many ways: financially, physically, socially, spiritually, or emotionally. But the good news is that Jesus can heal us everywhere we hurt. And He says in John 16:24, "Ask and you will receive, and your joy will be complete."

Seek God for any need you have. Don't just try to fix situations yourself or run to other people for help; go to God. Go to the source of all good things. Your prayer is powerful, even if you have not done everything right. When we pray, God answers us without reproach or faultfinding (James 1:5 AMPC). He understands our weaknesses, and we can go boldly to the throne of grace and receive help in plenty of time to meet our need (Hebrews 4:15–16).

God has a special place in His heart for the poor and needy, and He will hear and answer you. He even promises that you will see victory and be glad. Stay full of hope and expectation, because He has heard your prayer, and your answer is on the way.

*Father, thank You that You care for the poor and needy and You make them glad. Your goodness is more than I deserve, but I boldly ask for it in Jesus' name.*

# GOD'S SAVING GRACE

*Hasten, O God, to save me; come quickly, Lord, to help me. May those who want to take my life be put to shame and confusion; may all who desire my ruin be turned back in disgrace.*

**PSALM 70:1–2**

Scripture states over and over that God will deal with our enemies, so why do we waste our time in anger and seeking revenge? We don't even need to worry about our enemies. All we need to do is pray as David did—straightforward, bold prayers for God to help us and deliver us from them. In order to receive answers to this kind of prayer, we must cast our anxiety on God and let Him take care of us (1 Peter 5:7).

We cannot pray for God to take care of us and expect Him to do it while we have anger hidden in our hearts. But if we will forgive our enemies and pray for them as God instructs us to, we can depend on Him to bring our enemies to their knees and be ashamed of what they attempted to do to us.

God loves His children tenderly, and He does not take it lightly when anyone comes against them, especially if it happens with no cause. If you have enemies or are dealing with people who have hurt you without cause, you can rest assured that God will deal with them, and He'll lift you up and make your life joyful. Trust in the Lord, for He is good, and He is waiting to be good to you.

*Father, I release my enemies to You, and I wait on You for vindication. Help me quickly, Lord, and restore my joy.*

# PRAISE AND GRATITUDE

*From birth I have relied on you; you brought me forth from my mother's womb. I will ever praise you.*

**PSALM 71:6**

In today's scripture, the psalmist encourages us to praise God continually. Once we seriously start praising Him, our burdens and our troubles seem to weigh less heavily on us. This is part of the power of being thankful. As we give thanks to God for what's good in our lives, it helps us not to focus excessively on our problems. I believe God wants us to be grateful people, filled with gratitude not only toward God, but also toward others.

When someone does something nice for you, let that person know you appreciate them and what they did. Have you ever thanked the people who pick up your trash? The last time you ate at a restaurant, did you thank the server for filling your coffee cup? I could go on and on, but that's my point: We need to develop an attitude of gratitude toward the people in our lives.

Another way to express gratitude is to show appreciation toward your family members, especially your spouse. I appreciate Dave, and even though we've been married a long time, I still tell him I appreciate him. He's patient with me, and he is thoughtful.

Just a few words of thanks are a great way to bless God and others. When you express appreciation, it's good for the other person to hear it, but remember that it also releases joy in you. You enrich both your life and another person's life when you show gratitude for anything, big or small.

*Lord, I desire to have a thankful and praise-filled heart. Holy Spirit, I ask You to remind me every day of what I need to be grateful for.*

# YOU WILL ALWAYS
# HAVE HOPE

*As for me, I will always have hope; I will praise you more and more.*
**PSALM 71:14**

The psalmist says, "I will always have hope," and we can always have hope too. We can learn a lot about hope by looking at God's creation, and when I think of today's scripture, it reminds me of the rivers He has made. Like a river that never runs dry, hope continues to flow to those who belong to God. We can never exhaust it. God has an unending supply of hope for those who trust in Him. Because God is eternal, hope in Him is also eternal. Every day of your life, you can go to Him and He will give you fresh hope, just as fresh water flows in a beautiful river.

Proverbs 23:18 echoes Psalm 71:14, saying: "There is surely a future hope for you, and your hope will not be cut off." If your hope is in anyone or anything other than God, chances are that it will dry up. There will come a time when you can no longer find hope in it. But with God, you will always have hope, and as the psalmist says in today's verse, that's a reason to praise Him more and more.

*Thank You, God, that because I am Yours, I will **always** have hope. I praise You!*

# PRAISE GOD FOR HIS RIGHTEOUS DEEDS

*My mouth will tell of your righteous deeds, of your saving acts all day long—though I know not how to relate them all. I will come and proclaim your mighty acts, Sovereign Lord; I will proclaim your righteous deeds, yours alone.*

**PSALM 71:15-16**

What would happen if we replaced all complaining and murmuring with praise to God? I believe amazing things would take place. It is difficult to get through one day without complaining, let alone a lifetime. God wants to hear our praise, not our report on all the negative things we feel are happening to us.

We can purpose to look for all the good things God has done and is doing in our lives and talk about them. We can rehearse them to God when talking with Him and telling others of them. Our prayers should not only be about asking God for something; they should also be filled with praise and thanksgiving for all that He has already done.

Philippians 4:6 teaches us to pray *with thanksgiving*. If we are complainers, we will only keep complaining, even if God gives us something we are asking for. Let's learn to praise God even in the midst of our troubles, for that is when praise is most powerful. If we cannot praise Him in the valleys of life, then we won't praise Him on the mountaintops either. God is good all the time, not just when we like our circumstances. Let's tell of His mighty deeds and His saving acts.

*Father, You are righteous and You do righteous acts. I praise You for all Your goodness to me. I want my mouth to be filled with gratitude, not complaints. Please help me. Thank You.*

# ENVY

*Surely God is good to Israel, to those who are pure in heart. But as for me, my feet had almost slipped; I had nearly lost my foothold. For I envied the arrogant when I saw the prosperity of the wicked.*

**PSALM 73:1-3**

In Psalm 73, the psalmist Asaph was beginning to feel as though he had served God in vain, because the wicked seemed to fare better than he did. He said they have no struggles, their bodies are healthy and strong, and they have no burdens (vv. 4–5).

He also said that even though he had kept his heart pure and washed his hands in innocence, he had been afflicted and that every morning brought new punishments (vv. 13–14). It sounds like Asaph was not having a very good day! He was focusing on his problems and the final destination of the wicked without considering God's faithfulness to him.

He finally saw the light and realized that saying everything he thought would not have been good (v. 15). When his heart was grieved and his spirit was embittered, he said he was "senseless and ignorant," like a "brute beast" before God (vv. 21–22). He was repentant and realized that he was much better off than the wicked even though their circumstances seemed better than his did. He remembered that God was always with him, holding his hand (v. 23).

*Father, when I am tempted to envy the wicked, help me remember that no matter how many material goods they have, I am more blessed than they are because I have You.*

# WE DON'T NEED
# TO BE JEALOUS

*This is what the wicked are like—always free of care, they go on amassing wealth.*

PSALM 73:12

We can almost feel the jealousy in today's scripture as the psalmist Asaph writes about the wicked. We may be surprised to realize that people in Old Testament times struggled with jealousy for some of the same reasons we wrestle with it today—other people's seemingly easy, carefree lives and their financial blessings.

Jealousy "rots the bones," according to Proverbs 14:30. This is a strong statement and one that I don't want to be a victim of. Anytime you feel jealous or envious, the best course of action is to go to God quickly and ask Him to help and comfort you regarding the situation. Ask Him to show you how blessed you are and help you understand that you have no real reason to be jealous. God has a unique plan for each of us, and it is the very best plan for us. Don't compare yourself, your life, or your problems with anyone else's.

If we can trust God and know that He will give us what is right for us, then we don't need to be jealous of anyone else. I don't want anything God doesn't want me to have, and neither should you.

*Lord Jesus, I don't want to live with jealousy, comparing myself to others. Help me to discover the individual plan you have for me and work with You to become the best person You have created me to be.*

# WHEN YOU DON'T KNOW WHAT TO DO

*You guide me with your counsel, and afterward you will take me into glory.*

**PSALM 73:24**

Needing to make a decision and not knowing what to do can easily lead to confusion, which is not from God (1 Corinthians 14:33 NKJV). Proverbs 3:5 says we are not to lean on our own understanding but to trust the Lord with all our heart and mind (AMPC).

If we trust God with our mind, then our thoughts will be filled with hope, not frustration. Proverbs 3:6 goes on to say, "In all your ways know, recognize, and acknowledge Him, and He will direct and make straight and plain your paths" (AMPC).

During times of indecision, try to quiet your mind and see what is in your heart, because that is where you'll find your true desire and passion. After praying and waiting on God, you may have to step out to find out what you are to do. Sometimes the only way to know is to move toward something and see if God opens the door and you have peace about it. If not, at least you have learned what *not* to do. Many people do not know what the right thing is until they see what fits and what they like.

Another thing that helps is considering everything involved in what you are thinking about doing. You may want a new car, but if you don't want to make payments every month for several years, making the purchase is not wise.

*Father, I want to make decisions that put me in the center of Your will. Help me and guide me each step of the way. Help me not to be so afraid of doing the wrong thing that I end up doing nothing.*

# DESIRE GOD MORE THAN ANYTHING

*Whom have I in heaven but you? And earth has nothing I desire besides you. My flesh and my heart may fail, but God is the strength of my heart and my portion forever.*

**PSALM 73:25-26**

Have you ever known anyone whose main goal in life seemed to be the pursuit of the things this world offers, perhaps money, designer clothes, a nice home, a sporty car, or the latest electronic devices? I am talking about a person whose primary focus is accumulating things, one who puts all their time and energy into worldly possessions and spends no time developing a relationship with God or meaningful relationships with other people. Individuals who seek the things of the world more than anything else end up lonely and sad. The very things they think will fulfill them actually leave them feeling empty.

Though the psalmist Asaph lived centuries ago, before sports cars and electronic devices, people in his day also sought worldly goods over relationship with God. Perhaps this is why he felt compelled to write to God in today's scripture that "earth has nothing I desire besides you."

Nothing in this world compares to knowing God and living in intimate relationship with Him. No matter what you choose to pursue and value in your life today, pursue Him first and value Him most. He is all you need, and you will find your greatest fulfillment in Him.

*Help me, Lord, to focus on growing in my relationship with You more than on acquiring the things this world offers. Like Asaph, I desire nothing on earth more than I desire You.*

# IT'S OKAY NOT TO BE OKAY

*O God, why have you rejected us forever? Why does your anger smolder against the sheep of your pasture? Remember the nation you purchased long ago, the people of your inheritance, whom you redeemed—Mount Zion, where you dwelt.*

**PSALM 74:1–2**

Today's scripture gives us the impression that the psalmist Asaph isn't having a very good day, and that's okay. Every day of life isn't perfect, and there are times when it is good to be honest with God or someone else about the way you feel. Most of the time, if one Christian asks another how they are, the answer is "Fine," but they are not always fine. They say they are fine, because they think they are expected, as Christians, to be fine all the time. Asaph felt as though God was rejecting him forever and that He was angry with him, and he wrote about it.

We should not complain constantly, but there is a way to be honest about how we are feeling without being negative. Trust God always, but don't be phony or pretend to be fine when the truth is that you aren't fine at all.

Sometimes the best way to rid yourself of negative feelings is to talk them out. The psalmist David did this regularly with God, and it was okay. He was also a man of great faith. Don't feel that you always have to be fine, marvelous, amazing, and wonderful, or that you cannot admit when you are having a rough time and your emotions are not joyful. Even Jesus said, "My God, my God, why have you forsaken me?" (Matthew 27:46). He also said, "Into your hands I commit my spirit" (Luke 23:46). Even though He felt forsaken, He knew that He wasn't.

*Father, I am grateful that I can always be honest with You about how I feel, yet at the same time never stop trusting You.*

# GOD ALWAYS PROVIDES

*It was you who split open the sea by your power; you broke the heads of the monster in the waters. It was you who crushed the heads of Leviathan and gave it as food to the creatures of the desert. It was you who opened up springs and streams; you dried up the ever-flowing rivers.*

**PSALM 74:13–15**

In today's scriptures, the psalmist Asaph writes of God's great power and provision. He notes that God even fed Leviathan (a symbol of Israel's enemies) to the animals of the desert. Asaph had admitted earlier in this psalm that he felt forsaken, but now writes of God's mighty power and goodness. God parted the Red Sea and let the Israelites cross over unharmed, yet He drowned the Egyptians in the same sea. He provided for the Israelites in the wilderness in miraculous ways, and He will also provide for you and me.

When you are tempted to sin, He will provide a way out of temptation (1 Corinthians 10:13). And according to 2 Corinthians 9:8, He will provide all that you need: "And God is able to bless you abundantly, so that in all things at all times, having all that you need, you will abound in every good work."

God also provides forgiveness for our sins: "You, Lord, are forgiving and good, abounding in love to all who call to you" (Psalm 86:5). And He also promises to give us strength when we need it (Psalm 138:3; Isaiah 40:31). He says to "ask, and you will receive, that your joy may be full" (John 16:24 NKJV).

*Father, it is so good to know that Your provision is waiting for me in all areas of my life and that all I need to do is ask and receive it by faith. Thank You.*

# TALK ABOUT WHAT
# GOD HAS DONE

*We praise you, God, we praise you, for your Name is near; people tell of your wonderful deeds.*

**PSALM 75:1**

When you get together with others, perhaps for a family gathering or lunch or coffee with friends, what do you talk about? Would anyone refer to you as the type of person mentioned in today's scripture, one who tells of God's "wonderful deeds"? You always have a choice regarding what to talk about, and you can choose to speak words that encourage others and glorify God or words that cause others to feel deflated and that do not honor God. Telling others what God has done will strengthen and encourage them, and it is a way to give God praise.

Consider making a list of everything God has done for you. It should be a long list that includes not only the big things He has done in your life, but the seemingly smaller blessings too, because those matter a lot. Making such a list will help you achieve a new level of contentment in your life and help you to be very thankful. It will probably also amaze you! In addition, it will give you something to talk about next time you spend time with people you love.

*Help me, Lord, to be a person who tells others about what You have done and are doing in my life. I want my words to give You praise.*

# DO NOT BOAST

*To the arrogant I say, "Boast no more."*

PSALM 75:4

God's Word warns us of the dangers of pride. Pride is what causes us to boast about our own accomplishments when we should be thanking God and giving Him glory. We are to humble ourselves under God's mighty hand, and in due time He will lift us up (1 Peter 5:6).

The apostle James writes, "As it is, you boast in your arrogant schemes. All such boasting is evil" (James 4:16). We should let others praise us and not praise ourselves (Proverbs 27:2).

When someone compliments you, receive it graciously and thank them, but at the end of the day take all the compliments you receive and offer them to God, telling Him that you know you can do nothing good without His help.

Remembering that we are nothing without Jesus is the best way to keep from boasting and taking credit that belongs to God. Anything we can do that is worthy of praise is only because we have received it from God.

I once heard that it is yet to be seen what God could do through a man or woman who would give Him all the glory. If people compliment you often because of some skill or talent you have, be sure to remember that God is the One who gave it to you. If you do, then you will be able to keep it and perhaps even see it increase.

*Father, thank You for each ability You have given me. Any compliment I receive, I now give it back to You, because I know I can do nothing apart from You.*

# HOW TO RESPOND WHEN YOU ARE JUDGED CRITICALLY

*It is God who judges: He brings one down, he exalts another.*

**PSALM 75:7**

People judged the apostle Paul concerning his faithfulness. Apparently, some people thought he had not been faithful, but Paul was not the least bit disturbed by their opinions. He said, "I care very little if I am judged by you or by any human court; indeed, I do not even judge myself. My conscience is clear, but that does not make me innocent. It is the Lord who judges me" (1 Corinthians 4:3–4).

Prayerfully, we can all get to the place where Paul was, so that when we are judged we won't worry about it or let it steal our peace. We waste much time being overly concerned about what other people think of us or trying to defend ourselves. Paul did neither; he simply trusted God to take care of his reputation.

Jesus was certainly not concerned about His reputation. He was frequently judged by those who had no understanding of who He was or what He had come to earth to do, but He didn't waste His time being upset by it, nor did He ever try to defend Himself. He knew that God was His defense and Vindicator, and He is ours also.

*Father, I love You, and I thank You that You are my defender and Vindicator. I trust You to take care of my reputation.*

# GOD SAVES THE AFFLICTED

*The land feared and was quiet—when you, God, rose up to judge, to save all the afflicted of the land.*

**PSALM 76:8–9**

God loves His children, and the time will come when He will judge those who mistreat and afflict them. According to today's scripture, God saves the afflicted. Sometimes He waits longer than we can understand, but I believe that is because He is trying to deal with those who mistreat others and bring them to repentance. If they continue to refuse to repent and keep oppressing and afflicting God's children, He will eventually pronounce judgment on them.

All people should have a reverential fear of God. Although He is kind, there are also times when He is severe in how He deals with people. Romans 11:22 says, "Note then the kindness and the severity of God: severity toward those who have fallen, but God's kindness to you, provided you continue in his kindness. Otherwise you too will be cut off" (ESV).

We love to think of the kindness of God, and kindness is His nature, but because He is also just, the time will come when He will deal severely with those who continue in disobedience. He does it for their own good, hoping that because kindness didn't get their attention and inspire them to change, severity will. We should diligently pray for people who are repeatedly disobedient to God and who mistreat, oppress, and afflict others. Pray for them to see the light concerning their behavior and that they will repent, be forgiven of their sin, and learn to treat people according to God's will.

*Father, I pray for all those who afflict Your children, and I ask that You deal with them in such a way that they will repent and be saved.*

# SEEK GOD WHEN YOU NEED HELP

*I cried out to God for help; I cried out to God to hear me. When I was in distress, I sought the Lord; at night I stretched out untiring hands, and I would not be comforted.*

**PSALM 77:1-2**

Matthew 7:7 says, "Ask and keep on asking and it will be given to you; seek and keep on seeking and you will find; knock and keep on knocking and the door will be opened to you" (AMP).

The words of today's scripture indicate to me that the psalmist Asaph is refusing to give up. He says he will not be comforted until God helps him. Others in the Bible had this same attitude. Abraham persisted in prayer for Sodom (Genesis 18:16–33), Moses persisted in prayer for the Israelites (Exodus 32:11–13), and Hannah was persistent in prayer for a son (1 Samuel 1:9–18). God likes it when we refuse to give up. I prayed for my father's salvation for more than forty years, and three years before he passed away, he received Christ, and Dave and I had the privilege of baptizing him.

Jesus told His disciples that "they should always pray and not give up" (Luke 18:1). The apostle Paul also encourages us to persist, saying that we should not grow weary in doing good (Galatians 6:9). It is not the person who does what is right once or twice that becomes victorious, but the ones who believe His Word and persevere in living their lives according to it.

If you are at a place where you feel like giving up on something or someone, be encouraged to be persistent. You will reap if you don't faint and give up.

*Father, thank You for reminding me to be persistent. There are times when I grow weary and feel like giving up, but with Your help I will persevere until I see victory. Amen.*

# WHEN YOU HAVE A BAD DAY

*Will the Lord reject forever? Will he never show his favor again?...Has God forgotten to be merciful? Has he in anger withheld his compassion?*
**PSALM 77:7, 9**

Today's scriptures sound to me as though the psalmist was not having a great day. He was very bold and honest with God about how he felt. However, if you read the rest of Psalm 77, you will find that right after he asks these hopeless-sounding questions, he begins to remember the deeds of the Lord and His miracles of long ago. He considers all His works and meditates on His mighty deeds (77:10–12).

We can easily see from this that the answer to a bad day is to remember the good things God has done for you in the past. I think we often remember what we should forget and forget what we should remember. We forget how good God has been and all the times He has brought us through difficulties in the past, and we remember the prayers we think He hasn't answered, the difficulties we face that we don't understand, and the situations we think are not fair.

I encourage you today to be honest with God about how you feel, but lavishly praise Him for all the good things He has done in your life. And remember that if He did it once, He can do it again. Your breakthrough is on its way, so don't despair. Remember the good things, and more good things will follow.

*Father, I may be going through a hard time right now, but I know that You are faithful and that You will bring me through it and give me victory.*

# GOD WORKS THROUGH PEOPLE

*You led your people like a flock by the hand of Moses and Aaron.*

**PSALM 77:20**

God led the Israelites out of Egypt and through the wilderness to the Promised Land, but He did it through Moses and Aaron. God works through people—not necessarily through special, qualified, gifted people, but through available people. We should make ourselves available for God to use us in the lives of others and be open to those God sends to help us.

If you think you are not qualified for God to use you, just look at some of the people He used in the stories of the Bible. David was a shepherd; Rahab was a harlot; Ruth was a former worshipper of a foreign god; Jacob was a trickster, a schemer, and a liar; the disciples included fishermen, a tax collector, and a doctor. These were ordinary, flawed people just like you and me. And as they are examples to us, we can be examples of how God's strength is made perfect in our weaknesses (2 Corinthians 12:9).

Always remember that God can use the most unlikely person to speak a timely word to you or to help you when you need it. He even used a donkey to speak to a prophet (Numbers 22:28).

Pride can cause us to miss a word from God or even a miracle, as happened to a man named Naaman, whose story is in 2 Kings 5:1–19. I hope you will always be humble enough to accept whomever God sends to minister to you and also keep your heart open to being used by God in any way He wants to use you to bless others.

*Father, I want You to use me, and I want to receive from whomever You send to help me. Help me not to let pride cause me to miss my miracle. Amen.*

# HOW TO GET WHERE GOD WANTS TO TAKE YOU

*Then they would put their trust in God and would not forget his deeds but would keep his commands. They would not be like their ancestors—a stubborn and rebellious generation, whose hearts were not loyal to God, whose spirits were not faithful to him.*

**PSALM 78:7-8**

Despite God's continual gracious and miraculous provision for the Israelites as they traveled through the wilderness to the Promised Land, today's scripture tells us that they were very stubborn and rebellious. I define *stubborn* as obstinate or difficult to handle or work with, and *rebellious* as resisting control or correction, unruly, or refusing to follow ordinary guidelines. These two negative attitudes caused almost all the Israelites to die in the wilderness instead of completing the journey to the Promised Land (Numbers 26:65).

This same cycle is repeated and recorded many times in the Old Testament, and we can repeat it in our own lives if we insist upon being stubborn and rebellious. God has many blessings in store for us, just as He had good things in store for the Israelites in the Promised Land. To enjoy all the blessings He wants to pour out in our lives, we need to learn to give up our own ways and be pliable and moldable in His hands. As long as we are stubborn and rebellious, we will remain in the wilderness of stubbornness and rebellion and stay outside of the good things He wants to give us. He has great promises for you, promises He longs to see fulfilled in your life.

Let Him do a thorough work of humility and adaptability to His will in you so that you can leave your "wilderness" behind and enter your Promised Land.

*Help me, Lord, to be humble before You, eager to adapt to Your ways instead of stubbornly demanding my way.*

# THOUGHTS LEAD
# TO ATTITUDES

*But they continued to sin against him, rebelling in the wilderness against the Most High.*

**PSALM 78:17**

If you read all of Psalm 78, you will see that the Israelites had a bad attitude as they made their journey through the wilderness toward the Promised Land. I am certain that their bad attitudes started with negative thoughts. Thoughts lead to words, and words lead to emotional moods, attitudes, and actions. We know that the Israelites' bad attitudes caused them to complain and speak negatively to and about their leaders, Moses and Aaron, which ultimately led to total rebellion.

We are wise to remember that our thoughts are the raw materials for our attitudes. If we think loving thoughts toward people, we will have an attitude of love toward them, and we will speak kindly and lovingly toward them. We will also express our love for them through our actions. This example of love and kindness is positive, but the same principle applies to negative thoughts, words, and attitudes.

In any situation, you can have a good attitude or a bad one, and it will begin with your thoughts. Choose positive thoughts today!

*Lord, help me choose to think godly thoughts so I will have godly attitudes.*

# GRACE FOR EACH DAY

*Yet he gave a command to the skies above and opened the doors of the heavens; he rained down manna for the people to eat, he gave them the grain of heaven.*

**PSALM 78:23–24**

Today's scriptures mention that God fed the Israelites manna, but it doesn't mention that every morning He gave them only enough for one day, except for on the sixth day, when He sent a double portion of manna to provide for the Sabbath. We know this from Exodus 16:4–5, and it teaches us one of the ways of God—that He gives us what we need each day and asks us not to worry about the next day.

Jesus says: "Therefore do not worry about tomorrow, for tomorrow will worry about itself. Each day has enough trouble of its own" (Matthew 6:34). This is true, but each day also has its own grace and mercy. Lamentations 3:22–23 declares: "The steadfast love of the Lord never ceases; his mercies never come to an end; they are new every morning; great is your faithfulness" (ESV).

When God gave the Israelites just enough manna for each day, it was His way of teaching them to trust Him. He wanted to test them to see if they would obey His instruction not to gather more than they needed each day. He wants you and me, like the Israelites, to trust Him to provide what we need when we need it—and not to worry about tomorrow.

*Lord, I choose to trust You for all the grace I need today. Help me not to look too far ahead but to rely on You to give me exactly what I need each day.*

# GOD MAKES ALLOWANCES FOR OUR WEAKNESSES

*Their hearts were not loyal to him, they were not faithful to his covenant. Yet he was merciful; he forgave their iniquities and did not destroy them. Time after time he restrained his anger and did not stir up his full wrath. He remembered that they were but flesh.*

**PSALM 78:37-39**

If you are feeling guilty about something you've done wrong, let today's scriptures sink deep into your soul. God is merciful, and He forgives us even though we don't deserve to be forgiven. I love the statement that God remembers that we are "but flesh." He knows we have weaknesses, and He understands them. Of course, He expects us to admit and repent of our sins, and when we do, He extends His mercy. Receive mercy and forgiveness right now if you need it.

God loves you at this very moment, no matter who you are or what you have done. He may not like everything you do, but He never stops loving you. Let God's love heal your brokenness. Receive it freely as a gift and be thankful for it. One way you can show your gratitude is to extend to others the same mercy and forgiveness God gives to you.

*Father, thank You for Your mercy and forgiveness. Help me also to be merciful and quick to forgive.*

# THE POWER OF THE BLOOD

*He struck down all the firstborn of Egypt...But he brought his people out like a flock; he led them like sheep through the wilderness.*

**PSALM 78:51-52**

Just before God miraculously delivered the Israelites from their four hundred years of bondage in Egypt, an angel swept through the nation of Egypt and smote their firstborn. The only way for a family to escape this loss was to sprinkle the blood of a lamb on the side posts and tops of their doorframes (Exodus 12:1–7, 12–13). When God saw the blood, the angel of death passed over that household and no plague came on the people living there.

Jesus is called the Lamb of God (John 1:29; 1 Corinthians 5:7), and He shed His blood at Calvary. When we receive Him as Lord and Savior, we also receive the benefits His blood purchased on our behalf—cleansing, healing, protection, deliverance, and much more. We are spared from spiritual death and receive eternal life. We can thank God each day that the blood of His Son has been applied to us and say by faith: "I believe the power of Jesus' blood covers my home, my family, my physical body, and all that pertains to me."

*Thank You, Jesus, for shedding Your precious blood and for all the benefits that belong to me because of it.*

# THE POWER OF PRAISE

*Then we your people, the sheep of your pasture, will praise you forever;
from generation to generation we will proclaim your praise.*

**PSALM 79:13**

Praising and thanking God is one of the most powerful things we can do. Our praise helps us defeat the devil. He wants us to blame God for our problems and to murmur and complain about our lives, and when we do this, it weakens us. However, we can overcome evil with good (Romans 12:21). We confuse the devil when he launches an attack against us and we meet the attack head-on with praise and gratitude for God's goodness.

Whatever you might have to be upset about today, you have more to be thankful for. Praise God for His goodness, and teach the generation you are training to do the same. God wants us to educate our children and grandchildren about how to walk with Him. We can do this with our words, but we can do it more effectively through our example.

*Father, I have so much to be thankful for, and I repent for all the
times I have complained instead of offering You the sacrifice of
praise. Help me be a good example to all those around me as
I praise You at all times, in every situation.*

# GOD CAN FIX ANYTHING THAT IS BROKEN

*Restore us, O God; make your face shine on us, that we may be saved.*
**PSALM 80:3**

Is anything broken in your life—perhaps your marriage, a relationship with a child, your finances, your health, or your self-image? God is a God of restoration, which means He can take anything broken and make it like new.

It is never too late for God to work in your life. All you need to do is ask Him to do it and be willing to follow His guidance and direction. God said through Jeremiah, "But I will restore you to health and heal your wounds…because you are called an outcast, Zion for whom no one cares" (Jeremiah 30:17).

God can take the broken pieces of our lives and make something amazing out of them if we will give Him a chance to do so. I encourage you to turn over to God anything that is broken and be filled with hope, for He surely is a God of restoration.

*Father, thank You that You restore things in my life that are broken. I'm glad it is not too late for You to work in my life and make things like new.*

# GOD ISN'T IN A HURRY

*How long, Lord God Almighty, will your anger smolder against the prayers of your people? You have fed them with the bread of tears; you have made them drink tears by the bowlful.*

PSALM 80:4-5

The Israelites had not been faithful to God, and because of that, their enemies had gained access to their lives and made them miserable. The people had cried out to God, but He took His time answering them. Why would He do this? Sometimes, if He delivers people from the consequences of their sin too quickly, they don't learn the lessons they need to learn and they keep repeating the same pattern in their lives.

We find this to be true even with our own children. As much as we love them, there are times when we need to let them suffer for a while so they learn by experience the wisdom of being obedient.

Trust God's timing in your life. We are usually in a hurry, but He isn't. He prefers a good and lasting outcome rather than a quick one. As humans, we don't like to wait, and we want everything right now, but our God is patient, and His ways are always higher than ours.

*Father, I do get tired of waiting, but I want to trust Your timing in my life. Help me to be patient and know that You will do what is best for me.*

# WORSHIP GOD ONLY

*You shall have no foreign god among you; you shall not worship any god other than me.*

**PSALM 81:9**

The first of the Ten Commandments is "You shall have no other gods before me" (Exodus 20:3). A god is something we worship. We can worship just about anything, and throughout history people have done so. They have worshipped the sun, trees, various animals, carved images and idols, wealth, success, people, and the list goes on. I have traveled to many foreign countries and seen people worship just about everything you can think of. The fact that all cultures find something to worship is proof that people were created to worship. But God created us to worship Him, and worshipping anything or anyone else is wrong.

We are to give God the place that is due Him, which is first place in our lives. He should be first in our thoughts, time, conversation, money, and in every other area. Jesus says that as we seek first His Kingdom, all other things will be added to us (Matthew 6:33).

It is amazing to me that people worship things and people who are dead and have no life in them when they could choose to worship Jesus, who conquered death and is alive. I urge you not to be deceived into worshipping anything other than God alone. Ask yourself what you give your time to, and you will quickly find what is most important to you—that is, what you worship. God created you, you belong to Him, and all worship belongs to Him alone.

*Father, I don't want to make the mistake of worshipping or idolizing anything or anyone but You. Help me keep You first in my life at all times. Thank You.*

# SPEND TIME WITH GOD

*I am the Lord your God, who brought you up from the land of Egypt.*
*Open your mouth wide and I will fill it...But I would feed Israel with the*
*finest of the wheat; and with honey from the rock I would satisfy you.*
**PSALM 81:10, 16 AMP**

We can see in today's scriptures that God wants to give us the very best and to satisfy us completely. He wants us to find in His presence great peace, joy, and everything else we need. The key to receiving these blessings is spending time with Him.

Everyone on earth has the same amount of time each day, and some people regularly spend time with God while others do not. I believe that when people say, "I don't have time to spend with God," it's simply an excuse.

The truth is that we make time for what is most important to us. At this moment, you are as close to God as you want to be. What you sow, you will reap. If you want a bigger harvest, you can simply sow more seed. If you want a closer relationship with God, spend more time with Him. This may require adjustments in your schedule or better time management, but God will help you do whatever you need to do to spend time with Him. He wants to spend time with you too. Include Him in all you do, and talk to Him throughout the day as you go about whatever you are doing.

*Lord, help me to make whatever changes I need to make in my*
*schedule in order to spend time with You.*

# GOD'S WAYS ARE BETTER

*But my people would not listen to me; Israel would not submit to me.*
*So I gave them over to their stubborn hearts to follow their own devices.*
**PSALM 81:11–12**

God's ways and thoughts are higher than ours (Isaiah 55:8–9). If we follow Him and do as He instructs, we will have lives worth living. However, if we persist in stubbornness and rebellion, He will eventually give us over to our own ways.

Sometimes God has to give us what we think we want in order to prove to us that it is not what we want at all. I remember wanting to be part of a popular social group at a church I attended, and I finally got what I wanted through people-pleasing and insincerity. But when God called me into ministry, those people turned against me, and I quickly discovered that they only wanted me as long as I pleased them. They had no interest in God's call on my life, nor did they encourage me to pursue it.

Have you ever wanted something and, once you got it, discovered it wasn't best for you? We can ask God for what we want, but we should be satisfied and content with what He gives us, because He always does what is best for us and we should trust Him. Never want anything—besides God—so much that you cannot be happy without it.

*Father, I want to be content with what You give me and never think*
*I cannot be happy unless I get what I want. Help me trust You*
*completely, knowing that You will always do what is best for me.*

# GOD DEFENDS THOSE IN NEED

*Defend the weak and the fatherless; uphold the cause of the poor and the oppressed. Rescue the weak and the needy; deliver them from the hand of the wicked.*

**PSALM 82:3-4**

Many people are hurting in different ways, but no matter who you are or what your source of pain is, you can rejoice because God is your defender. He sees your hurt, He knows who your enemies are, and He has a plan for your defense and deliverance.

Satan will tell you that God doesn't love you and that you have no one to help you, but remember that Satan is a liar. God is on your side, and He is fighting for you. If you look seriously with faith in your heart at our scriptures for today, you will realize that you have no need to fear.

Proverbs 3:5 says: "Trust in the Lord with all your heart, and lean not on your own understanding" (NKJV). Don't try to reason concerning what God will do or when He will do it. Just know that He will do what is best for you at just the right time. While you wait, you can rest in Him, knowing that He will never forsake you.

*Father, I love You. I am grateful that You are my defender and that You will deal with my enemies. Help me stay at peace while I wait on You.*

# GOD HEARS
# AND HE ANSWERS

*O God, do not remain silent; do not turn a deaf ear, do not stand aloof,
O God.*

**PSALM 83:1**

God definitely hears our prayers and answers them. He may not
answer on our schedules or in the way we think is best, but His
way is always better than our way. God loves for us to pray and
invites us to ask for things that are exceedingly and abundantly
above anything we could think, ask for, or imagine (Ephesians
3:20). Are you asking for big things? Things that seem almost
impossible for God to do? If not, why not start today? Remember
that all things are possible with God (Matthew 19:26).

We talk to God in prayer, but He also talks to us. The psalmist in today's verse asks God not to remain silent. God speaks,
but we must learn to listen or perceive what He says to us. God
sometimes shouts, but He usually whispers. He speaks through
His Word, our desires, other people, open or closed doors, and
even through our circumstances.

You will never learn to hear from God if you are afraid of making mistakes. Learning to hear His voice is like learning anything
else, and you won't do it perfectly all the time. We often learn
more from our mistakes than we do from our successes. You may
think you have never heard God speak to you, but I can assure
you that He has; you may simply need to learn to recognize His
voice. Ask God to teach you to hear Him. Then read and study
His Word and step out in faith until you learn how to discern
His voice.

*Father, I need to hear You speaking to me. Teach me in this area and
guide me to the right resources so I can learn. Thank You.*

# GAINING STRENGTH THROUGH TRIALS

*As they pass through the Valley of Baka, they make it a place of springs; the autumn rains also cover it with pools. They go from strength to strength, till each appears before God in Zion.*

**PSALM 84:6–7**

The Valley of Baka is the valley of mourning, the place where we experience trials and suffer. But it can also become a place we grow spiritually and gain strength. Although it is an unpleasant place, it can become a place of life-giving springs. I have heard that many times, we will realize that what we thought was our greatest enemy turned out to be our best friend. This is because we go deeper in God during times of difficulty.

James 1:2 says that we should consider it joy when we fall into various trials and temptations. Why? Because although these times are uncomfortable, they are the places where we grow and gain strength. One of the most difficult times in my life occurred when people I thought were my best friends turned against me and betrayed me. I was deeply hurt, but it did teach me to never trust people more than I trust God. We must know human nature and realize that human beings have no ability to be perfect and will disappoint us, just as we disappoint others.

What have you learned as a result of the difficult times you have been through? Anytime you are in a hard place, remind yourself that it will work out for your good and look for the place of springs in the Valley of Baka.

*Father, help me find the blessing in every trial. Let me gain strength as my faith is tested and turn every difficult place into a place of blessing. Thank You.*

# GOD'S PRESENCE

*Better is one day in your courts than a thousand elsewhere; I would rather be a doorkeeper in the house of my God than dwell in the tents of the wicked.*

**PSALM 84:10**

God has promised us that He will never leave us, and that He will be with us always (Deuteronomy 31:6). We should learn how to appreciate the presence of God in our lives. He is never more than a thought away. One day with God is worth more than thousands with anyone else, and His presence brings us fullness of joy (Psalm 16:11).

Learn to seek God's face—His presence—rather than His hand, and you will find His hand is always open to you. Seek Him for who He is, not merely for what He can do for you. His presence satisfies your soul like nothing else. The psalmist David said that it was the one thing he would seek above all else (Psalm 27:4).

What are you seeking? What do you want? If you seek God first, then everything else you desire will come with His presence. Keep Him first and all other things will be added to you (Matthew 6:33). Tell Him numerous times every day that you need *Him* more than what He can do for you, and take time to simply enjoy His presence.

*Father, I'm sorry for all the times I have sought Your gifts instead of seeking You. Help me recognize Your presence and learn to enjoy it more than anything else.*

# EXPECT ABUNDANT LIFE

*For the Lord God is a sun and shield; the Lord bestows favor and honor; no good thing does he withhold from those whose walk is blameless.*

**PSALM 84:11**

Everyone goes through good times and difficult times in life. When we face challenges or seasons of suffering, being able to maintain a good attitude through the difficulty is a virtue, and it is very important. But continual suffering is not God's will for anyone. The apostle Paul wrote that he knew "what it is to be in need" and "what it is to have plenty" (Philippians 4:12). We will go through difficulties in this life, but we can and should expect God's deliverance from them, along with a return to the abundant life Jesus died to give us (John 10:10).

Today's scripture represents God's heart toward us. He is a God who gives us favor and honor, and we can trust that He will not withhold any good thing from us. During times when we don't get what we want when we want it, God has a good reason. Perhaps the timing isn't right, maybe we are not mature enough to handle it yet, or God may have something better in mind for us. When He seems to be withholding something, it is never because He doesn't want us to be blessed. That thought simply isn't consistent with who He is.

*Thank You, God, that You want to bless me. Help me to go through difficulties with a good attitude, expecting You to deliver me and restore abundant life to me.*

# THE GOD OF SECOND CHANCES

*Restore us again, God our Savior, and put away your displeasure toward us. Will you be angry with us forever? Will you prolong your anger through all generations?*

**PSALM 85:4–5**

God graciously forgave and restored the Israelites many times after they disobeyed Him. He is a God of second chances—and more if needed. Are you feeling bad because you keep making the same mistake over and over? If so, don't draw away from God; press toward Him. He remains faithful even when we are faithless (2 Timothy 2:13).

God's mercy and unlimited forgiveness are beyond our understanding, and they are beautiful. I encourage you to receive both today and be at peace with God. Guilt is a useless and wasted emotion. Once we have repented of a sin, God forgives it and forgets it. He not only removes the sin but also the guilt that went with it. For many years I asked for forgiveness but kept the guilt. I finally realized that feeling guilty was my way of punishing myself. But Jesus has already taken our punishment, and all that is left for us to do is receive His gift of forgiveness and go on with life.

God does become angry, but He doesn't stay angry. He restores and revives His people so that we might rejoice in Him. Today can be a new beginning for you if you let it. It is not too late for you, even if you feel you have made too many mistakes. Where sin increases, grace increases even more (Romans 5:20).

*Father, thank You for giving me a second chance and more if I need them. You are good. I'm sorry for my sins. I ask for Your forgiveness, and I receive it and let go of guilt. May Your will be done in my life.*

# RIGHTEOUSNESS AND PEACE

*Mercy and loving-kindness and truth have met together; righteousness and peace have kissed each other.*

**PSALM 85:10 AMPC**

I love today's scripture because it teaches us that in order to have God's mercy, we must face truth, and that peace only comes from understanding righteousness with God. Jesus says that if we continue in His Word, then we will know the truth and it will set us free (John 8:32). Some people avoid the truth because it is often painful to face. However, it is the only thing that makes us free. Once we face truth, we can ask for and receive God's mercy.

In order to have peace with God, we must understand what it means to be in right standing with God through faith in Christ. When we know we are made right with God and that He loves and accepts us, we can have and enjoy peace with Him. If we don't have peace with Him, we cannot enjoy peace with ourselves or with other people.

Jesus, who was perfect and knew no sin, became sin that we might be made the righteousness of God in Christ (2 Corinthians 5:21). Receive your right standing with God through faith, and it will be life-changing. You need not always feel that something is wrong with you, because God sees you as right through your faith in Jesus. We don't do everything right, but God's righteousness has been given to us as a gift, and the more we believe it, the more our actions will be right also.

*Father, thank You for mercy, righteousness, and peace. These are wonderful blessings from You, and I appreciate them and want to walk in them fully. Teach me to receive and enjoy the gifts You have given to me.*

# PRAISE AND PETITION

*Hear me, Lord, and answer me, for I am poor and needy. Guard my life, for I am faithful to you; save your servant who trusts in you. You are my God; have mercy on me, Lord, for I call to you all day long.*

**PSALM 86:1-3**

The psalms are filled with David's taking his petitions (requests) to the Lord while at the same time praising Him for His goodness. Today's scriptures show just one of many examples of this. Prayer is not a last resort; it should be our first course of action in every situation. We are told to pray with thanksgiving (Philippians 4:6), and the combination of petition and praise is powerful beyond anything we can imagine.

Remembering and rehearsing all the good things God has done for us in the past invites Him to do even more in the future. I encourage you to take some time today and write down at least five prayers you recall God answering, and praise Him for doing so.

You cannot ask God for too much, so pray about everything that is on your heart. He is able to do "exceedingly abundantly above all" you can dare to hope, ask, or think (Ephesians 3:20 NKJV). Life becomes exciting when we learn to pray in faith and wait and watch for God to answer. This is an aspect of life that I enjoy greatly.

*Father, thank You for hearing and answering my prayers. You are great, and I praise You for all You have done, are doing, and will continue to do for me. I love You.*

# AN UNDIVIDED HEART

*Teach me your way, Lord, that I may rely on your faithfulness; give me an undivided heart, that I may fear your name. I will praise you, Lord my God, with all my heart; I will glorify your name forever.*

**PSALM 86:11–12**

Jesus said that the most important commandment is that we should love the Lord with all our heart, soul, mind, and strength, and that the second most important is for us to love our neighbor as ourselves (Mark 12:30–31). God wants us to have a heart fully set on Him, not a divided heart that only partially belongs to Him and partially belongs to someone or something else. We may be interested in other things, but God should always take first place.

I've known many people who try to work in ministry while also working at a business or in another career, and this doesn't work well. Eventually they must decide what they will give themselves to. People become worn-out if they try to be fully committed to two or more things. You might own a side business and be in ministry, but you would need to have someone run the business while you focus on God. I find that He takes all my time if I am going to properly do the job that He has given me.

Jesus knew the purpose for which He came to earth, and He focused on only that. When He called His apostles, they left everything else and followed Him. Be single-minded and set your heart fully on God, and He will be able to use you in great ways.

*Father, help me always have an undivided heart that is filled with You first and foremost. You are the most important thing in my life, and I need You. You are my life.*

# ARE YOU AN IMITATOR OF GOD?

*But you, Lord, are a compassionate and gracious God, slow to anger, abounding in love and faithfulness.*

**PSALM 86:15**

Today's scripture, like many others in Psalms, gives us insight into God's nature and character. Let's look at each word that describes Him. He is compassionate, not unfeeling or distant. He is gracious, not harsh or rude. He is slow to anger, not quick-tempered or easily angered. And He is "*abounding* in love and faithfulness" (emphasis mine), not limited in terms of how loving or faithful He will be. This description of God helps us understand who He is, but He has many other wonderful qualities in addition to these.

Ephesians 5:1 teaches us to be "imitators of God" (AMPC), and we should desire to be like He is. He sees the desires of our hearts and will help us become more and more like Him in our behavior. We can do this because His power and character are in us. Begin to imitate God in your life, doing what you believe He would do in situations, instead of what you feel like doing, and you will be amazed.

*Father, help me to know You for who You really are and to imitate You in every area of my life.*

# WHEN YOU NEED COMFORT

*Give me a sign of your goodness, that my enemies may see it and be put to shame, for you, Lord, have helped me and comforted me.*

**PSALM 86:17**

When people are hurting, one of the first places they turn to in the Bible is the Book of Psalms, because it brings comfort. In today's scripture, the psalmist David says that God has comforted him, and God will comfort us too.

God tells us in His Word that those who mourn will be comforted (Matthew 5:4), so if you are sad about anything, ask for and receive God's comfort. When we receive comfort from Him, then we can comfort others "with the comfort we ourselves receive from God" (2 Corinthians 1:4). In fact, I think one of the most important ministries Christians can have is the ministry of comforting those who mourn.

The world promises us pain and hurt, but God promises us deliverance and comfort. Don't just assume you will get comfort; ask for it. James 4:2 says we have not because we ask not, so ask and ask and ask. You cannot ask for too much.

God can comfort you in a way no one else can. He knows everything about you and exactly what you need. You are very special to God, and He will always give you comfort when you need it.

*Father, thank You for Your comfort. No one can comfort me as You do. Bring people who need comfort across my path so I can give them the comfort that You have given to me.*

# SELAH

*Glorious things are spoken of you, O city of God!* Selah

**PSALM 87:3 NKJV**

Throughout Psalms (and in Habakkuk), in some Bible translations, we see after certain verses the word *selah*, which means "pause, and calmly think of that." We see it in today's scripture and also in Psalm 87:6. This phrase lets us, as readers, know that we have reached a good place to stop, consider, and slowly digest the meaning of what we have just read. We may take time to pray or meditate on the verse or passage we have read, or we may think about how it applies to our lives or a certain situation.

Jeremiah writes about stopping to feed on and digest the words of God. He says, "Your words were found and I ate them, and Your words became a joy to me and the delight of my heart" (Jeremiah 15:16 AMP). To use a figure of speech, we need to "chew" on the scriptures, rehearsing specific words or phrases in our minds and taking time to think about and process them. Sometimes, we read the Bible for *quantity*, hoping to get through a certain number of chapters or pages, when we should read for *quality*. Whatever passage you are reading, let me encourage you to read in a manner that allows the Word to go down into your innermost being and feed your spirit.

*Father, I honor Your Word, and I ask You to help me take my time as I read it, so it will affect the deepest parts of me.*

# HOPE IN PRAYER

*But I cry to you for help, Lord; in the morning my prayer comes before you.*

**PSALM 88:13**

Throughout Psalm 88, the psalmist speaks of his troubles. He feels overwhelmed with them, as though he is drawing near death. We too feel overwhelmed at times and cry out to God for deliverance. Psalm 88 includes eighteen verses, and in all but verse 13, the psalmist seems to be miserable and despairing of his circumstances.

I love the fact that in the midst of what seems to be utter darkness in his life, he still has hope in prayer. He has not stopped praying, because he knows his help can only come from God, and he apparently believes that God will help him if he asks Him to. I want you to know today that, when you call on Him, God will help you too.

The psalmist is not happy about how long God is taking to respond to him, but he still believes that only God is the answer to his problems. I want to encourage you: No matter how long you have waited on God for your answer to come, remain hopeful of answered prayer. God is faithful, and He will answer you at just the right time. Even though you may have many troubles, find things to be thankful for and voice your gratitude to God. Thanksgiving is powerful, especially during seasons of waiting and times of trouble.

*Father, help me not to give up hope regarding receiving help from You. I know that You alone can help me, and it is to You that I cry out in prayer. I wait on You to answer me.*

# GOD'S LOVE

*I will sing of the Lord's great love forever; with my mouth I will make your faithfulness known through all generations.*

**PSALM 89:1**

Numerous times in Psalm 89, the psalmist mentions God's love and faithfulness. These two attributes are important to remember. God is love, and He is faithful. He can never deviate from either of these qualities, for they are aspects of who He is.

No matter what you may be going through at this time in your life, always remember that God loves you and that He is faithful. God will not leave you without help forever. Your faith may be tested at times, but God will always come through if you continue trusting Him. As the psalmist does, I encourage you to speak often about God's love and faithfulness. In your prayers, talk to Him about these qualities, and talk about them in your conversations with other people.

When you are trying to help someone who is going through difficulty, nothing is more powerful than reminding them that God loves them, that He is faithful, and that He will not leave them stranded or alone in their troubles. Encourage them to keep trusting Him, no matter how long it takes for His answer to come.

*Father, thank You for reminding me that You love me and that You are faithful. I trust You to deliver me from my troubles, and I wait on You to do so.*

# THE GOD OF JUSTICE

*Righteousness and justice are the foundation of your throne; love and faithfulness go before you.*

**PSALM 89:14**

Notice in today's scripture that the psalmist mentions justice and righteousness as the foundation of God's throne. Certainly, He is a just and righteous God. Justice is just one of His amazing and admirable character traits. He brings justice as we wait on Him and trust Him to be our Vindicator when someone or something has hurt, offended, or wronged us. In the face of cruel accusations, Job makes this powerful statement about God: "I know that my Redeemer and Vindicator lives, and at the last He will take His stand upon the earth" (Job 19:25 AMP).

When we face a situation that is unjust or when we need to be vindicated, God never asks us to take matters into our own hands. He simply asks us to pray and forgive—and He does the rest. He makes even the injustices and the pain we suffer work for our good (Romans 8:28). He justifies, vindicates, and recompenses us. He pays us back for our pain if we follow His commands to forgive our enemies, and He even gives us double for our trouble (Isaiah 61:7; Job 42:10). Refuse to live in unforgiveness, and trust God to bring justice for you and to reward you for any mistreatment you have endured.

*Lord, I declare today that You are a just God and that You are my Vindicator. I will pray and forgive, trusting You to do the rest.*

# THE RIGHT KIND OF FEAR

*Who...is like the Lord, a God greatly feared and reverently worshiped in the council of the holy [angelic] ones, and awesome above all those who are around Him?*

**PSALM 89:6-7 AMP**

We should have the wisdom to fear walking out into the middle of oncoming traffic, into a fire that is out of control, into the path of a tornado, or into other such situations. But other kinds of fear are negative, detrimental to us, and to be resisted and overcome—except one, and it is more valuable than we might imagine. I am talking about the reverential fear of God, which is the kind of fear the psalmist writes about in today's scriptures.

The fear of God is an awe-inspiring, respectful type of fear that gives Him honor above all else. It says, "I know God is all-powerful and that He means what He says. He is good. He loves me, and He will always take care of me." The emphasis is on reverence and awe, not our common modern-day understanding of fear. The fear of God will set us free from wrong and tormenting fears. We can literally trade one kind of fear for another; we can give up all negative fear and embrace a type of fear that is good for us.

The fear of the Lord is not intended to make us afraid that God will harm us. God is always good, but through our own foolishness, we can open doors for the devil by disobeying the Lord. For this reason, Scripture urges us to have a reverential fear of God. This attitude toward Him will keep us on the right path in life.

*Help me, God, to resist all kinds of fear, except one. Help me to embrace fully the fear of the Lord—the reverential fear and awe of You.*

# ETERNITY

*A thousand years in your sight are like a day that has just gone by, or like a watch in the night.*

**PSALM 90:4**

God lives outside of time, and He sees everything from an eternal perspective. To Him, a thousand years is like one day, but to us one day can seem like a thousand years, especially if we have a problem and we are waiting on God for deliverance and help.

We should learn to think more like eternal beings than temporal ones, for that is what we are. We will leave this earth eventually, but we won't stop existing; we will simply pass into another realm and continue throughout eternity with God. *Forever* is something we cannot grasp with our finite minds, but we will live forever, and the best part of our lives will begin when we leave this earth and get to our heavenly home.

If you are waiting on God right now for something, I encourage you to believe that God is working and to not be so focused on how long it seems to be taking. Go ahead and enjoy your life while God is working on your problem. He will bring your answer, and He won't be late.

*Father, I look forward to living in Your presence forever. When I get in a hurry, remind me that I am an eternal being and that Your timing in my life is perfect.*

# DON'T WASTE YOUR TIME

*Teach us to number our days, that we may gain a heart of wisdom.*
**PSALM 90:12**

Each day God gives us is precious, and once it is gone, we can never get it back. A day wasted is a day lost, so I encourage you to make your time count. For example, don't waste a day in anger, unforgiveness, or self-pity. None of these negative emotions helps us in any way, and they are a complete waste of time.

We all have twenty-four hours in a day, yet some people seem to accomplish so much in that period of time, while others do nothing. I urge you to think about what you are doing with the time God has given you and make it useful, not useless. Today you have an entire day to make other people happy, to be thankful for all God's blessings, or to finish a project you have intended to finish for months.

According to Psalm 118:24, "This is the day the Lord has made" (NKJV), so do something worthwhile with it. Today's scripture says, "Teach us to number our days, that we may gain a heart of wisdom." Wise people do now what they will be happy with later. I encourage you to do something with the time you have today that you will be satisfied with tomorrow.

*Father, thank You for the reminder not to waste my time. Time is a blessing You have given me, and it is a valuable one. Help me use mine wisely and do all that You want me to do while I am here on the earth.*

# GOD'S FAVOR

*May the favor of the Lord our God rest on us; establish the work of our hands for us—yes, establish the work of our hands.*

**PSALM 90:17**

God's favor is a wonderful blessing. When His favor is on you, people will want to do things for you without even knowing why. Grace is said to be God's undeserved favor, which means He does things for us that we do not and cannot deserve. He does them because He is good and wants to grant us His favor.

I lived half my life not knowing what divine favor was. I occasionally asked a person if they could *do* me *a* favor, but I never knew that I could pray and ask God to give me favor. Once I learned about it, I started seeing God's favor in my life in little and big ways.

Often, when our ministry team traveled overseas to hold crusades, we saw God give us favor to obtain permits people told us were impossible to get, and we watched various denominations come together in unity to help with and attend our event. In addition to that, the property on which our building sits was for sale for quite a while. One year prior to the time we purchased it, someone offered the owner the exact same amount of money we did, and he turned it down. But because of God's favor, when we made the same offer a year later, he agreed to it.

Living with God's favor is exciting. It is just plain fun to watch God open doors that no one except God could open for you. Pray for and expect favor, and you will see amazing things happen in your life.

*Father, thank You for divine favor. I am excited to watch You give me favor as I go through my daily life.*

# A PLACE OF REST AND PROTECTION

*He who dwells in the shelter of the Most High will remain secure and rest in the shadow of the Almighty [whose power no enemy can withstand].*

**PSALM 91:1 AMP**

Psalm 91 is a powerful chapter of the Bible, and it speaks of God's protection. Today's scripture teaches us that God offers us a place of shelter, which some translations refer to as a "secret place" (KJV, NKJV) where we may dwell in safety, security, and peace. This shelter is the place of rest in God, a spiritual place where fear and worry are vanquished and peace reigns. It is the shelter of God's presence. When we spend time praying and seeking God, dwelling in His presence, we are in the secret place, or shelter, of the Most High.

This refuge God makes available to us is a hiding place, a private place, a resting place. It is our shelter when we are hurting, overwhelmed, or feeling weary or discouraged. It is a dwelling place where we are secure and at ease beneath the shadow of the Almighty. Notice that the Amplified Bible says that God, the Almighty, has power "no enemy can withstand." We experience the sheltering of God against our enemy when we are mistreated or persecuted, when we are in great need, or when we feel we simply cannot keep moving forward in life.

God invites you today to take refuge under the protective shadow of His wings, and He wants you to remain there always.

*Lord, I choose to dwell in the shelter You offer me today and always. Thank You for this safe, secure, peaceful place.*

# WHAT WILL YOU SAY OF THE LORD?

*I will say of the Lord, "He is my refuge and my fortress, my God, in whom I trust."*

**PSALM 91:2**

David writes often of God's goodness and His character. In today's scripture, David refers to God as his refuge, his fortress, and his God, in whom he trusts. Notice also that before David describes God, he writes "*I will say* of the Lord" (italics mine). Perhaps we should also regularly ask ourselves, "What am I saying of the Lord?"

We need to *say* godly words, not just *think* godly thoughts. We may think, *I believe many good things about the Lord*, but are we *saying* those good things? Often, we claim to believe something, yet the opposite comes out of our mouths.

We need to speak aloud the goodness of God. We need to do it at proper times and in proper places, but we need to be sure we do it. I cannot encourage you strongly enough to make verbal confessions of God's goodness part of your daily fellowship with Him. Verbalize your thanksgiving, your praise, and your worship. Say aloud what is in your heart about God. It will glorify Him and bless you!

*Help me, Lord, to pay attention to what I say about You and to speak words that honor You and strengthen me.*

# ANGELIC PROTECTION

*If you say, "The Lord is my refuge," and you make the Most High your dwelling, no harm will overtake you, no disaster will come near your tent. For he will command his angels concerning you to guard you in all your ways; they will lift you up in their hands, so that you will not strike your foot against a stone.*

**PSALM 91:9–12**

Angels are heavenly beings that do God's bidding, according to Psalm 103:20, which means that He dispatches them to help, protect, or otherwise minister as He sees fit. Throughout the Bible, people encountered angels for various reasons. Jacob wrestled with an angel in Genesis 32:22–32 and Hosea 12:4. The angel Gabriel announced Jesus' impending birth to His mother, Mary (Luke 1:26–33), and two angels sat in the empty tomb after Jesus' resurrection (John 20:11–12). In Revelation 5:11–12, the apostle John sees many angels praising God, saying, "Worthy is the Lamb, who was slain, to receive power and wealth and wisdom and strength and honor and glory and praise!"

We can see that angels carry out a variety of functions. According to today's scriptures, the Lord promises angelic protection and deliverance to those who trust in Him by taking refuge in Him and living in Him as their dwelling place. Having angelic protection does not mean we will never experience any trial or affliction. It means we are protected from whatever the enemy ultimately plans for us as long as we keep our trust in God and believe and speak of Him in accordance with His Word.

*Thank You, God, for the assurance of Your angelic protection.*

# ALL GOD WANTS IS YOUR LOVE

*"Because he loves me," says the Lord, "I will rescue him; I will protect him, for he acknowledges my name."*

**PSALM 91:14**

Jesus says the first and most important commandment is for us to love God with all our heart, soul, mind, and strength (Mark 12:30). In today's scripture, we see again that God promises many wonderful blessings to those who love Him. He is not asking for our perfection; He wants our love.

He promises to rescue us, protect us, answer our prayers, be with us in trouble, deliver us, honor us, and give us long life if we will only love Him (Psalm 91:15–16). Jesus says that if we love Him, we will obey Him (John 14:15). Clearly, obedience is part of our love for God, but it is important to remember that God will do all these wonderful things for us even if we make mistakes, as long as we truly love Him.

Tell the Lord several times each day that you love Him. I never tire of my husband or children telling me they love me, and God never tires of hearing it either. Throughout God's Word, He reminds us that He loves us, and we should love Him in return. Love the Lord with all your heart, make Him first in your life, and enjoy all the benefits of having a close, intimate relationship with Him.

*Father, I do love You very much. I appreciate You for who You are. I appreciate all the promises You have given me in your Word, and I appreciate all You do for me. You are good, and You are the most important thing in my life.*

# PRESENCE, DELIVERANCE, HONOR, AND SATISFACTION

*He will call on me, and I will answer him; I will be with him in trouble, I will deliver him and honor him. With long life I will satisfy him and show him my salvation.*

**PSALM 91:15–16**

Today's scripture relates to yesterday's verse, which says, "'Because he loves me,' says the Lord, 'I will rescue him; I will protect him, for he acknowledges my name'" (Psalm 91:14). The psalmist is writing about angelic protection, and it is important to know that this protection does not mean we will never experience trial or affliction. It means we are protected from whatever the enemy ultimately plans for us as long as we keep our trust in God and believe and speak of Him in accordance with His Word.

Remember that Psalm 91:14 sets us up to receive certain promises from God *because of our love for Him*. In that context, the Lord says that He will answer us when we call on Him. He then makes several promises I'd like for us to focus on today, because they show us that our deliverance doesn't always happen immediately; they represent a pattern and a progression God often takes us through.

It took many years for me to see this pattern: God is with us in our trials and troubles, then He begins to deliver us out of them, and afterward He honors us. Then He satisfies us with long life and shows us His salvation. As we go through this progression, we will develop greater trust, peace, and joy in the Lord. Going through things with God helps us to develop a more intimate relationship with Him. Isn't that what you want? I certainly do.

*Thank You, Lord, for Your promise that because I love You, You will be with me in my trials, You will deliver me, You will honor me, and You will satisfy me with long life and show me Your salvation.*

# THE RIGHTEOUS FLOURISH

*The righteous will flourish like a palm tree, they will grow like a cedar of Lebanon.*

**PSALM 92:12**

When we flourish, we develop in a healthy and vigorous way. This kind of growth is a promise to the righteous. The righteous are those who trust God and believe His promises. Through faith in Christ, we are viewed as righteous, meaning that God sees us as being in right standing with Him (2 Corinthians 5:21).

A cedar tree can grow as much as a foot per year. Because of its rich foliage and beauty, it is a very desirable tree. This psalm promises that a righteous person will flourish and grow like a cedar. I love growth in God, and I delight in becoming more and more like Jesus all the time.

Our verse for today tells us that the righteous will be fruitful, healthy, and beautiful, and will flourish and show quick growth. This sounds good to me, and I am sure it does to you also. Keep these promises in mind as you press on to serve God with all your heart. You will grow today as you serve and love Him with all your heart.

*Father, thank You for growth in You. I want to be more like Jesus. You have given me the Holy Spirit to transform me into His image, and I want to submit to Him in all things. Please help me do so.*

# BE PLANTED IN GOD'S HOUSE

*Planted in the house of the Lord, they will flourish in the courts of our God.*

**PSALM 92:13**

We flourish best if we are planted in a church or body of people, rather than moving from place to place, not being connected with or accountable to anyone. God's idea of church is not for us to simply go each week, sit on a pew, and watch other people do things; He wants us to be involved. Each person should participate, and everyone should contribute.

Being planted is equivalent to being committed to something. When we are committed, we do what we should do whether it is convenient or inconvenient, easy or hard.

You don't have to stay in one group or church for your entire life. Sometimes it is right to move to another place where God wants you to serve or grow in a different way, but don't be the kind of person who never sticks with anything for very long. Finish what you start.

*Father, I ask You to help me know what You want me to be committed to and then stay planted in that place or thing until You are finished with it. I want to finish what I start. Thank You.*

# BEARING FRUIT IN OLD AGE

*They will still bear fruit in old age, they will stay fresh and green, proclaiming, "The Lord is upright; he is my Rock, and there is no wickedness in him."*

**PSALM 92:14–15**

Although we age each year, we don't have to get old. Age is a number, but old is a mindset. God wants us to bear fruit and remain vital, no matter what our age is. Don't listen to the devil when he whispers, "You are too old to do that," or "You are too old to try something new."

Each stage of life is beautiful and meant for a purpose. We are to remain vibrant and available to the Lord for His purpose at every point in life. I am in the latter years of my life, so I am very glad to know that I can still bear fruit. As a matter of fact, I believe that some of my best years are ahead of me.

We grow wiser as we age and gain experience. In many ways, the more years we add to our lives, the more valuable we become to others because of what we have learned going through life. If you are feeling useless or uncertain about your purpose, let me assure you that God has plenty for you to do. Make yourself available and start taking opportunities that pass before you, and soon you'll find a perfect fit for yourself.

*Father, I pray that You will help me know how I can serve and bear good fruit. I want to be useful, not useless.*

# STRONG AND MIGHTY GOD

*Mightier than the thunder of the great waters, mightier than the breakers of the sea—the Lord on high is mighty.*

**PSALM 93:4**

When we think of ocean breakers, we see in our mind's eye powerful surges and the spray of water pummeling cliffs or coastal rock formations. We can almost hear the rush and crash when we envision this scene. The great waters and breakers of the sea are mighty forces of nature, but as the psalmist points out in today's scripture, God is even mightier. His power and strength are far greater than anything on earth. In fact, they are limitless.

At times in your life, you may face situations that seem impossible. No amount of human strength can change them or make them right. Without God, all anyone can rely on is human strength, which often fails. In 2 Chronicles 32:8, Judah's King Hezekiah says this about the king of Assyria, who was considered very strong and who had a mighty army with him: "With him is only the arm of flesh, but with us is the Lord our God to help us and to fight our battles." When the people of Judah heard this, they "gained confidence from what Hezekiah the king of Judah said."

What was true for the people of Judah is true for you. The Lord is with you to help you and to fight your battles. No person or thing is mightier than He is.

*Thank You, mighty God, that You are greater than anyone or anything on earth and that You will help me and fight my battles for me.*

# GOD SEES AND HEARS

*Does he who fashioned the ear not hear? Does he who formed the eye not see?*

**PSALM 94:9**

We sometimes feel alone, and although we are praying and asking God to help us, we are not sure that He is listening or that He sees our pain and misery. But He does. God is omnipresent, which means He is everywhere all the time, so He sees you and everything that is going on in your life. He also hears all your prayers, and as you continue trusting Him, you will receive answers.

God cares that you are hurting, and He has crafted a plan and a timing for your deliverance. All you need to do is wait patiently and expect Him to show up at any moment with your answer. Think of other times when you have felt the way you feel right now. Remember how God answered you, and trust Him to do it again.

We know that God can answer anything He chooses, and we don't understand why He waits so long sometimes, but we trust that His timing is perfect in our lives. As you go through your day today, keep saying to yourself, "God is working." This will keep you encouraged, and it will feed your faith and keep it strong.

*Father, thank You that You are working in my life right now even if I cannot feel it or see any change. Help me trust that Your timing in my life will be perfect.*

# FINDING PEACE DURING DIFFICULT TIMES

*Blessed [with wisdom and prosperity] is the man whom You discipline and instruct, O Lord, and whom You teach from Your law, that You may grant him [power to calm himself and find] peace in the days of adversity, until the pit is dug for the wicked and ungodly.*

**PSALM 94:12–13 AMP**

We sometimes reach a tipping point in our lives when we recognize we are under so much pressure that we are on the verge of losing our peace and are about to start behaving badly. In today's scriptures, the psalmist writes of the Lord granting a person "[power to calm himself and find] peace in the days of adversity" (Ps. 94:13). Here are some steps that will hopefully help the process:

*Step 1:* Slow down (or stop), take a deep breath, and regroup.

*Step 2:* Regain your perspective. Be realistic about what is really happening.

*Step 3:* Resist the devil at his onset, when you first realize he is pressuring you.

*Step 4:* Cast your care on God and let Him show you what He can do. Keep saying, "God, I let this go. I trust You!" until you feel yourself calming down.

*Step 5:* Think about what you are thinking about concerning the things that frustrate you and stop thinking about it. Instead, think about something good and positive.

*Step 6:* Exercise self-control and manage your emotions instead of letting them control you.

*Step 7:* Ask yourself if you can delay or delegate any of the things that are causing you stress, and make a plan to do so.

*I thank You, God, for the peace You give and for granting me the ability to calm myself and find peace in the midst of troubling situations.*

# DON'T WORRY

*When anxiety was great within me, your consolation brought me joy.*

**PSALM 94:19**

God is the God of all comfort (2 Corinthians 1:3). When we are anxious or worried, we should pray immediately and ask for His comfort. Paul teaches us: "Be anxious for nothing, but in everything by prayer and supplication, with thanksgiving, let your requests be made known to God," and His peace will keep your heart in Jesus (Philippians 4:6–7 NKJV).

In Psalm 37 David writes that even though the wicked prosper, it will only last for a short time (vv. 9–10). We should not fret (worry) but trust in God and keep doing good, and we will inherit blessings (vv. 1–4). Anxiety causes us to waste today worrying about tomorrow, but Jesus says, "Therefore do not worry about tomorrow, for tomorrow will worry about itself. Each day has enough trouble of its own" (Matthew 6:34).

God gives us grace for each day, but He will not give us tomorrow's grace today, so go ahead and enjoy this day that God has given you, and don't waste it worrying about things you cannot fix or change.

*Father, worry is a great temptation for me. I ask You to help me realize how useless it is and to replace all my worry and anxiety with trust in You.*

# PRAISE BEFORE PETITION

*Come, let us sing for joy to the Lord; let us shout aloud to the Rock of our salvation. Let us come before him with thanksgiving and extol him with music and song.*

**PSALM 95:1-2**

We should remember to praise, worship, and give thanks to God before we begin making our petitions, or requests, of Him. Sadly, we are often so eager to tell the Lord what we need Him to do for us that we forget to remember all the wonderful things He has already done. God already knows what we need before we ask Him (Matthew 6:8), so we don't need to spend an excessive amount of time on telling Him.

Ask God for what you need and want, but make sure your prayers are full of thanksgiving. Paul's prayers were filled with thanksgiving. I believe that giving of thanks is the power behind answered prayer. Philippians 4:6 tells us that instead of being anxious, we should pray about all things with thanksgiving. "With thanksgiving" is the most important part of the prayer.

Dave and I do a lot for our children, and they frequently tell us how thankful they are and how much they appreciate what we do. Their expressed gratitude makes us want to do more, but if they were not thankful, soon we would lose our desire to do as much as we do for them. If people are not thankful for what they have, they won't be thankful for what they get. Be generous in expressing your gratitude and appreciation to God at all times, and enter His presence with thanksgiving, not with petition.

*Father, You are so good to me, and I always want to express my gratitude for all You have done. Help me not to rush into Your presence with my petitions without remembering to first be thankful.*

# LIVE IN THE PRESENT

*For he is our God and we are the people of his pasture, the flock under his care. Today, if only you would hear his voice…*

**PSALM 95:7**

Notice that today's scripture says, "*Today*, if only you would hear his voice" (italics mine). We need to understand that God wants us to focus on each day as it comes and to learn how to be people of the present. The choices we make today determine whether we will enjoy every moment in our lives or waste them by being anxious or upset. Sometimes we end up missing part of today because we feel guilty about yesterday or carry regrets over something in the past, or we are too concerned about tomorrow. We need to keep our minds focused on what God wants us to be doing now.

I believe that anxiety is caused by trying to mentally or emotionally get into things that are not here yet (the future) or focus on things that have already been (the past). We often spend our mental time in the past or in the future, instead of living in the moment we have now.

When we don't truly give ourselves to what we are doing at the moment, we become prone to anxiety. If we live in the now, we will find the Lord there with us. Regardless of the situations life brings our way, God has promised never to leave us or forsake us but to always be with us (Hebrews 13:5; Matthew 28:20). Don't waste your precious time now worrying about yesterday or tomorrow. Live today!

*Thank You, God, for this present moment. Help me not to dwell on yesterday or become too wrapped up in what could happen tomorrow, but to enjoy today.*

# HEARING GOD'S VOICE

*Today, if only you would hear his voice, "Do not harden your hearts as you did at Meribah, as you did that day at Massah in the wilderness."*

**PSALM 95:7-8**

People often complain that they don't hear from God. I think there are times when we do hear God's voice, but we harden our hearts to it because we don't want to do what He is telling us to do.

Each time God speaks to us and we harden our hearts, it becomes more difficult to hear Him the next time He speaks. Hearing God is important, but obeying what He has spoken to us is more important. We cannot have selective hearing, meaning that we listen to God when He says something we like and pretend not to hear Him when we don't like it.

Is there anything God has instructed you to do that you have not done? If so, now is the time to be obedient. Everything God tells us to do or not to do is only and always for our benefit. Obeying God is the wisest thing we can do, because it leads us into the good life He wants us to live.

*Father, I'm sorry for the times You have spoken to me and I have stubbornly turned a deaf ear. Forgive me and help me to be obedient each time I hear Your voice.*

# WE WILL REAP WHAT WE SOW

*Let all creation rejoice before the Lord, for he comes, he comes to judge the earth. He will judge the world in righteousness and the peoples in his faithfulness.*

**PSALM 96:13**

Words, thoughts, and actions are seeds we sow, and they eventually bring a harvest in our lives. God's Word teaches us that we will reap what we have sown (Galatians 6:7). The day will come when God will judge the earth, and His judgment will be righteous. On that day, we will all have to give an account of what we have done (Romans 14:12).

Those who believe in Jesus Christ and have received Him as Savior and Lord will not be judged in terms of whether or not they will go to heaven, but they will be judged and rewarded accordingly for their works. However, those who have rejected Jesus during their lifetime will be facing a very different kind of judgment. They have spent their lives doing as they please, and on Judgment Day, they will reap the results of what they have sown.

Those who believe in Christ look forward to that day. They rejoice to see it come, but unbelievers will not rejoice. On that day, they will regret their decision to reject Jesus during their lifetime. Let us pray daily for those who have rejected Jesus, that they might be saved and spend eternity with Him.

*Father, I pray for all those who have rejected Jesus as their Savior and have walked in their own will instead of following You. I pray they will believe and receive Jesus before it is too late. Send the perfect laborer into their path to speak a timely word to them.*

# LOVE GOD AND HATE EVIL

*Let those who love the Lord hate evil, for he guards the lives of his faithful ones and delivers them from the hand of the wicked.*

**PSALM 97:10**

If we love God, we should love what He loves and hate what He hates. He hates wickedness, evil, and injustice, and we should too. God does not hate wicked and evil people, but He hates the works they do. If we truly hate what is evil, we will be careful to avoid it.

The world is filled with wickedness, but those who love God must resist it and stand firm in righteousness. Don't compromise and do the things that evil people do. If they reject you because of your stand for God and His righteousness, don't worry about it, because God will never reject you. It may be difficult in this lifetime when we are persecuted for righteousness' sake, but God's Word tells us that we are blessed when this happens to us (Matthew 5:10–12).

As today's scripture says, God will guard and deliver those who hate evil from the hand of the wicked. He will bless and reward you as you endure persecution for His sake. People may reject you, but God is with you.

*Father, help me stand strong when people persecute me because I hate evil and choose to walk in Your ways. Amen.*

# GOD HAS DONE MARVELOUS THINGS

*Sing to the Lord a new song, for he has done marvelous things; his right hand and his holy arm have worked salvation for him.*

**PSALM 98:1**

God has done "marvelous things" in our lives, as today's scripture says. But too often we focus only on what we want Him to do that He still has not yet done, and we fail to see or remember all that He *has* done. I encourage you today to take time to recall some of the great and marvelous things He has done in your life.

Today I remember that God has sent Jesus to pay for our sins. He has given us mercy, been patient with us, shown us kindness when we did not deserve it, and given us hope. Hope is powerful, and we should rejoice because we have it. When we have hope, we cannot be defeated. We hope for what we don't yet see but believe is ours by faith. We believe we will receive the desires of our heart at just the right time. Hope expects these blessings. It looks for God to show up at any moment and once again do something marvelous.

You never know what God may do today—perhaps something amazingly astonishing, something so great you will have difficulty finding the right words to tell others about it. I love to watch the Lord work in my life and yours, for He does indeed do marvelous things.

*Father, You have done marvelous things in my life. I am sorry about how often I forget what You have done and complain about what You have not done yet. I trust that You will do all that needs to be done in my life at just the right time. Thank You.*

# NO MORE FEAR OR WORRY

*The Lord reigns, let the nations tremble; he sits enthroned between the cherubim, let the earth shake. Great is the Lord in Zion; he is exalted over all the nations.*

**PSALM 99:1-2**

If we could truly understand how much God loves us and how great He is, we would never suffer from fear or worry again. It seems that each day the devil presents us with something to worry about or something to be afraid of, but we have the privilege of turning away from his lies and turning toward God.

What are you worried about today? What are you afraid of? Is any of it greater than your God? He desires that we enjoy peace…amazing peace, a peace that assures us that no matter what we are facing or dealing with, in the end God will cause it to turn out for our good.

Our troubles are tools God uses to help us mature spiritually. We grow in faith as we learn to pray and then believe that whatever He gives us is His perfect will in the moment we are in. Let me assure you that whatever you are going through today will come to an end. And when it does, you will be stronger than you were before, and you will be closer to God.

*Father, when I am hurting, help me trust that You are with me and that You are working good in the midst of my difficulty. Strengthen me, Lord, and let me glorify Your name.*

# OUR GOD LOVES JUSTICE

*Let them praise your great and awesome name—he is holy. The King is mighty, he loves justice—you have established equity; in Jacob you have done what is just and right.*

**PSALM 99:3-4**

Let's remember how great and awesome God's name is, as we read in our scripture for today. In the Old Testament, God was called by many names, and each one represented something wonderful about His character. For example, Jehovah-Rapha means the Lord our Healer; Jehovah-Jireh, the Lord our Provider; El Shaddai, the Lord God Almighty; and El Elyon, the Most High God. There are many other names of God, and they are all beautiful.

In the New Testament, we have the name of Jesus. That name is "the name that is above every name" (Philippians 2:9), and we are blessed to be able to use His name in prayer.

Let's also remember based on today's scripture that God loves justice. I love that He loves justice, because it means He makes wrong things right. If someone unfairly mistreats you, He will bring justice in your life. I have been the recipient of God's justice on many occasions, and it is awesome.

God also establishes equity, which means He is fair and impartial. He treats each of us with equity. Life is not fair, but God is. I was abused in my childhood, and there was nothing I could do about it, but I learned to trust God for justice and equity, and I have seen it come to pass in my life. If you have been mistreated, ask God for justice and wait on Him. He will give you many blessings for your former trouble.

*Father, thank You for Your beautiful name and for justice and equity. It is comforting to know that You will make right the wrongs that have been done to me.*

# THE POWER OF JOY

*Shout for joy to the Lord, all the earth. Worship the Lord with gladness; come before him with joyful songs.*

PSALM 100:1-2

If the devil wasn't afraid of our joy, he wouldn't work so hard to take it away from us. Even though we may not be able to find joy in our circumstances, we can always find joy in Jesus. He gives us hope, and when we have hope we cannot be defeated. Hope opens the door for joy.

Nehemiah 8:10 says that the joy of the Lord is our strength. The joy of the Lord is a different type of joy than joy in our circumstances, because it is always available. No matter what, you can have joy today. Just look at what you do have and stop looking at what you don't have.

You have the hope of eternal life. If you research how many promises of God are in the Bible, you will find thousands of promises on which you can stand in times of trouble, knowing that God's Word is always true.

Smile and laugh as much as possible, because the more joy you have, the more powerful you are.

*Father, help me to pay more attention to You than I do to my problems. Help me be filled with joy as I trust You to take care of everything that concerns me.*

# FIND THINGS TO BE THANKFUL FOR

*Enter his gates with thanksgiving and his courts with praise; give thanks to him and praise his name.*

**PSALM 100:4**

Being ungrateful is a symptom of a lack of spiritual maturity, and prayer often goes unanswered because of an ungrateful heart. A heart that is not thankful often expresses itself through bad attitudes and negative speech. There are people who are grumblers, murmurers, critics, faultfinders, and complainers. You have probably encountered people like this, and I have too, but we must be careful not to grumble, complain, or find fault with others. We need to be the kind of people who are thankful for what God is doing.

If we want to see God at work in our spouse, our children, our finances, our circumstances, or our job, we can start by being grateful for what we already have, and we can use our words to express our gratitude.

The Holy Spirit once impressed on me the idea that when people pray and ask God for things but don't have a thankful heart, it's a clear indication that they are not ready for something else, because they won't be thankful for that either. Part of the enemy's plan is to keep us dissatisfied with something all the time.

God's answer to ingratitude is for us to fill our lives with thanksgiving and praise. Look for something today to be thankful for, and offer a prayer of praise and thanksgiving for it.

*Father, help me watch for things to be thankful for and to be diligent in thanking You for them.*

# A BLAMELESS HEART

*I will be careful to lead a blameless life—when will you come to me? I will conduct the affairs of my house with a blameless heart.*

**PSALM 101:2**

Today's scripture mentions a blameless life and a blameless heart. Does the idea of living a blameless life and having a blameless heart seem impossible to you? I think all of us would have to admit that we do not consider our lives and hearts blameless or completely without fault.

Second Chronicles 16:9 says that "The eyes of the Lord run to and fro throughout the whole earth to show Himself strong in behalf of those whose hearts are blameless toward Him" (AMPC). When I first read this verse years ago, I thought, *I had better straighten up, because I am certainly not blameless*. But then I learned that to be blameless in God's sight does not mean to perform perfectly and never make the tiniest mistake. It simply means to have a sincere, heartfelt desire to obey God's Word and to live in a way that pleases Him.

If you truly want to live according to God's Word and your heart is to please Him, then you have a blameless heart and are just the type of person in whom God wants to show Himself strong. And You can count on God to show Himself strong on your behalf.

*Thank You, Lord, that I can walk blameless before You because I sincerely want to please You in every way.*

# MAKE A DECISION TO DO WHAT IS RIGHT

*I will not look with approval on anything that is vile. I hate what faithless people do; I will have no part in it. The perverse of heart shall be far from me; I will have nothing to do with what is evil.*

**PSALM 101:3-4**

The world we live in today is filled with all kinds of evil, and as God's children, we must make a firm decision not to compromise righteousness and take part in evil things that go on around us. Be careful who you choose as friends, and steadfastly resist the temptation to do anything you know is not God's will.

In today's verse, the psalmist David declares that he will have no part in anything that is evil or vile, and he will not do what faithless people do. He made a firm decision to disapprove of and avoid it all. God's Word tells us that temptation will come to us (Luke 17:1). Satan sets traps that are designed to lure us into temptation. Pray daily that you will not be deceived when temptation is great.

It is useless to pray that you will not be tempted because you will be, and so will I. Even Jesus faced temptation, but He never sinned (Hebrews 4:15). The apostle Paul writes that God "will not let you be tempted beyond what you can bear," but that He will provide a way out for us (1 Corinthians 10:13). Stand firm. Be strong. And be a godly example for others to follow.

*Father, help me never to compromise morally in order to fit in with anyone if they are doing ungodly things. Help me resist the temptation to compromise and to always stand strong for what is right.*

# GOD GIVES GRACE
# TO THE HUMBLE

*Whoever slanders their neighbor in secret, I will put to silence; whoever
has haughty eyes and a proud heart, I will not tolerate.*

**PSALM 101:5**

God hates pride. Clearly, David hates it too, because he states in
today's scripture that he will not tolerate someone with a proud,
arrogant heart. Pride is something we need to be quick to recognize in our lives, and we will notice it in our thoughts, words, and
attitudes. Every human being will have to confront pride at various times in life. Pride makes us think we are better than others,
it causes us to judge and criticize, and it makes us unwilling to
listen to and respect other people's ideas and opinions. It can even
keep us from loving and appreciating people or from developing
relationships that would be a blessing to us. These are just a few
of the problems pride creates.

God helps and "gives grace to the humble," but He "resists the
proud" (1 Peter 5:5 NKJV). I believe one reason He resists helping those who are proud is that they don't think they need help.
They are independent, but God wants us to be totally dependent
on Him.

If we want to humble ourselves "under God's mighty hand"
(1 Peter 5:6), we need to learn to say, "Apart from Jesus I can
do nothing," based on John 15:5, and realize that everything
we have, everything we are, and everything we can do comes
from Him.

*Lord, keep me from pride and help me to live a humble life, realizing
that apart from You, I can do nothing.*

# JUST BE YOURSELF

*Hear my prayer, Lord; let my cry for help come to you. Do not hide your face from me when I am in distress. Turn your ear to me; when I call, answer me quickly.*

**PSALM 102:1–2**

I love the boldness we see in Psalms. It sets an example we can follow. When the psalmist prayed, he was authentic. He didn't try to sound super spiritual, but he was honest with God about how he felt and what he wanted.

God wants us to be the same way. When you pray, be yourself—your everyday, plain self. Are you at the end of your rope, feeling like you can't take any more? Then you too can tell God you need an answer quickly. He will answer you at just the right time—perhaps not as quickly as you want Him to, but He likes when you are honest with Him and pour out your true feelings.

The religious leaders and Pharisees of Jesus' day were phony. They prayed lengthy, perfect-sounding prayers, but their hearts were far from God (Luke 20:45–47). Be real, genuine, and authentic, and you will get answers from God much quicker than you would trying to sound eloquent. We don't need to try to impress God; we just need to be honest with Him. After all, He already knows how we feel and what we need.

*Father, help me always to be authentic and genuine when I come to You in prayer. I never want to be phony or try to impress You with fancy words.*

# HOPE FOR THE AFFLICTED

*You will arise and have compassion on Zion, for it is time to be gracious and show favor to her; yes, the appointed time [the moment designated] has come.*

**PSALM 102:13 AMP**

According to Merriam-Webster.com, to be *afflicted* is to be "grievously affected or troubled (as by a disease)." An affliction can be physical, but it can also be mental, emotional, or spiritual. Those who are afflicted and going through very difficult situations need God's compassion, grace, and favor. Because He is merciful and compassionate, they can expect God to show compassion to them and deliver them. According to 1 Corinthians 10:13, He does not allow more to come to us than we can bear.

If you are afflicted in some way today, you can be confident that at the exact right moment, God will arise, be gracious, and have compassion on you. Whenever you experience a difficult or trying time, be encouraged that God sees your situation. Know that as long as you put your trust in Him, you will see victory in His timing and according to His way. Stay in faith and be patient. God won't be late.

*Thank You, Father, for being gracious to me and showing me compassion.*

# GOD NEVER CHANGES

*In the beginning you laid the foundations of the earth, and the heavens are the work of your hands. They will perish, but you remain; they will all wear out like a garment. Like clothing you will change them and they will be discarded. But you remain the same, and your years will never end.*

**PSALM 102:25-27**

Everything in the world is subject to change, but God is always the same. People change, and new things wear out, but we can always depend on God. He is the same "yesterday and today and forever" (Hebrews 13:8).

James 1:17 tells us that "every good and perfect gift" comes from God. He is the source of all good things. Isaiah 40:8 tells us that "the word of our God endures forever." It is wonderful to know we can always trust that God will do what He says He will do.

Are you trusting God for something that His Word promises He will do? If so, then don't give up, no matter how long it takes, because it is impossible for Him to not be faithful.

Paul wrote to Timothy and told him that even if we are faithless, God remains faithful, for "He cannot deny Himself" (2 Timothy 2:13 NKJV). Relax and put all your trust in God. He will never leave you without the help you need in order to do whatever you need to do.

*Father, I need Your strength and help today and every day. I'm glad that You never change, and that I can always depend on You to be with me and help me. Thank You.*

# GOD FORGIVES OUR SINS
# AND HEALS OUR DISEASES

*Praise the Lord, my soul; all my inmost being, praise his holy name.
Praise the Lord, my soul, and forget not all his benefits—who forgives
all your sins and heals all your diseases.*

**PSALM 103:1–3**

It is important that we do not forget all the benefits with which
the Lord blesses us. Praise Him for them regularly and thank Him
often. Even in the midst of other activities, we can praise God
in our innermost being, thanking Him for everything He does
for us.

He forgives all our sins, and that is marvelous. He also heals
all our diseases. This does not mean that He heals all of them
miraculously, but I do believe that all healing comes from God.
God still does miracles today, but He also uses medical technol-
ogy and medicine, which I believe He gave human beings the
wisdom to create.

Sometimes we pray for healing, and it comes quickly. At other
times it takes much longer than we would like. In December
2017, I became very sick. I was diagnosed with severe adrenal
fatigue and told to rest for eighteen months. The recovery actually took longer than eighteen months, but thankfully I now feel
very well. Over the years, God has healed me from many different
things, and I trust Him for healing no matter how long it takes
or how it comes.

*Father, I believe You are the Creator of all healing, and I trust You for
healing. I am grateful that You forgive all my sins, and I praise and
thank You.*

# A YOUTHFUL MINDSET

*Who satisfies your desires with good things so that your youth is renewed like the eagle's.*

**PSALM 103:5**

The idea of having our youth "renewed like the eagle's" probably sounds good to most people, because certain aspects of staying young are appealing to us. For example, I don't know anyone who enjoys getting wrinkles or arthritis. We would prefer to keep our skin, our joints, and our organs from growing old and developing the problems that sometimes come with advancing age.

Age is a number. Getting old is a mindset. I believe we can age with a youthful mindset as our bodies grow older, and to me, this is one way our youth can be renewed like the eagle's. An important key to a youthful mindset is to continue to do everything we can do and enjoy it, while also making the adjustments we need to make.

My husband, Dave, is an avid golfer. He *loves* playing golf, practicing golf, watching golf, and even reading about golf. I once asked him how he thought it would affect him if he reached a point where he can't play golf. He replied, "I've already thought about it and made up my mind to be happy anyway and to find other things to do." Dave's comment represents a healthy mindset toward aging, one that will allow him to be happy in any stage of life.

Today, I hope you will decide to have a positive attitude and a youthful mindset toward growing older, so you can enjoy doing all the things you can do, even if you need to make some adjustments to do them.

*Father, thank You for every stage of my life. As I grow older, help me to develop a youthful mindset and to find ways to enjoy the life You have given me. Give me grace to make any adjustment I need to make to continue to live each day to the fullest.*

# WHEN YOU BECOME ANGRY

*The Lord is merciful and gracious, slow to anger, and abounding in mercy.*

**PSALM 103:8 NKJV**

Today's scripture reminds us that the Lord is "slow to anger," but you and I do not always follow this example. We can become angry quickly. When we do become angry, though, we know that we can be "angry, and yet do not sin" (Ephesians 4:26 NASB).

The feeling of anger is not a sin; it is what we do with our anger that determines whether it becomes sin or not. To feel anger when we are mistreated is human nature. But the person who can control their anger is said to be stronger than someone who "takes a city" (Proverbs 16:32).

Forgiveness is the answer to anger. It is a gift God has given us to keep us safe from the trouble anger causes if we let it fester. Being angry and holding unforgiveness against someone is very destructive, but being quick to forgive solves both of those problems.

You may think the person who hurt you doesn't deserve to be forgiven, but the point is that you deserve peace, and you can have it by forgiving. When you forgive someone who has wronged you, you are doing yourself a favor. Hating someone is like taking poison and hoping your enemy will die; it doesn't work. When we forgive, God can go to work solving the problem, but as long as we remain angry, the door stays open for the devil to work.

*Father, help me not to stay angry when I do become angry. Help me to be quick to forgive. I don't want unforgiveness to open a door for the devil to work in my life.*

# OUR SINS ARE PAID FOR

*As far as the east is from the west, so far has he removed our transgressions from us.*

**PSALM 103:12**

I believe God gives each of us abilities and corresponding energy to fulfill His plans and purposes for our lives. If you feel low on energy, you may be surprised to know this, but it could be the result of faulty thinking in some area of your life. Negative thoughts—fear, bitterness, guilt, discouragement, resentment, unforgiveness, and others—always steal energy.

Some of the most energy-draining kinds of thoughts we think are about past mistakes, failures, and sins, which produce guilt and condemnation. The enemy loves to fill our minds with thoughts of past failures we cannot do anything about. But we can choose how we will think about these things. We can dwell on the past and what we have lost, or we can think about the future and the opportunities in front of us. We can focus on our sins, or we can think about God's grace, demonstrated by sending Jesus to pay for our sins and remove them completely.

We cannot pay for our sins with feelings of guilt, because Jesus already paid for our sins when He died on the cross. His sacrifice is good for all time (Hebrews 10:10). There is nothing we can add to what Jesus has done. We can only receive with humility and gratitude the complete forgiveness He offers and refuse the guilt—because we know our sins are removed as far as the east is from the west.

*Thank You, God, for sending Jesus to suffer and die for my sins. I know that I am forgiven completely, and I have no guilt or condemnation for past failures and sins.*

# PUT YOUR ANGELS TO WORK

*Bless (affectionately, gratefully praise) the Lord, you His angels, you mighty ones who do His commandments, hearkening to the voice of His word.*

**PSALM 103:20 AMPC**

We all have guardian angels who will work on our behalf, protecting and helping us, if we give them the right material to work with. That material is the Word of God. Today's scripture says they hearken (listen) to His Word, and we can assume they don't listen to or work according to our complaining or murmuring.

God's Word tells us repeatedly in a variety of ways how powerful the words of our mouth are and how careful we need to be about what we say. It was interesting for me to find out from today's scripture that my words also affect what my angels can or cannot do for me.

I want my angels to be able to do all they can do for me, and I am sure you feel the same way, so we should be wise in what we say. For example, instead of saying, "I can't do that," we should say, based on Philippians 4:13, "I can do all things that God wants me to do through Christ, who gives me strength." Don't say, "I'll never have any money," but say, "God supplies all my needs according to His riches in glory by Christ Jesus" (Philippians 4:19). Let your angels work for you, and you will experience more good things in your life.

*Father, thank You for giving me angels who work on my behalf and who hearken to Your Word. Grant me the wisdom to speak words of life that my angels can use.*

# GOD HAS DONE MARVELOUS THINGS

*How many are your works, Lord! In wisdom you made them all; the earth is full of your creatures. There is the sea, vast and spacious, teeming with creatures beyond number—living things both large and small.*

**PSALM 104:24-25**

I have mentioned before that I enjoy watching documentaries about nature. They remind me of the greatness of God and how marvelous He is. The variety of animals, fish, insects, birds, flowers, and trees is beyond amazing. I watched one program about the colors of animals, and it was quite intriguing. If we simply think of the peacock and how majestic it looks when its tail feathers are spread out, it leaves us in awe. The peahen does not have flamboyant tail feathers like the male has; peacocks have them to impress the peahens during mating season. Many other kinds of male birds have stunning colors they display, along with dances designed entirely to impress and attract the females for mating purposes.

We enjoy all the colors in nature, but we usually don't even think about how amazing they are. Think about how dull life would look if there were no colors and everything was black and white or gray. God does many wonderful things simply for our enjoyment, yet we often fail to appreciate them.

God has also given animals instincts that urge them to take specific actions at specific times. Some fish and other animals travel thousands of miles each year to the exact same spot for the sole purpose of giving birth in that place. When their young are old enough, they return to where they were born—and repeat the cycle the following year. All I can say is that God is amazing.

*Father, when I think of all the things You do each day just to keep the earth in good running order and to feed all the animals in the world, I cannot doubt that You will also take care of me. Thank You.*

# BELIEVE FOR GOOD

*When you open your hand, they are satisfied with good things.*

**PSALM 104:28**

When you think about the days ahead of you, are you confident that God has good things in store for you, or do you think, *Well, things have never worked out for me in the past, so I'm not sure anything will go well in the future.*

Let me remind you of 2 Corinthians 5:17: "Therefore, if anyone is in Christ, he is a new creation. The old has passed away; behold, the new has come" (ESV). As a new creation in Christ, you don't have to allow the old things that happened to you to continue to influence your thinking or affect your life. The old things have passed away. You're a new person with a new life in Christ. You can begin to have your mind renewed by studying God's Word and learning about His good plan for you. Good things are going to happen to you, and you can start believing that you will be "satisfied with good things," as we read in today's scripture.

Even if your reality is filled with negatives, you can still have a positive attitude toward it. In every situation, trust God and know that He loves you. Believe that He works good out of *all* things (Romans 8:28).

Rejoice! It's a new day, a day for good things.

*Thank You, Lord, that everything old in my life has passed away. I am a new creation in Christ, and I look forward to the good things You have in store for me.*

# CHOOSE YOUR THOUGHTS CAREFULLY

*I will sing to the Lord all my life; I will sing praise to my God as long as I live. May my meditation be pleasing to him, as I rejoice in the Lord.*

**PSALM 104:33–34**

In today's scriptures, the psalmist writes about the greatness of God and declares that he will sing to and praise God all his life. We should make the same commitment. No matter how many problems you may have right now, you have much more to praise God for. Take time often to think of the majestic things God has created, and it will help you realize that He has no problem handling your difficulties.

We meditate on something most of the time. Our meditation consists of the thoughts that run through our mind either purposely or randomly, and they are important. David prays in Psalm 19:14 that his words and meditations would be pleasing in God's sight, and here the psalmist prays the same prayer.

Literally thousands of thoughts run through our minds, and the more we can train ourselves to choose what to meditate on instead of just meditating on whatever falls into our minds, the better off we will be. Our thoughts turn into words and actions and determine the quality of our life, so they are very important. I urge you to consider what you think about and make sure your meditations are pleasing to God.

*Father, I will praise You all my life for all the marvelous things that You do, and I ask You to help me meditate only on things that are pleasing to You.*

# SEEKING AND LONGING FOR GOD

*Seek and deeply long for the Lord and His strength [His power, His might]; seek and deeply long for His face and His presence continually.*

**PSALM 105:4 AMP**

Throughout the Book of Psalms, we see that David deeply longs for the Lord. He could have longed for other things—just as you and I can—but his deepest yearning was for God.

In Psalm 27:4, David writes: "*One thing* I ask from the Lord, *this only* do I seek: that I may dwell in the house of the Lord all the days of my life, to gaze on the beauty of the Lord and to seek him in his temple" (italics mine). The only thing he wanted was to be in God's presence. If he couldn't have that, nothing else mattered. That's a deep longing!

I believe your heart, like David's, longs for God. The way to satisfy this great hunger and thirst is to seek Him. You seek Him by reading His Word, praying, spending time with Him, thinking about Him, talking about Him, and acting in ways that glorify Him. He promises in Jeremiah 29:13, "You will seek me and find me when you seek me with all your heart." You aren't likely to find God in a way that fulfills your heart's deep longing by casually glancing around for Him, but you *will* find Him if you seek Him deliberately, diligently, and with all your heart.

There is no better way to spend your time and energy than by seeking God, and there is no better place to be than in His presence. That's where your deepest longing will be satisfied.

*Father, I deeply long for You. Help me to seek You and Your presence above all else.*

# PATIENT AND POSITIVE

*And he sent a man before them—Joseph, sold as a slave. They bruised his feet with shackles, his neck was put in irons, till what he foretold came to pass, till the word of the Lord proved him true.*

**PSALM 105:17-19**

Today's scripture reminds us of Joseph and the unjust treatment he received from his brothers. They sold him into slavery and told his father that a wild animal had killed him. Meanwhile, a wealthy man named Potiphar purchased Joseph and took him into his home as a slave. God gave Joseph favor everywhere he went, and soon he found favor with his new master.

Joseph kept getting promoted, but then he ended up being falsely accused of having an affair with his boss's wife and ended up in prison.

Joseph tried to help others the entire time he was in prison. He did not complain, but he was patient and had a positive attitude in his suffering, and God eventually delivered him and promoted him to the point where no one else in Egypt had more authority than Joseph, except Pharaoh himself.

God also vindicated Joseph with his brothers, and he displayed a godly attitude by refusing to mistreat them, even though they deserved it. He said that what they had meant for his harm, God had worked out for his good—that they were in God's hands, not his, and that he had no right to do anything but bless them (Genesis 37–45). We can expect similar results when we stay patient through suffering and keep a positive, forgiving attitude.

*Lord, when I go through times of suffering or difficulty, help me stay patient and positive and be willing to forgive those who have treated me wrongly.*

# BE LED BY GOD

*He spread out a cloud as a covering, and a fire to give light at night.*

**PSALM 105:39**

When the Israelites were delivered out of Egypt and on their way to the Promised Land, God led them by a cloud during the day and a pillar of fire at night (Exodus 13:21). When the cloud settled, they had to stop traveling, and when the cloud moved, they had to move and follow it (Numbers 9:22). Sometimes the cloud remained in place for a long time, and at other times it did not. But whenever the cloud moved, the Israelites had to be ready to move also.

This represents how we need to be ready to follow God, even if it requires changes we did not plan to make. Some people find change exciting and adventurous, but others hate change and resist it steadfastly. Change is part of life, and when circumstances change, the first thing we need to do is embrace the transition, because resisting it will only make life more difficult.

Following God is not boring, because we never know what He will do or ask us to do. One change we all must face is letting go of things that God is finished with, or stopping things we should not do any longer. I encourage you to follow God, because even though His ways are not our ways, they are best.

*Father, I want to follow You and not stubbornly hold on to things that You are finished with. Teach me to follow You at all times. Thank You.*

# ENJOY THE JOURNEY

*We have sinned, even as our ancestors did; we have done wrong and acted wickedly. When our ancestors were in Egypt, they gave no thought to your miracles; they did not remember your many kindnesses, and they rebelled by the sea, the Red Sea.*

**PSALM 106:6-7**

Today's scriptures represent only two verses of many in Psalm 106 that remind us of how the Israelites behaved as God led them out of Egypt toward the Promised Land. Among acting out other bad attitudes, including complaining and rebellion, they became self-centered and demanding. This warns us of the dangers of a greedy heart, because such a heart is never satisfied—and that is an unsafe spiritual condition.

Although God had led the Israelites out of bondage in Egypt and had destroyed Pharaoh and his army, who were chasing after them, the Israelites were not satisfied (see Psalm 106:8–25). No matter how much He provided for them, they always wanted more. They were on the way to the Promised Land, but they were not enjoying the journey. Many times, we have the same problem.

If people are not careful, they can waste their entire lives wanting what they do not have. No matter what their place in life, they always want something else. They keep murmuring and grumbling to God about what they want. When He gives it to them, they start complaining again because they want something more.

The Israelites eventually got what they asked for, but they were not ready to handle it. Ask God to give you a heart that is satisfied and content at every point along your life's journey and one that is able to handle increase when it comes. Instead of complaining, learn to enjoy where you are on the way to where you are going.

*Father, thank You for leading me into a good place. Help me to enjoy the journey and to be satisfied with every gift You give me.*

# REMEMBERING BUILDS TRUST

*Then they believed his promises and sang his praise. But they soon forgot what he had done and did not wait for his plan to unfold.*

**PSALM 106:12-13**

God miraculously delivered the Israelites from almost unbearable conditions in slavery in Egypt. As He led them into freedom, they "believed his promises and sang his praise." But before long, they forgot about God's amazing deliverance. Even after He led them to settle in a land of peace and abundance, they complained and grumbled (Psalm 106:24–25).

People today can be tempted to be just like the Israelites in the Old Testament. God can do something incredible for us, something that causes us to know His Word is true, and we can soon forget His promises and begin to doubt His Word.

If you have been frustrated lately and found yourself complaining, if you have lost your peace and joy, ask yourself this question: *Am I believing God's Word?* The only way to rest in God's promises and to live in His joy and peace is to believe His Word.

Perhaps you could take time today to list the situations that have caused you to know that God's Word is true and trustworthy. Remember how He has come through for you or worked miracles in your life. Think about how you praised Him when He worked on your behalf. Let those remembrances stir your faith to believe God and to trust Him in fresh new ways for whatever you face today.

*Father, help me not to forget any of the wonderful things You have done for me, but to remember them and to give You praise.*

# IS WHAT YOU THINK YOU WANT WHAT YOU REALLY WANT?

*In the desert they gave in to their craving; in the wilderness they put God to the test. So he gave them what they asked for, but sent a wasting disease among them.*

**PSALM 106:14–15**

I mentioned yesterday the Israelites in the wilderness. Just as they did, we often crave things that will not be good for us, but God allows us to have them in order to teach us a lesson. We may think we want something and beg God to give it to us, only to find out we are not ready to handle the responsibility that comes with it.

People frequently tell me they wish they had a ministry like mine. When they say this, most of the time they are only looking at the fact that I am on television or have the privilege of preaching to large crowds. They have no idea of all the hard work that goes on behind the scenes or the thousands of hours I spend preparing messages and writing books. They don't know about the critical judgment that people in the public eye are likely to receive.

Be wise about wanting what someone else has, and realize that with every privilege comes a corresponding responsibility. You can ask God for anything you want, but it is wise to also say to Him, "Please don't give it to me unless it will be best for me."

*Father, I want Your will in my life more than I want my own will. Give me what is best for me, not simply what I think I want.*

# THE PAIN OF ENVY

*In the camp they grew envious of Moses and of Aaron, who was consecrated to the Lord. The earth opened up and swallowed Dathan; it buried the company of Abiram.*

**PSALM 106:16–17**

The world is filled with trouble, and not one of us can avoid it. Just think of the people who are sick, or parents whose children have terrible diseases, or people who need jobs and don't have them. There is enough trouble in the world without causing trouble for ourselves, which is exactly what we do when we envy other people.

God gives each of us what He knows we can handle. Although His decisions may not always seem fair to us, we should remember that He does not make mistakes. He knows what He is doing, and we should trust Him in that.

If God doesn't choose you for something you want, the best course of action is to be happy for the person He did choose and know that He will promote you at the right time. Being jealous or envious doesn't change God's mind; it only makes you miserable. So be content with what you have and stay happy.

*Father, help me to be content with what You have given me and not ever to be jealous or envious of others. Amen.*

# STAY PURE

*They mingled with the nations and adopted their customs. They worshipped their idols, which became a snare to them.*

**PSALM 106:35–36**

We live in the world, but we are not to think and behave as the world does (John 17:16). God's children are a set-apart people. We belong to Him and should stay pure for His use. The Israelites were warned to have nothing to do with the idolatrous nations around them, but they disobeyed and mingled with them. They worshipped their idols, and this became a snare (a trap) for them.

Sometimes saying no to ungodly things is difficult, but if we do it, we will later enjoy the fruit of having been obedient to God. It is important to stay pure and not have a mixture of the godly and the ungodly in our life. We cannot belong to God halfway and belong to the world halfway. According to 1 John 2:15–17, we should not love the world or the things in it. If we do love the world, these verses tell us, then love for the Father is not in us.

We can certainly enjoy the things in the world that are not sinful, but we cannot love them more than we love God or allow them to pull us away from Him. God requires first place in our lives, and if we don't give it to Him, we will end up in a trap that Satan has designed for our destruction.

*Father, help me to be in this world without becoming worldly. I want to stay pure for You and for Your use. Help me not to compromise and get mixed up with the wrong people or wrong things.*

# SPEAK GOD'S TRUTH

*Let the redeemed of the Lord say so, whom He has redeemed from the hand of the adversary.*

**PSALM 107:2 AMP**

You and I have been "redeemed from the hand of the adversary." But this doesn't mean the devil will leave us alone. When you realize that the enemy is trying to harass you with negative thoughts or worries, you can allow him to succeed, or you can stand up to him. One way to stand against him is to remember how God has redeemed you and to say so, as today's scripture instructs. In other words, open your mouth and begin to confess all that God has done for you in Christ.

Satan places anxious, negative thoughts in our minds, sometimes actually bombarding our minds with them. He hopes we will receive them and begin speaking them. If we do, he then has material to actually create in our lives the very circumstances he has caused us to be worried about.

Once we recognize ungodly thoughts, we can take authority over them, ask for God's help, and determine to live the good life God wants us to live, not the life the enemy wants us to live.

Let me encourage you not to be the devil's mouthpiece. Don't speak the lies he puts into your mind. Find out what God's Word promises you and begin to declare His truth. As we speak His Word in faith, we wield a mighty sword that exposes and defeats the enemy's tactics and lies.

*Lord, when the enemy brings negative thoughts into my mind, help me to remember to stand against them by speaking Your Word, which always defeats him.*

# GOD'S HEALING WORD

*He sent out his word and healed them; he rescued them from the grave.*

**PSALM 107:20**

I have said probably thousands of times, "Jesus heals us everywhere we hurt." I have experienced this personally, and I have seen Him heal countless other people in all kinds of ways. I *know* there is healing in the Word of God, and it has the power to change your life completely.

As a result of sexual abuse during my childhood, I developed many wrong mindsets that kept me hurt and wounded. But as God's Word renewed my mind (Romans 12:1–2), I began to think differently and speak differently. Eventually, my attitudes and behavior also changed. Anyone who lives according to His Word can expect the same kind of results.

Do you need healing in some way? Are you tired of carrying the burden of pain, shame, guilt, anger, fear, or other negative emotions? Would you like to put the pain of the past behind you and be led into a wonderful future? Then make God's Word a priority. Spend time reading and studying it. Think about it and believe it. Confess it (speak it aloud) and remind yourself of it often.

No matter who has wounded or offended you, no matter what you have done or what has been done to you, God is your healer. And His Word has the power to heal you *everywhere* you hurt.

*Father, thank You for Your Word. As it renews my mind, help me to experience its healing power.*

# THE AMAZING MERCY
## OF GOD

*He stilled the storm to a whisper; the waves of the sea were hushed.
They were glad when it grew calm, and he guided them to their desired
haven. Let them give thanks to the Lord for his unfailing love and his
wonderful deeds for mankind.*

**PSALM 107:29–31**

Throughout Psalm 107 we read accounts of the Israelites rebelling
against God, having trouble, repenting, and God being merciful
to them and restoring their blessings. Our God is indeed merciful, and truly His mercies are new every morning, as Lamentations 3:22–23 promises. Consider this beautiful scripture in its
entirety: "The steadfast love of the Lord never ceases; his mercies
never come to an end; they are new every morning; great is your
faithfulness" (ESV).

When we wake up each day, a fresh supply of God's mercy is
available to us. I am so thankful that God's mercy never runs out,
and I am sure you are too.

Let us give thanks to the Lord for His unfailing love and His
wonderful deeds for us. We could never thank God too often
for His mercy, forgiveness, and kindness to us. We should never
forget these blessings, but always keep in mind that we would be
destroyed if it were not for God's kindness and favor.

*Father, thank You for mercy and Your unfailing love. Thank You for
Your extreme patience with me and for restoring me over and over
again. I ask that my mouth would always be filled with thanksgiving
for You.*

# THE GOD OF INCREASE

*He blessed them, and their numbers greatly increased, and he did not let their herds diminish.*

**PSALM 107:38**

God is a God of increase. Whatever we give to Him, He gives back to us multiplied many times over. God wants us to grow and increase in all areas of life—in wisdom, humility, holiness, finances, good health, and knowledge of Him.

One of the most important ways in which He wants us to increase is love. First Thessalonians 3:12 says, "May the Lord make your love increase and overflow for each other and for everyone else, just as ours does for you."

The Lord also "gives strength to the weary and increases the power of the weak" (Isaiah 40:29). God is a God of increase, but Satan wants to diminish us. He comes only to steal, kill, and destroy (John 10:10). He wants to make us feel little and have little lives, but God wants to do exceedingly and abundantly above and beyond all we could ask, hope, or think (Ephesians 3:20).

As you wait on God, expect Him to do great things in your life, and expect increase. Don't let the devil make you feel little or diminished, and when he tries, remember that he is a liar (John 8:44).

*Father, thank You for bringing increase into my life in every area. Help me recognize and resist Satan when he is trying to diminish me.*

# GOD IS FAITHFUL

*For great is your love, higher than the heavens; your faithfulness reaches to the skies.*

**PSALM 108:4**

How great is God's love? It is too great to measure, higher than the heavens. Paul prayed that the people to whom he ministered would know the height, depth, length, and breadth of God's love for them (Ephesians 3:17–19). When we know how much God loves us, it solves the problem of fear and insecurity. It makes us bold, and we are not so afraid of making mistakes that we won't step out in faith and take advantage of the opportunities God gives us.

I urge you to meditate on how much God loves you. Not only is His love higher than the heavens, but the psalmist David says that His "faithfulness reaches to the skies," indicating that it is too great to be measured. Even when we are faithless, God remains faithful (2 Timothy 2:13). God will never let us down. He may not do everything we ask Him to do, but if He doesn't, it is because He has something better in mind.

God will never leave you or forsake you. He is with you at this very moment. He is never more than one thought away. All you need to do to bring Him into your presence is to think about Him or to say something to Him. God is always working on your behalf, and He has great things planned for you.

*Father, thank You for Your love and faithfulness. Knowing that I can always depend on You allows me to enter Your rest instead of worrying.*

# GOD GIVES VICTORY

*Give us aid against the enemy, for human help is worthless. With God we will gain the victory, and he will trample down our enemies.*

**PSALM 108:12–13**

Too often, when we are in trouble or have questions we need answered, we run to our friends for help. But we should always go to God first. He may use a person to help us or to speak a timely word to us, but if it doesn't originate with God, it will be useless.

God gives us victory over our enemies if we listen to and obey Him. He will fight for us, and while we wait, we can expect to see Him do great things and look forward to them. Ask God for help, pray for and forgive your enemies as God instructs, and avoid depending on human flesh, for God says clearly in today's scripture that "human help is worthless."

Dave and I have four adult children, and we love for them to come to us for advice. It shows that they respect and value our opinion. If they always went to other people for counsel, we would feel that they don't value our ability to help them. I imagine God is the same way. He is our Father, and He wants us to run to Him for all the help we need.

If you have asked God to help you but you don't see anything changing yet, don't be discouraged. As long as you keep believing, God is working.

*Father, I am thankful that You are always working on my behalf and that You will give me victory over my enemies.*

# PRAYER POWER

*My God, whom I praise, do not remain silent, for people who are wicked and deceitful have opened their mouths against me; they have spoken against me with lying tongues. With words of hatred they surround me; they attack me without cause. In return for my friendship they accuse me, but I am a man of prayer.*

**PSALM 109:1–4**

Prayer is the most effective way to defeat the devil. When we pray, we are calling on God's power to do for us what we cannot do for ourselves. The fervent, effective prayer of a righteous person avails much, making tremendous power available (James 5:16). Always remember that when you pray, tremendous power is made available, whether you feel anything or not. We pray by faith, not by feelings.

In today's scripture, the psalmist David was in a difficult place. He was surrounded by people who hated him and attacked him without cause, but he believed that as he prayed, God would work on his behalf, deal with his enemies, and give him victory.

Whatever you may be dealing with now or in the future, remember to pray before doing anything else. Sometimes people say, "Well I guess there is nothing left to do but pray." Prayer is not a last-ditch effort; it should always be our first line of defense.

*Father, forgive me for all the times I have tried to solve my own problems and failed. Help me to always remember to pray before doing anything else and to believe in the wonderful power of prayer.*

# COULD YOU BE A "HEALED HEALER"?

*For I am poor and needy, and my heart is wounded within me.*

**PSALM 109:22**

Today's scripture speaks of a wounded heart, and if your heart is hurting or wounded, I encourage you to receive God's healing so you can go on with your life, enjoy it, and fulfill the plans and purposes He has for you.

In Old Testament days, if a priest had a wound or a bleeding sore, he could not minister. I think we can learn from that today, because we have a lot of wounded people who are trying to minister and bring healing to others while they ignore their own wounds, which remain unhealed. These people are still bleeding and hurting. They are what I call "wounded healers."

But there are also "healed healers," and God loves to use people who have been hurt or wounded and then healed, because nobody can minister to someone better than a person who has been in the same situation as the person they are trying to help. Ask God to heal you everywhere you hurt so He can use you to help others. Ask Him to make you a healed healer.

*Father, thank You for Your desire and ability to heal every wounded heart, including mine. Heal me and use me to help others also find healing in You.*

# ENTERING GOD'S REST

*The Lord says to my lord: "Sit at my right hand until I make your enemies a footstool for your feet."*

**PSALM 110:1**

Today's scripture refers to entering the rest of God. We are invited to sit at His right hand in Christ until He deals with our enemies and makes them a stool for our feet. Being seated with Christ means we have entered God's rest. This is a special kind of rest that is not a rest *from* work, but a rest *while* we work and do what we need to do. We don't have to worry or be anxious, but we can trust that God is working on our behalf.

The writer to the Hebrews urged them not to fail to enter the rest of God while it was available, and he taught them that the way to enter it is through believing (Hebrews 3:19, 4:1–3). When we trust (believe) God's promises, it takes all the pressure off us. We trust that God is working even though we may not see or feel anything. "Faith is the assurance...of the things [we] hope for, being the proof of things [we] do not see and the conviction of their reality" (Hebrews 11:1 AMPC).

If you have experienced God's rest, you know how wonderful it is. But if you haven't, then once you do enter into it, you will be amazed at how much you can enjoy your life while God solves your problems. He isn't asking you to worry, fret, be anxious, or try to reason an answer. He simply wants you to believe He is faithful and will give you victory as you trust Him.

*Father, thank You that I can enter Your rest while You deal with my enemies. Thank You for teaching me all I need to know about entering it.*

# RULING OVER OUR ENEMIES

*The Lord will extend your mighty scepter from Zion, saying, "Rule in the midst of your enemies!"*

**PSALM 110:2**

We have an enemy, Satan (the devil), but God has given us power and authority over him (Luke 10:19). Satan does have power, but we have power and authority in Christ. Having authority is good, but for it to be effective, we must exercise it. Jesus spoke to Satan and told him to get behind Him (Matthew 16:23). In this instance, Satan was working through Peter, attempting to stop Him from going forward with God's plan of redemption for all humanity.

At other times, Jesus simply quoted the Word to Satan when He was being tempted to do things that would be against God's will (Luke 4:1–13). The Word of God is the most effective weapon we have against the enemy.

Satan is a liar, according to John 8:44, and any thought that comes into your mind that doesn't agree with God's Word is a lie from him and should be resisted immediately. The mind is the field on which we win or lose our battle with the devil. Renew your mind according to God's Word, and you will see and experience the good plan God has for your life (Romans 12:2).

By wielding the Word of God, you can rule in the midst of your enemies. Submit to God, resist the enemy, and the enemy will flee (James 4:6–7). God has placed all things under Jesus' feet (Ephesians 1:22), and because we are His body, these things are also under our feet. Lift up your head and live as a conqueror, because you are one.

*Father, thank You for giving me authority and power over my enemies. Help me remember to speak Your Word when the enemy attacks me and always to walk in obedience to You.*

# GOD OUR PROVIDER

*He provides food for those who fear him; he remembers his covenant forever.*

**PSALM 111:5**

Do you need provision in an area of your life, and you are not really sure where it will come from? Be encouraged, because in today's scripture God promises to provide for those who fear Him, meaning those who worship and honor Him with awe-inspired reverence. As long as we worship God, we can expect His provision.

Perhaps someone who has provided for you in the past has died, or you are losing your job, or you will soon be on a fixed income. If you are concerned about provision for any reason, mark Psalm 111:5 in your Bible. Meditate on it and even memorize it, because believing it is a key to having your needs met. If you have this promise in your heart, then when a need arises in your life, this verse will strengthen you and help you live in faith, not in fear.

Believe God's Word when He says He gives food and provision to those who reverently fear Him and worship Him. Whatever your situation may be, God will provide for you as you continue to worship and honor Him.

Worship is actually fun and energizing, while worry makes our hearts heavy and causes a loss of joy. Do not worry; worship and watch God provide for your every need.

*Thank You, Father, for meeting all my needs as I reverently fear and worship You.*

# THE BEGINNING OF WISDOM

*The fear of the Lord is the beginning of wisdom; all who follow his precepts have good understanding. To him belongs eternal praise.*

**PSALM 111:10**

The Bible teaches that those who walk in wisdom will be blessed, fruitful, and happy (Proverbs 2:1–24, 28:26). I like to define wisdom as the right use of knowledge, and to say that walking in wisdom is doing now what you will be happy with later.

According to Proverbs 3:1–18, wise people will be so blessed, in fact, that they will be envied. There is no such thing as wisdom without worship. But how do people become wise? Today's scripture says that the fear of the Lord, which means reverent, awe-struck worship, is the beginning of wisdom. In other words, reverence is foundational to having a successful life in God's eyes.

Many people today are seeking knowledge and information, and we have worlds of knowledge and information in the palm of our hand each day. All we have to do is punch a few buttons on our phone, and it is amazing what we can learn. Knowledge and information are good, but wisdom is far better. Knowledge without wisdom can cause people to be pompous or proud, which will ultimately be detrimental to them. Wise people are knowledgeable, but not all knowledgeable people are wise.

We should seek wisdom diligently and "search for her as you would hidden treasures" (Proverbs 2:4 AMP). Nothing is more important than wisdom, and it starts with reverence toward God.

*Lord, I ask today for wisdom, and I know that it begins with worship and godly fear of You. I worship You with all my heart.*

# DON'T FEAR BAD NEWS

*They will have no fear of bad news; their hearts are steadfast, trusting in the Lord.*

**PSALM 112:7**

Because the early years of my life were filled with abuse, I made the mistake of beginning to expect and be afraid of bad news. It seemed that nothing good ever happened to me, so I stopped hoping or thinking it would. Later in life, when my relationship with God was growing, I realized I constantly had an ominous feeling around me. I didn't understand this until God told me it was "evil forebodings."

I had never heard the term *evil forebodings*, but ran across a scripture that explained it to me: "All the days of the desponding and afflicted are made evil [by anxious thoughts and forebodings], but he who has a glad heart has a continual feast [regardless of circumstances]" (Proverbs 15:15 AMPC).

I had experienced so many disappointments in my life that I had begun to expect them and fear them. But we see in today's scripture that the righteous "will have no fear of bad news." The children of God trust Him and know He will meet their needs and guide them as they handle every situation that arises. Let me encourage you not to fear bad news, because God loves you and has a good plan for your life.

*Father, I am grateful that I don't have to fear bad news. Help me to always be confident that You will take care of me no matter what the circumstance may be.*

# GOD HONORS
# THE POOR AND NEEDY

*He raises the poor from the dust and lifts the needy from the ash heap;*
*he seats them with princes, with the princes of his people.*

**PSALM 113:7–8**

Human beings tend to view some people as better than others, but God values everyone equally. The poor and needy are often made to feel as though they belong to a lower class, but God will lift them up and cause them to sit in high places with people in whose presence they may have never thought they would be, called "princes" in today's scripture.

God has a special place in His heart for the poor, the needy, and the hurting. He wants to comfort them and elevate them to a place of dignity. God lifts up those who have been oppressed or treated unjustly, and He will give them a double portion for their former pain and oppression (Isaiah 61:7). If you feel you have been belittled, or if you are poor and needy, you can look forward to God promoting you to a place of honor.

God has you marked for blessings. He has planned your deliverance and your reward. Put your trust in Him and know that nothing in this world can drag you down unless you let it.

Lift up praise to God now and forever, because He is good and worthy of praise.

*Father, thank You for lifting me up and giving me honor among Your people.*

# THE GREATNESS OF GOD

*Tremble, earth, at the presence of the Lord, at the presence of the God of Jacob.*

**PSALM 114:7**

God is great and mighty, and we should tremble in His presence not because we are afraid of Him, but in reverence and awe, realizing how powerful He is. When I am invited to go to a church to minister the Word of God, I have a reverential fear of the pastor, and I want to be respectful. I do what I am asked to do and stick to the time frame I am given. I know the pastor has the power to either invite me back or never ask me again. Having a reverential fear of God means that we obey Him and want to please Him because we know that He has the power to bless our lives or to remove blessings if He so chooses.

It seems to me that few Christians have, or even understand, the fear of the Lord. The Bible says that "the fear of the Lord is the beginning of wisdom" (Proverbs 9:10). It also speaks of "perfecting holiness in the fear of God" (2 Corinthians 7:1 NASB). God has called us to live holy lives, but we can't do so without the reverential fear of Him.

God is great, and He wants to show His greatness in your life, but it's important to remember to ask Him to do so. As James 4:2 says, "You do not have because you do not ask God." Go to God's throne boldly and ask Him for more than you think is possible, remembering that all things are possible with Him (Matthew 19:26).

*Father, thank You for all You have done in my life. I ask You to do great things, and I also ask that You help me increase in holy living and teach me to reverently fear You.*

# GIVE GOD ALL THE GLORY

*Not to us, Lord, not to us but to your name be the glory, because of your love and faithfulness.*

**PSALM 115:1**

God does many wonderful things for us and through us, and we should be careful to give Him the glory (credit). It is a tragic mistake to begin to think that we are the cause or the source of our blessings. Don't think God is blessing you because of your goodness or abilities, but instead remember that He is blessing you in spite of your mistakes.

The best and quickest way to lose your blessings is to take credit for them. Give God all the glory, because He is not willing to share His glory with anyone else. First Corinthians 1:27–31 teaches us that God chooses the weak and foolish things of the world to work through, so no one may boast in His presence. We should also be careful not to give the credit due to God to any other person or thing. He is the source of everything that is good. Praise Him often and thank Him frequently for all He does in your life, and remember that apart from Him, you can do nothing (John 15:5).

I frequently remind myself that nothing good dwells in my flesh (Romans 7:18), and that without God, I am nothing and can do nothing. In the Amplified Bible, Classic Edition version of Psalm 36:11, the psalmist David writes, "Let not the foot of pride overtake me," and pride can easily overtake all of us. Pride chases us, always trying to find an entrance into our lives because Satan, the author of pride, knows that God exalts the humble, but pride brings destruction.

*Father, help me remain humble at all times and always to give You the glory that is due to You alone.*

# BLESSINGS ARE HEADED YOUR WAY

*May the Lord cause you to flourish, both you and your children. May you be blessed by the Lord, the Maker of heaven and earth.*

**PSALM 115:14–15**

God's desire is to bless you and your children. He is always good, and He has good things planned for you. Perhaps you have gone through a difficult and dry season; if so, you should expect things to change and get better.

Be full of hope always. This means that you expect something good to happen at any moment. God wants us to believe His promises, and I view our scriptures for today as one example of the promises we should expect to see fulfilled. You and your children will flourish and be blessed by God. Expect this for yourself and for your children. Speak it, and while you wait on God to do it, be a blessing to someone around you. By being good to others, you sow seed for your harvest.

When we as parents make godly decisions, our children inherit the blessings we receive from God. Then they follow our example and make godly choices in their own life. We face many decisions each day. Making godly decisions is important, because what we do today will determine our quality of life tomorrow.

Be wise and do now what you will be happy with later.

*Father, I am expecting good things to happen to me and to my children because You have promised me that they would. Help me be a blessing to others as I wait on You.*

# GOD HEARS

*I love the Lord, for he heard my voice; he heard my cry for mercy. Because he turned his ear to me, I will call on him as long as I live.*

**PSALM 116:1–2**

It is wonderful to fully believe that God hears us when we pray. He will hear and answer us unless we ask for something that is not according to His will.

Prayer is simply talking to God, and we don't have to try to make it sound eloquent; we can be ourselves. I encourage you to talk to God the way you would talk to a good friend, and talk about everything, because He is interested in all that concerns you. God loves to hear your prayers, and He wants to help you in everything you do, but often we do not have certain things because we do not ask for them (James 4:2). Just ask in faith, believing you receive what you ask for, and you will have it (Mark 11:24). Scripture doesn't say *when* it will come, but it *will* come if you don't give up.

Some people believe others can hear from God, but they doubt that they can. This is not true. The Holy Spirit lives inside all born-again believers. He knows God's will and enables us to hear from God in a variety of ways. Usually, God leads us by what 1 Kings 19:12 calls "a still small voice" (KJV). I often feel God speaks through a definite knowing in my heart of what is right or simply what I have peace about. If you want to hear from God, believe that you can hear from Him and that it is His will for you to do so.

*Father, give me confidence that I can hear from You and teach me how You speak to me. I want to hear from You and always be in Your will.*

# TRUST IN GOD BRINGS CONTENTMENT

*I trusted in the Lord when I said, "I am greatly afflicted."*

**PSALM 116:10**

I think it's safe to say that most people feel afflicted in some way over the course of their lives. The psalmist who wrote today's scripture certainly did, and so did the apostle Paul. Paul writes of some of his afflictions in 2 Corinthians 11:21–28. If we look at only two verses from that passage, we can see that he suffered greatly: "Five times I received from the Jews the forty lashes minus one. Three times I was beaten with rods, once I was pelted with stones, three times I was shipwrecked, I spent a night and a day in the open sea" (vv. 24–25). Yet, later in his life, Paul wrote: "I know what it is to be in need, and I know what it is to have plenty. I have learned the secret of being content in any and every situation, whether well fed or hungry, whether living in plenty or in want" (Philippians 4:12).

I believe what Paul was saying when he said he learned to be content was that he still trusted God even if he did not particularly like the situation in which he found himself. Therefore, his trust kept him in perfect peace. This is true for us too. When we truly trust in the Lord, we are content and peaceful.

Trusting God and refusing to complain during hard times greatly honors Him. There is no value in saying how much we trust God when all is well if, when we face difficulties, we can't say, "I trust You, Lord," and sincerely mean it.

*Teach me, Lord, to be content, even in the midst of challenges and afflictions. I trust You.*

# FULFILL YOUR VOWS

*I will fulfill my vows to the Lord in the presence of all his people.*

**PSALM 116:18**

We make a vow when we tell someone we will do something or we promise to do something. People take vows when they marry. These are commonly called marriage vows, and they should be taken seriously. Marriage vows are not to be made quickly or broken carelessly, and when marriage becomes difficult, we should do everything we can do to work things out and keep the vows we have made. God does not think a vow is unimportant. He knows that a vow is very important and should not be made unless a person fully intends to honor it.

We sometimes say we will do things but don't follow through. Many people today seem to think that failing to keep their vows (promises) is no problem. Glibly saying to someone "I'll call you soon, and we will go to lunch" may not seem important, but as far as God is concerned, we have vowed or promised to do something, and it is important that we keep our word and do it.

Dave and I diligently endeavor to do what we say we will do. I believe God blesses people who take their word seriously. He always keeps His Word; we expect Him to do so, and He expects the same from us. When we tell God we will do something, we should always follow through with it. If you have unfulfilled vows in your life, I urge you to fulfill them, and if needed, apologize for not doing so previously.

*Father, I am sorry for the promises I have made and not kept. Forgive me and help me to correct the ones that I can and to always keep my word from this time forward. Thank You.*

# PRAISE THE LORD

*Praise the Lord, all you nations; extol him, all you peoples. For great is his love toward us, and the faithfulness of the Lord endures forever.*
**PSALM 117:1–2**

Psalm 117 consists of only two verses, and we read similar words throughout Psalms. I have come to believe that any time God's Word says certain things repeatedly, they are important, and we need to pay close attention to them.

We enter God's gates with thanksgiving and come into His courts with praise (Psalm 100:4), so I believe thanksgiving and praise should always precede our requests. I can't ask God for something if I am not even in His presence, so I begin my morning prayer times with praise and thanksgiving. I pray in other ways throughout the day without doing that because I am not making a law out of it, but I do believe that our day should be filled with thanksgiving and praise, as well as prayers for ourselves and others.

Scripture says many times that God loves us and that His love is great and endures forever, and I believe we should also tell Him that we love Him throughout the day. I don't think we can say this too often. I never tire of hearing my husband tell me that he loves me, and I never tire of hearing God tell me that He loves me. I seriously doubt that He gets tired of hearing us tell Him we love Him.

Tell God today that He is good, that you appreciate all He does for you, that you love Him, and that you are relying on Him to help you in all you do.

*Father, I am thankful for You, and I praise You for all Your mighty works. I love You and I need You. You are good and You are faithful. I put my trust in You. Amen.*

# THE FEAR OF OTHER PEOPLE

*When hard pressed, I cried to the Lord; he brought me into a spacious place. The Lord is with me; I will not be afraid. What can mere mortals do to me?*

**PSALM 118:5–6**

The psalmist cried to the Lord, and He led him into a spacious (large) place. I often say I would rather believe God for a lot and get some of it than believe God for a little and get all of it. What kind of prayers do you pray? Are you bold enough to ask God for more than sounds reasonable to you? Ephesians 3:20 tells us that God is able to do exceedingly, abundantly, above and beyond "all that we [dare] ask or think" (AMPC).

The psalmist also believed that God was with him. For this reason, he had no need to fear. Let's believe we will have no fear in our lives. Fear is our enemy, and it desires to prevent us from making progress and to keep us living little lives filled with disappointment. We have nothing to fear as long as God is with us and we know that He loves us. He is greater than any enemy.

We should not fear other people because they are not greater than God is, and nothing anyone threatens to do to us will come to pass as long as we keep our trust in Him. If something unjust does happen, God will permit it only because He intends something better for us.

Many people forfeit their destiny due to the fear of other people. Don't let this happen to you. God is with you, He is for you, and you can live in a large place without fear.

*Father, thank You that I don't have to live in fear because You are always with me and You love me. Bring me into a large, spacious place where I can enjoy my life and be a blessing to many people.*

# TAKE REFUGE IN THE LORD

*It is better to take refuge in the Lord than to trust in humans. It is better to take refuge in the Lord than to trust in princes.*

**PSALM 118:8–9**

A refuge is a place of safety from danger or trouble, a place we can run to when we are afraid. God is the Christian's refuge. It is better to trust in God than to trust in human beings. I am not suggesting that we distrust people, but we must not put in them the trust that belongs to God. We should also realize that human beings can and may disappoint us or abandon us when we need them most. Thankfully, there are faithful people who stick with us no matter what, but we set ourselves up for emotional devastation if we look at anyone and think, *They will never hurt me.*

I was once hurt badly by a group of people I foolishly thought would never reject me. I was sure they would always be part of my life and ministry, but Satan deceived them, and they quickly turned their backs on me and accused me of things that were not true. It was a painful lesson, but one that has been important in my life and ministry. I have many wonderful people who help me. I trust them, but I never look at them and think, *You will be here forever; you will never disappoint or hurt me*, because I know this way of thinking would invite trouble. God is my refuge. People are my friends, my co-workers, and my helpers, but God is my refuge, and I pray He is yours too.

*Lord, help me never to give to other people the total trust that belongs only to You alone.*

# REJECT REJECTION

*The stone the builders rejected has become the cornerstone; the Lord has done this, and it is marvelous in our eyes.*

**PSALM 118:22–23**

Today's scriptures speak of the "stone the builders rejected." Jesus is that stone, but He has become the cornerstone of all we believe in. The cornerstone of a building is one on which the weight of the building rests, and Jesus is the rock on which the weight of everything rests. People rejected Him, but God raised Him up. When people reject you and me, we can reject their rejection and know that God will vindicate us and promote us as we follow Him.

Joseph's brothers rejected him, but God chose him to be a ruler and to have a place of tremendous power (Genesis 37, 39–41). David's brothers rejected him, but God anointed him to be a king (1 Samuel 16:6–13).

Rejection is extremely painful, as bad as physical pain, or perhaps worse. God has created us for acceptance, and rejection goes against everything in His plan for us, yet we all experience it. It often comes from those we love most, because Satan knows they are the ones who can influence and hurt us most. He uses the pain of rejection to try to get us to be people-pleasers instead of God-pleasers. The apostle Paul states in Galatians 1:10 that he would not have become an apostle of Jesus Christ if he had tried to be popular with people. How many people miss their destiny because they don't reject the rejection that comes to derail them? Probably more than we can count.

God accepts you, and that is what really matters, so when people reject you, pray for them and reject their rejection, because God has a plan for you that will succeed without them.

*Lord, help me to stand strong when people reject me, and help me to believe what You say about me more than I believe what they say about me.*

# TODAY IS A GIFT

*This is the day which the Lord has made; let's rejoice and be glad in it.*
**PSALM 118:24 NASB**

Do you ever make up your mind about what kind of day you will have before you even get out of bed? Perhaps you wake up grumpy or not looking forward to dealing with a boss or co-workers, and you dread the day ahead of you. Many people live this way, and to do so is to let your emotions control you instead of your managing them.

I believe the psalmist discovered the secret to living ordinary days with extraordinary enthusiasm. He simply viewed each day as a gift from God to him and decided and declared that since the Lord had made it, he would enjoy it and be glad. He made a decision that produced the feelings he wanted rather than waiting to see how he felt.

God's presence makes each day exciting if we have a godly perspective on life as a whole. Everything we do is sacred and amazing if we do it as unto the Lord and believe He is with us. Ask yourself right now whether you truly believe that God is with you even in the midst of very ordinary tasks. If your answer is yes, you can have an extraordinary day!

You may not have the most wonderful day on earth planned today, and you may need to do some things you don't enjoy, but you can still have a great day by choosing to receive it as a gift from God and to rejoice in it.

*Thank You, Lord, for this day. I receive it as a gift from You to me, and I **will** rejoice in it!*

# GOD WANTS YOU TO SUCCEED

*Lord, save us! Lord, grant us success!*

**PSALM 118:25**

Success comes in various forms. There are many people in the Bible who were successful and prosperous in their occupations, but there are also many who were not wealthy in terms of goods or finances, but were often abased. Yet these people were successful because they were rich spiritually.

There is nothing wrong with having money as long as the money doesn't have you. You might ask, "Joyce, doesn't the Bible say that money is the root of all evil?" No, it doesn't. It says that "the *love* of money is the root of all evil" (1 Timothy 6:10 KJV, italics mine).

Jesus says, "No one can serve two masters. Either you will hate the one and love the other, or you will be devoted to the one and despise the other. You cannot serve both God and money" (Matthew 6:24). We can, however, use money to serve God and to help people.

God wants us to be successful, and we should trust Him to give us only the material blessings He knows we can handle while still keeping Him first in our lives. We should want and seek spiritual success, which includes knowing and obeying God's Word, knowing Jesus, and following the guidance of the Holy Spirit. When we put our spiritual lives first, everything else God wants us to have will follow.

*Father, I seek You first and trust You to add to me whatever You want me to have. I believe You want me to be successful in all areas of life, and I trust You to teach me what success truly means.*

# HOW TO BE BLESSED

*Blessed and favored by God are those who keep His testimonies, and who [consistently] seek Him and long for Him with all their heart.*

**PSALM 119:2 AMP**

Psalm 119 is the longest of all the psalms and the longest chapter in the Bible, with 176 verses. It is full of praise and exhortation regarding God's Word. In today's scripture, we read about keeping God's "testimonies," which is the same as keeping His Word or His teachings.

What the psalmist is communicating in today's scripture is that in order to be blessed and experience God's favor, we must do two things. First, we must know His Word. It's not possible for God to say one thing but do another. He cannot lie, and He is always faithful in performing what He has promised. The more we know His Word, the more we know how we can expect Him to show Himself in our lives.

Second, we must seek God consistently with our whole heart. This begins by knowing His Word. I know many people who want their lives to get better, but they won't discipline themselves to learn God's Word and seek Him through it.

Spending time with God by studying the Word is your choice, and only you can make it. When you do choose to seek Him with your whole heart, it won't take long before your desires will begin to change, your life will begin to change, and God will become more important to you than anything else.

*Lord, I choose today to study, learn, and know Your Word. Help me to seek You through Your Word with my whole heart.*

# HELP ME NOT TO SIN AGAINST YOU, LORD

*I seek you with all my heart; do not let me stray from your commands.*
*I have hidden your word in my heart that I might not sin against you.*

**PSALM 119:10-11**

Anyone who wants to live a holy life must study God's Word diligently and allow it to fill their heart. The Word of God will speak to you when you are about to do something that is sinful. Also, when you are tempted to sin, you can speak and meditate on His Word, and it will strengthen you to resist the temptation you are facing.

I recently felt jealous of someone, and immediately the Holy Spirit reminded me that love is not jealous (1 Corinthians 13:4). It is important to me to walk in love because I know that this is the one new commandment that Jesus left us before He was crucified (John 13:34). Instead of letting the jealousy fester and take root in my heart, I started praying for God to help me love the person I was jealous of and pray for their continued blessing.

We cannot resist sin unless our hearts are filled with God's Word, which means we will need to make the effort to study, hear, read, and think about His Word daily. According to our verses for today, if we hide the Word in our hearts, we will not sin against God, nor will we stray from His commands. Time spent learning God's Word is an investment that pays rich dividends.

*Father, grant me the grace and discipline to make studying Your Word a priority in my life. I want to live a holy life, and I know I cannot do so without a heart filled with Your instructions.*

# SPEAK THE WORD

*Praise be to you, Lord; teach me your decrees. With my lips I recount all the laws that come from your mouth.*

**PSALM 119:12-13**

One of the greatest lessons God has taught me is the importance of speaking His Word aloud. According to Ephesians 6:17, His Word is a sword, and it is our number one weapon against our enemy, the devil. When the enemy attacks our mind or tempts us to sin, we can speak a portion of Scripture that applies to the situation we are facing. This will strengthen us, but it will also drive the enemy away.

In Luke 4:1, we read that the Holy Spirit led Jesus into the wilderness, where He stayed for forty days. During that time, Satan tempted Him in various ways. After these temptations, Jesus replied, "It is written," and He quoted a scripture relevant to each particular temptation. For instance, Satan showed Jesus all the kingdoms of the world and said, "I will give you all their authority and splendor; it has been given to me, and I can give it to anyone I want to. If you worship me, it will all be yours" (vv. 6–7). Jesus answered Satan by saying, "It is written: 'Worship the Lord your God and serve him only'" (v. 8).

You and I can follow Jesus' example in our lives. If you become angry, you can quote scriptures that tell you not to let your anger linger. If you feel selfish, you can quote scriptures on giving and being a blessing to others. Quoting Scripture aloud helps God's Word become deeply rooted in your heart. In addition, it summons your angels to work on your behalf, because they obey His Word (Psalm 103:20).

*Father, teach me to keep Your Word in my heart so I can speak it aloud and wield it as a two-edged sword when the devil tempts me or lies to me. Thank You.*

# WHEN YOU NEED COUNSEL

*Though rulers sit together and slander me, your servant will meditate on your decrees. Your statutes are my delight; they are my counselors.*
**PSALM 119:23–24**

I believe God's Word gives us the answer to any problem we have. It will counsel us when we need to know what to do or how to handle a specific situation. In addition, the Holy Spirit, who dwells inside of us, is our Counselor (John 14:16–17 AMP). There is nothing wrong with getting professional counseling if you need it and can afford it, but if not, the fact that God's Word and His Spirit will counsel you should give you comfort.

I think we run to other people too quickly and should give God a chance to counsel us before seeking help from another human being. If we do choose to see a professional counselor, we need His guidance concerning the right person for us.

I was sexually abused during my childhood, and when I began my journey of healing, I could not afford a professional counselor. But God counseled me and brought me to a place of wholeness and victory through His Word, and He will do the same for you if you need it. God's Word contains healing power. Spending time in His presence also brings healing. Be patient and trust that God's Word and His Holy Spirit are working in you to give you good counsel.

*Father, when I don't know what to do, thank You that You provide counsel and advice for me in any situation. Let me always seek counsel from You first and trust You to guide me to the next step I am to take.*

# ASK GOD FOR UNDERSTANDING

*Give me understanding [a teachable heart and the ability to learn], that I may keep Your law; and observe it with all my heart.*

**PSALM 119:34 AMP**

People often say that reading the Bible is confusing and that they don't understand what God is saying through it. Sometimes this is because they try to figure it out with their minds. We need to realize we are not smart enough to comprehend the mind of God, and we cannot always depend on our natural understanding (Proverbs 3:5). Moses explained to the Israelites that there are "secret things" known only to God (Deuteronomy 29:29). He said that when God revealed His will—meaning when He made things clear—those were the words they should obey. Likewise, all we need is to ask God to show us what we are to do and then follow Him when He reveals it to us.

The apostle Paul wrote: "I am telling the truth in Christ, I am not lying, my conscience testifies with me [enlightened and prompted] by the Holy Spirit" (Romans 9:1 AMP). He knew he was doing the right thing because his actions bore witness in his spirit, his inmost being.

Paul's attitude is the attitude we need. Before reading or studying God's Word, we should always ask the Holy Spirit to teach us and then depend on God to show us things in such a way that we know with an inner certainty that what has been revealed to our minds is correct. We may be tempted to reason in our minds and search for logical solutions, but discernment and revelation from God are always better than our own reasoning, and we can trust the Holy Spirit to guide us.

*Holy Spirit, I ask that You help me, guide me, and teach me every time I read the Word of God.*

# LEARNING THE HARD WAY

*Their hearts are callous and unfeeling, but I delight in your law. It was good for me to be afflicted so that I might learn your decrees.*

**PSALM 119:70-71**

As parents, we want our children to listen to what we tell them and to obey. If they don't, a loving parent will correct them in some way. Children must learn that disobedience has consequences and that those consequences are not pleasant.

God is our Father, and He also must correct us at times; the Bible tells us clearly that He does this because He loves us: "My son, do not make light of the Lord's discipline, and do not lose heart when he rebukes you, because the Lord disciplines the one he loves, and he chastens everyone he accepts as his son" (Hebrews 12:5–6).

In today's scriptures, the psalmist mentions that it was good for him when God afflicted him. We usually don't think any kind of correction is good for us as it's happening, but later we see (hopefully) that it helped us to obey God in ways that brought blessings to our life.

It is better if we simply obey God's Word and trust that what He tells us to do or not to do is for our good. But if we won't do that, He loves us enough to correct us so we can learn the consequences of not obeying Him.

*Father, teach me to obey Your Word. If I don't, then I welcome Your correction, knowing that You give it only because You love me and want the best for me.*

# WHAT THE BIBLE TEACHES ABOUT MEDITATION

*Oh, how I love your law! I meditate on it all day long.*

**PSALM 119:97**

In today's scripture, the psalmist writes of meditating on God's law, meaning His Word, "all day long." To meditate on something is simply to turn it over and over in your mind and even mutter it softly. I'd like to share three significant observations about meditation with you today.

1. God's Word indicates that meditation is more than a quick reading or pausing for a few brief reflective thoughts. The Bible presents meditation as serious pondering done by serious, committed followers who are willing to concentrate deeply.

2. Meditation is ongoing and habitual. Joshua 1:8 and Psalm 1:2 say that the godly person meditates on God's law "day and night."

3. Meditation is not a religious ritual. In some biblical passages where the term occurs, the writer goes on to point out the results. Joshua 1:8 says those who meditate on God's Word "will be prosperous and successful." And Psalm 1:3 says that "whatever they do prospers."

Meditating on God's Word does take time and attention, and it requires silencing the noise of life temporarily as you give yourself to deeper study of God's Word. You will be amazed how much power meditation releases in your life. The more you meditate on God's Word, the more you will be able to draw readily upon its strength.

*Lord, I pray that You would give me the desire to meditate on Your Word so it will become deeply established in my heart and readily available to me when I need it.*

# GOD DOES WHAT IS BEST FOR YOU

*Sustain me, my God, according to your promise, and I will live; do not let my hopes be dashed.*

**PSALM 119:116**

We all experience disappointment, such as when we want and expect something to happen and it doesn't. We feel as the psalmist must have felt when he wrote the words of today's scripture—as though our hopes have been dashed. The answer to disappointment is to trust God to always do the best thing for us. Just because you and I want something doesn't mean it is right for us.

We are individuals, and God has a personalized plan for each of us. What is right for someone else may not be best for you. I encourage you not to fight against life. Learn to relax in God, and when you do feel disappointed, shake it off and keep going.

You can be comforted when you experience disappointment by knowing that God loves you and has a wonderful plan for your future. If He doesn't give you what you ask for, you can be confident that the reason is that He has something better in mind. His plan will unfold little by little, and you will soon realize how much He loves you as He works in your life.

*Father, when I am disappointed, help me remember that I can receive comfort from You and that You will always do the best thing for me as I trust You.*

# UNDERSTANDING OF GOD'S WORD UNFOLDS

*The unfolding of Your [glorious] words give light; their unfolding gives understanding to the simple (childlike).*

**PSALM 119:130 AMP**

God's Word contains tremendous treasures—truths that will change our lives, encouragement to follow God's will to a life of purpose and blessings, and powerful life-giving secrets that God wants to reveal to us. These are made known to those who ponder, study, think about, practice mentally, and meditate on the Scripture.

Today's scripture teaches us that understanding of God's Word is a process of "unfolding." There is no end to what God can show us from just one particular biblical phrase or one verse of Scripture. We can study a scripture one time and see one nugget of truth in it. Then when we study it again, we see something about it that we did not even notice previously. Studying God's Word is like looking at a diamond; every time we look at it, we see a new facet.

The Lord keeps revealing His secrets to those who are diligent about studying the Word. Don't be a person who settles for building your spiritual life on someone else's understanding of the Scriptures. Study the Scriptures yourself. Allow the Holy Spirit to guide and encourage you through them. Let the truth and power of God's Word bless your life.

*Lord, as I study and meditate on Your Word, continue to unfold its treasures to me.*

# DEVOTE YOUR THOUGHTS TO GOD'S WORD

*I rise before dawn and cry for help; I have put my hope in your word. My eyes stay open through the watches of the night, that I may meditate on your promises.*

**PSALM 119:147–148**

In today's scriptures, we can sense the psalmist's commitment to God's Word. In modern language, we would say he "gets up early and stays up late" to meditate on God's promises. Reading or hearing the Word is good, but when we also devote our thoughts to it, as the psalmist did, we begin to understand it more deeply. The Word of God is filled with power, and it has the ability to change us. Just as good, nutritious food must be chewed well and swallowed for us to benefit from it, so the Word of God must be taken in and digested to become part of us. We do this in our minds, by thinking about it and focusing on it, not allowing ourselves to be distracted while we spend time in it.

I encourage you to make a habit of choosing a Bible verse and meditating on it throughout the day, or perhaps for a week or more at a time. To choose a verse, you might think of one that is particularly meaningful to you, or you might think of a topic that is important to you right now, such as prayer, healing, or managing your finances. Then look up verses about that subject online or in a concordance. This way, biblical truth will become rooted in your heart and become more meaningful to you.

*Lord, I want to devote my thoughts to Your Word and to make time in my schedule to seriously study it. Help me, I pray.*

# CALL ON THE LORD
# IN YOUR DISTRESS

*I call on the Lord in my distress, and he answers me. Save me, Lord, from lying lips and from deceitful tongues.*

**PSALM 120:1–2**

We all have times such as the psalmist had, when people slander us and say things about us that are not true. It hurts us when this happens, but God will help us if we turn to Him for deliverance. Call on the Lord in your distress. Don't try to take revenge on those who are slandering you, but remember that vengeance belongs to God (Romans 12:19).

God will give you justice in due time. While you wait, it is important not to speak unkindly about the person who hurt you. Instead, pray for them and be sure you completely forgive them. These things are necessary for us to do in order for God to do His part. Obedience releases God's blessings in our life.

Our first impulse when someone tells lies about us is to defend ourselves, but Jesus never did that. People said all kinds of things about Him that were not true, and He simply waited on God for justice. You can go ahead and enjoy your life while God does the work that only He can do.

*Father, it hurts when people lie about me, but I want to wait on Your justice. Help me to forgive and to wait for You to deliver me.*

# GOD WATCHES OVER YOU

*He will not let your foot slip—he who watches over you will not slumber;*
*indeed, he who watches over Israel will neither slumber nor sleep.*

**PSALM 121:3-4**

Realizing that God watches over us at all times is very comforting. There is never one moment when He doesn't have His loving eye on us. God doesn't sleep, so even when we are asleep, He is watching us.

God is our protector and our hiding place. He is the place we run to when we are hurting, in trouble, or in any kind of danger. I encourage you to think several times a day, *God is watching me right now*. Remembering His watchful eye over me comforts me. It helps me to realize that nothing is hidden from God, and it increases my desire to live a life that pleases Him.

Are you afraid of anything right now? If so, just remember that God is watching over you. He is with you. If you are hurting physically or emotionally, He is with you to comfort you. All you need to do is ask Him for what you need. God loves you very much, and He delights in meeting your needs and giving you the desires of your heart.

*Father, it is wonderful to know that You are always watching over me and that You will protect me. Help me remember that You see me at all times.*

# GOD PROTECTS YOU

*The Lord will keep you from all harm—he will watch over your life; the Lord will watch over your coming and going both now and forevermore.*
**PSALM 121:7-8**

A friend of mine was once sitting in a lawn chair in a boat reading about how God gives His angels charge over us to guard us (Psalm 91:11). The boat hit a big wave, her lawn chair tipped over, and she bumped her head. She had a headache but was not seriously injured. She asked the Lord why He didn't protect her from that and felt that He said, "You are not dead, are you?"

We spend too much time looking at what God doesn't do and not enough time focusing on what He does do. Think of how seriously my friend could have been injured; maybe God allowed her to fall to teach her that sitting in a lawn chair in a moving boat is not wise. I often think about how many people are driving cars at the same time. Relative to the amount of traffic in the world, there are not too many accidents. God is protecting us.

We don't know how much God protects us from, but today's scriptures say that He watches over us and will not let harm come to us. These promises are for His children, and we can thank Him that even if accidents happen, they are not as bad as they could have been.

We also have God's promise that "all things work together for good" to those who love Him and want His will (Romans 8:28 NKJV), so if something happens that doesn't seem good at first, we can trust God to work something beneficial out of it ultimately.

*Father God, thank You for Your protection. Help me realize how much You do to prevent and protect me from harm. When something happens that is not good, help me remember that You will work it out for good.*

# ARE YOU SECURE OR INSECURE?

*Pray for the peace of Jerusalem: "May those who love you be secure. May there be peace within your walls and security within your citadels."*

**PSALM 122:6-7**

Insecurity in people is a problem that seems to have reached epidemic proportions. God wants His people to be secure in His love and acceptance, and He wants us to be bold, not fearful. The apostle John writes that "perfect love casts out fear" (1 John 4:18 NKJV), and perfect love is the love of God.

Insecurity is tormenting. It holds people back from the good things God has prepared for them. Insecure people often lead lonely lives. They are so afraid of rejection that they isolate themselves, thinking it will keep them from being hurt, yet they hurt themselves by keeping others at a distance.

Insecure people interpret the actions and words of others in negative ways and take things personally when they should not. For example, an insecure person might imagine that someone doesn't like them because that person didn't speak to them at a party, but that may not be the case at all. Maybe the person didn't even see them. People who struggle with insecurity won't apply for a promotion that is available at work because they fear being turned down.

The cure for the insecure is to receive and abide in the love of God. Know that He is always with you, and that if you fail at something you try to do, it doesn't make you a failure. It simply means that you should either try again or try something else.

*Father, I want to be secure in Your love for me and to be bold as I walk through life. Help me live without insecurity so I can have the life You want me to enjoy.*

# SEEK GOD'S MERCY

*Have mercy on us, Lord, have mercy on us, for we have endured no end
of contempt. We have endured no end of ridicule from the arrogant, of
contempt from the proud.*

**PSALM 123:3-4**

Have you endured contempt from people who don't understand
you or who don't like you or your decision to serve God? Have
you endured ridicule from those who are arrogant and proud,
who know nothing about you, yet presume to judge you harshly?
Most of us have encountered situations such as these. Jesus did,
and as His servants, we are not above our Master.

Cry out to God for mercy, as the psalmist does in today's scriptures. God's mercy will comfort you and give you the grace to
forgive the people who have hurt you. God will deal with them
according to His own timing, and while you wait on Him to do
it, you can enjoy your life.

Don't believe what people say about you more than you believe
what God says about you in His Word. People judge only what
they see from the outside, but God sees and judges what is in the
heart (1 Samuel 16:7). John 15:25 says that people hated Jesus
without a cause, and I think this is one of the saddest verses in
the Bible. Jesus came to love, help, deliver, and save, yet people
had contempt for Him and ridiculed Him in their arrogance. His
Father delivered and rewarded Him, and He will also deliver and
reward you.

*Father, it hurts me when people hate and ridicule me, but they
hated and ridiculed Jesus too. Have mercy on me, O God, have
mercy on me.*

# GOD IS ON YOUR SIDE

*If the Lord had not been on our side—let Israel say—if the Lord had not been on our side when people attacked us, they would have swallowed us alive when their anger flared against us; the flood would have engulfed us, the torrent would have swept over us.*

**PSALM 124:1–4**

I don't know what you are going through right now or what you may deal with in the future, but I do know that God is on your side, and because of that you have nothing to fear. The apostle Paul asks in Romans 8:31–32: "What, then, shall we say in response to these things? If God is for us, who can be against us? He who did not spare his own Son, but gave him up for us all—how will he not also, along with him, graciously give us all things?" These scriptures give us the answer we need in order to remain peaceful while we go through difficult things: God is for us.

We are "more than conquerors" through Christ who loves us (Romans 8:37). When are we conquerors? Right in the middle of our trials, when we look like sheep being led to the slaughter. It is comforting and empowering to know that we are more than conquerors when everything appears to be against us and it seems there is no way we can win (Romans 8:36–37).

Always remember that God is on your side and you will come out on top. You will have the victory.

*Father, help me remain steadfast during trials, knowing that You are with me and that I am more than a conqueror through Christ. Thank You.*

# HELP FOR THE PAIN
# OF THE PAST

*Our help is in the name of the Lord, the Maker of heaven and earth.*

**PSALM 124:8**

All of us have a past, and most people have a mixture of positive experiences and negative experiences in their past. I don't know anyone who doesn't grapple with certain painful issues from days or years gone by. Perhaps you were teased mercilessly as a child and still feel insecure or sensitive because of that old pain. Maybe someone you loved left you without explanation. Maybe someone you trusted betrayed you. Maybe someone violated you physically or emotionally. Or perhaps you made a mistake about which you still feel guilty. Whatever the source of your hurt, always remember that God loves you, and you do not have to continue living in the pain of the past. You don't have to spend your life mourning over something you can't do anything about.

God wants to heal what has been damaged and restore what was lost through every hurt, injustice, and mistake in your life. Today's scripture is a powerful reminder that our help is not in ourselves or in other people, but in God. He will help you in any way you need help. In fact, He's waiting to help you, so ask for His help today.

*Thank You, Father, for the reminder that my help is in You. I look to You today for help in healing the pain of my past.*

# LIVE WITH EXPECTANCY

*Those who trust in and rely on the Lord [with confident expectation] are like Mount Zion, which cannot be moved but remains forever.*

**PSALM 125:1 AMP**

The amplification of today's scripture teaches us that to "trust in and rely on the Lord" is to have "confident expectation" in Him. Everyone and everything on earth will let us down at some point, and only God is worthy of our confident expectation, because He will never disappoint us.

To live with expectation is not the same as living with a sense of entitlement, which is an attitude that says we *deserve* everything. We don't deserve anything from God, but because of His great love and mercy toward us, He desires that we live in holy expectancy, believing He will give us His very best at the proper time and in the proper way.

Even if you have had a problem or a need for a long time, the situation can change if you will do your part. Your part is to believe God's Word, obey Him, sow good seeds, have a vision of breakthrough, and think and speak in agreement with God's Word. Your part is also to be faithful and persistent in your expectation, continuing to trust and rely on God.

*Lord, fill me today with confident expectation and give me the grace to persist in it until I receive the very best that You have for me.*

# GOD WILL RESTORE
# WHAT YOU HAVE LOST

*When the Lord restored the fortunes of Zion, we were like those who dreamed. Our mouths were filled with laughter, our tongues with songs of joy. Then it was said among the nations, "The Lord has done great things for them."*

**PSALM 126:1-2**

When we trust God, our sadness always turns to joy because He is a deliverer and a restorer. Perhaps you have waited a long time and feel that nothing has happened, but I encourage you to keep believing, because as long as you believe, God can work on your behalf.

What do you need restored in your life? There was a time when I needed restoration of confidence, security, self-worth, the belief that I was loved, boldness and courage, and the list could go on. I can honestly say that one by one God has restored everything the devil stole from me through sexual abuse. I often felt that nothing would ever change, and then suddenly, God gave me a breakthrough in some way.

This has happened throughout my life and still happens today. God is a God of restoration, and He can actually make us better than we were before we were wounded or disappointed. Put your hope in Him and expect something good to happen to you today.

*Father, I trust You to restore all I have lost. Grant me patience to wait peacefully and be filled with hope that You are working in my life.*

# TEARS TURNED INTO JOY

*Restore our fortunes, Lord, like streams in the Negev. Those who sow with tears will reap with songs of joy. Those who go out weeping, carrying seed to sow, will return with songs of joy, carrying sheaves with them.*

**PSALM 126:4–6**

Psalm 126 speaks of those who "sow with tears," and sometimes this is what we need to do. It means that while we are still hurting, we keep doing the right thing—keep helping others, keep praying, and keep studying God's Word. As we do, we sow seeds for an eventual harvest. I used to wonder why God wouldn't give me the ability to solve my own problems or help myself, but at the same time I was hurting, He would give me the ability to help others. Then I learned that He wants us to reach out to others, and when we do, we are sowing seed for our future harvest.

Those who sow in tears will reap sheaves (a harvest) with songs of joy. Nothing is more joyful than experiencing a reversal of bad circumstances and having them turn into something good. It is exciting and makes us happy.

The Bible says that weeping endures for a night, but "joy comes in the morning" (Psalm 30:5 NKJV). Admittedly, it often takes more than one night for our problems to be solved, but this Psalm teaches us a principle: God always comes through and gives us victory. Your problems will end, and your sorrow will turn to joy.

*Father, I am grateful that I can depend on You to turn my weeping into joy. You are good, and You always bring good things. I wait on You and put my trust in You.*

# GOD IS IN CHARGE OF YOUR REPUTATION

*Unless the Lord builds the house, the builders labor in vain. Unless the Lord watches over the city, the guards stand watch in vain.*

**PSALM 127:1**

When we try to build our lives and our reputations in our own strength, we are leaning on the arm of flesh (ourselves and other people). We work hard to do everything we think will cause us to be successful from a worldly perspective. But today's scripture indicates such effort is in vain. The Lord is the One who builds our lives and our reputations, according to His good plans for our lives.

Philippians 1:6 assures us that "He who has begun a good work in you will [continue to] perfect and complete it until the day of Christ Jesus [the time of His return]" (AMP). God will complete the good work He has begun in you and me. We can be certain of this.

God is the One who started the good work in you, and He is the One who will finish it. We should always do the part He gives us to do, but we should never try to do anything without leaning entirely on Him. We need to be patient and rest in Him as He accomplishes what needs to be done instead of intervening according to our own ideas when things are not happening as quickly as we would like or in the way we would like. There are certain responsibilities we need to fulfill in our lives, and there are certain things only God can do. Take the pressure off yourself by leaning on the arm of the Lord instead of the arm of the flesh.

*Lord, help me to be patient as You complete the good work You have begun in me.*

# DON'T WASTE YOUR TIME WORRYING

*It is vain for you to rise early, to retire late, to eat the bread of anxious labors—for He gives [blessings] to His beloved even in his sleep.*

**PSALM 127:2 AMP**

Today's scripture, written by Solomon, reminds us that worrying is an absolute waste of our time. When we read it, we think of someone who can't sleep because they are so anxious. Being upset tires us out, steals our joy, wastes a lot of emotional energy, can harm our health, and does not change one thing. Jesus says we can't add even one hour to our life by worrying (Matthew 6:27). Yet we often worry, worry, worry, which gets us nowhere. Usually, the things we worry about are situations we are powerless to change; that's why we are upset about them. When faced with something only God can fix, we are wise to stop trying to fix them and to rest in Him, knowing He will do exactly what needs to be done at exactly the right time.

One of Jesus' messages to us can be summarized by saying "calm down and cheer up" (John 14:27, 15:11). I believe these two actions combined serve as a one-two knockout punch to the devil. When you realize you can't fix everything, you calm down, and when you know God can, you cheer up.

*God, help me to calm down and to cheer up, knowing You can and will fix what I cannot.*

# CHILDREN ARE A BLESSING

*Children are a heritage from the Lord, offspring a reward from him. Like arrows in the hands of a warrior are children born in one's youth.*

**PSALM 127:3–4**

If you have children, you may have wondered on occasion, as I did, if they really were a blessing, because they gave you trouble. Maybe they were being rebellious or stubborn or doing things that they knew would get them in trouble, but they would not listen to you.

Three of my four children gave me reason to be quite concerned at different times, but each one has turned out to be a tremendous blessing to Dave and me. Our two sons, who were challenging at times, now run the day-to-day business of the ministry. One of my daughters has a teaching ministry and is doing well. The other daughter works for me and helps me with literally everything from ordering my vitamins to doing my filing.

I could not imagine life without my children. They are a wonderful blessing and the joy of my heart. If you are struggling with a child right now, just remember that when they grow up, they will feel differently about things than they do now, and that eventually you will rejoice in the great blessing they are to you.

*Father, thank You for my children. Help me when I struggle with them to remember that every child goes through things while they are growing up. I thank You for Your promise that, according to Proverbs 22:6, if I train them up in the way they should go, they won't depart from it when they are older.*

# THE BLESSINGS OF OBEDIENCE

*Blessed are all who fear the Lord, who walk in obedience to him. You will eat the fruit of your labor; blessings and prosperity will be yours.*

**PSALM 128:1–2**

Obedience to God brings reward. We should obey Him because we love Him, not just to gain a reward, but He does promise blessing and prosperity to those who fear Him and walk in obedience to Him. The word *prosperity*, mentioned in today's scriptures, does not simply mean an accumulation of wealth, but it refers to an ongoing state of success in all areas of life. If we have money but are poor spiritually, then we lack what is most important in life.

Think of how wonderful it would be to have good health, be spiritually prosperous, have a good social life with plenty of really great friends, be peaceful emotionally, and have abundant finances. I think this kind of arrangement sounds like "blessings and prosperity." If we are obedient to God, we can expect to be blessed and prosperous. Disobedience to God brings the opposite of what obedience yields in our lives. Those who disobey God will not be blessed, nor will they prosper.

Obedience to God is the way we prove our love for Him (John 14:15). I encourage you to examine your heart and see if there are areas in your life in which you know you are being disobedient to God. If so, repent, receive His forgiveness, and start obeying Him right away.

*Father, I am sorry for any disobedience in my life. I ask You to forgive me and help me walk in Your will in the future. I love You and I want to honor You by being obedient to You.*

# DON'T LET THE DEVIL WIN

*"They have greatly oppressed me from my youth," let Israel say; "they have greatly oppressed me from my youth, but they have not gained the victory over me."*

**PSALM 129:1–2**

God loves us, but the devil hates us, and he is our enemy. He attacks us relentlessly in a variety of ways, hoping to wear us out and convince us to give up. But, the psalmist says in today's scriptures, "They have not gained the victory over me." You and I should be determined to have the same testimony.

Even in death, we still have victory. Christians are the only people on earth who are better off dead. Think about it: According to the apostle Paul, "To live is Christ and to die is gain" (Philippians 1:21), and "Death has been swallowed up in victory" (1 Corinthians 15:54). We are eternal beings, which means we do not die in terms of ceasing to exist. We simply leave our earthly bodies and go to heaven, a much better place. If Satan cannot defeat us even in death, we need not fear him in any area of life.

The only way the devil can win is for us to give up and stop believing in Jesus. I urge you never to do that, no matter how difficult your circumstances are or how long they persist. Our faith is the victory that overcomes the world (1 John 5:4). Always remember that we win in the end.

*Father, help me remain strong in faith as I go through difficulties in this life. I want to be able to say with the psalmist that my enemies have not gained victory over me.*

# GOD HAS SET ME FREE

*Plowmen have plowed my back and made their furrows long. But the Lord is righteous; he has cut me free from the cords of the wicked.*

**PSALM 129:3-4**

"Plowmen have plowed my back" is a metaphor that refers to being treated cruelly. We can imagine a person lying facedown on the ground with a plow running back and forth across his back, and it seems excruciating. The New Living Translation of today's verse says, "My back is covered with cuts." This mental picture reminds us of times when we feel that trials and tribulations are beating us up relentlessly.

However, we should never forget what the psalmist says: Because the Lord is righteous, He cuts us free from the cords of the wicked. God is a God of justice and righteousness, and He is our deliverer and rescuer. He will not leave us helpless in our difficult times.

Keep in mind that no matter what the devil tries to do to you, he will not win in the end. Remain steadfast in your faith and continue trusting God, because help is on the way.

God has heard your prayers, and He has a good plan for your life. Even though you may be experiencing difficult times at the present, everything will work out for good if you keep your trust and confidence in God (Romans 8:28).

*Father, I love You and I appreciate being able to put my trust in You. I need You to deliver me from those who treat me cruelly. Help me remain steadfast and continue trusting You.*

# FROM THE DEPTHS
# OF MY HEART

*Out of the depths I cry to you, Lord; Lord, hear my voice. Let your ears be attentive to my cry for mercy. If you, Lord, kept a record of sins, Lord, who could stand?*

**PSALM 130:1–3**

It is a good thing that God does not keep a record of our sins, because if He did, none of us could stand before Him. He is merciful, and He always hears our cry for mercy. He especially hears and pays attention to a sincere cry that comes from the deepest part of our heart.

In today's scriptures, I hear a cry of desperation, a cry coming from a place of deep repentance for sin. We probably all ask God to forgive our sins, but there are times when the sorrow we feel over our sins is so deep that we cry out to God for mercy. It comes from a deeper place than usual.

I am grateful that God is gracious and that He forgives our sins. I am grateful for His mercy, and I am sure you are too. Let us rejoice that He keeps no record of our sins, and that once we repent of them, He not only forgives them, but He forgets them and remembers them no more (Hebrews 8:12).

*Oh God, You are so very good. Thank You for Your mercy and forgiveness, which have no limits. Thank You that when I cry out to You, You hear me and come to my aid. You will never leave me nor forsake me, and I praise You for Your goodness.*

# DON'T JUST WAIT; WAIT PATIENTLY

*I wait [patiently] for the Lord, my soul [expectantly] waits, and in His word do I hope.*

**PSALM 130:5 AMP**

Many times in life, we find ourselves having to wait. We can just wait and let time pass, or we can wait well and make the most of our time. If we want to wait well, we will wait patiently, expectantly, and in hope, as today's scripture indicates.

Patience is extremely important for people who want to glorify God and enjoy their lives (James 1:4). If people are impatient, the situations they encounter will cause them to react emotionally, which probably won't be good. When pressured by circumstances, we need to follow the psalmist's example in Psalm 130:5 and wait patiently and expectantly for the Lord.

The next time you have to wait on something or someone, rather than becoming impatient, try talking to yourself a little. Tell yourself, "Getting upset will not make this go any faster, so I might as well find a way to enjoy the wait." Then perhaps say, "I am developing patience as I wait, so I am thankful for this situation." When you speak in such ways, you are acting on the Word of God rather than reacting with impatience to an unpleasant circumstance.

*Father, when I have to wait on something, help me not to react emotionally or become impatient, but to wait well—patiently, expectantly, and in hope.*

# WE WILL NEVER UNDERSTAND EVERYTHING

*My heart is not proud, Lord, my eyes are not haughty; I do not concern myself with great matters or things too wonderful for me.*

**PSALM 131:1**

Years ago, I spent a lot of time trying to understand everything that was going on in my life and why God did or didn't do certain things. The more I reasoned about these situations, the more confused I became. Satan delights in provoking us to try to understand things we are not meant to understand, but "God is not the author of confusion" (1 Corinthians 14:33 NKJV).

According to today's scripture, some things are "too wonderful" for us to understand. Only God can understand them, because He knows the end from the beginning (Isaiah 46:10). He knows all things, and we only know in part (1 Corinthians 13:9–12). If we knew everything that God knows, we wouldn't need Him, so we should understand that there will always be things that we cannot and will not understand. Trusting God will involve some unanswered questions.

People who are proud think they should know everything, but those who are humble don't worry about what God doesn't show them. They simply put their trust in God and believe that if they need to know something, He will tell them.

Stop trying to understand things that God does not intend for you to understand right now, and you will enjoy a lot more peace.

*Father, forgive me for trying so hard to reason out everything in my life and for thinking that I should know everything. There are things that only You can understand, and I want to humble myself and be happy knowing only what You want me to know.*

# CHOOSE CONTENTMENT

*But I have calmed and quieted myself, I am like a weaned child with its mother; like a weaned child I am content.*

**PSALM 131:2**

If we are discontent and generally dissatisfied with life, we easily become upset and frustrated. But if we choose to be content no matter what is going on, our emotions remain balanced and stable. Our thoughts greatly impact our moods. Some thoughts improve our moods and increase our level of contentment, while others send our moods spiraling downward, making us unhappy and discontent. We can think ourselves into being happy, and we can think ourselves into being sad. In addition, the way we speak to ourselves also affects our emotions and moods, so if we talk to ourselves properly, we can stay content and emotionally stable.

Notice in today's scripture that the psalmist David writes, "I have calmed and quieted myself." This tells us that he made a choice to manage his emotions instead of allowing them to control him. We can all make this same decision for ourselves. We can choose to be content, completely satisfied in our God, who loves us and always works for our good. Even when we don't have everything we want, we can trust God to provide what is right and best for us in His perfect timing.

*Father, I choose today to calm myself and to be content. Thank You for all You have given me and done for me. I trust You and am completely satisfied in You.*

# GOD'S DWELLING PLACE

*Lord, remember David and all his self-denial. He swore an oath to the Lord, he made a vow to the Mighty One of Jacob: "I will not enter my house or go to my bed, I will allow no sleep to my eyes or slumber to my eyelids, till I find a place for the Lord, a dwelling for the Mighty One of Jacob."*

**PSALM 132:1–5**

David had a great passion to build a house in which God would dwell. As the situation turned out, God did not allow him to build it. Instead, the responsibility for building it went to David's son, Solomon. Today we don't have to build houses for God to dwell in because believers are His home. First Corinthians 6:19–20 says: "Do you not know that your bodies are temples of the Holy Spirit, who is in you, whom you have received from God? You are not your own; you were bought at a price. Therefore honor God with your bodies."

When I think about the fact that God chooses us to be temples, or homes, for Himself, by the Holy Spirit, it amazes me. He dwells in us and guides us; He teaches us truth, convicts us of sin, and convinces us of righteousness (John 14:17, 16:7–15). If we will simply listen to and obey the Holy Spirit in us, we will have powerful and enjoyable lives.

Because our bodies are temples of God, we should take good care of ourselves by eating properly, exercising, getting enough rest, and doing everything we can do to benefit ourselves physically. God wants to do a lot through us, and we should always remember that He is never far away. He is with us and in us, all the days of our lives.

*Father, thank You for living in me by the Holy Spirit. Help me honor You by taking good care of myself. I want to follow Your lead and cooperate with the work You want to do through me.*

# GENERATIONS OF BLESSING

*The Lord swore an oath to David, a sure oath he will not revoke: "One of your own descendants I will place on your throne. If your sons keep my covenant and the statutes I teach them, then their sons will sit on your throne for ever and ever."*

**PSALM 132:11–12**

As parents, we want our children to inherit what we have worked for. The psalmist David, as a father, was no different. He desired for his sons to sit on his throne, and in today's scriptures, God promised him that they would if they followed His commands.

If we teach and train our children properly, and if they follow the will of God, they will inherit what we work for. It is my desire that my ministry continue long after I am gone. I have asked God to give me this, and our two sons currently run the day-to-day business of Joyce Meyer Ministries. Also, three of our grandchildren work on our staff, and I believe they will carry on the work that God has allowed me to begin.

Let me encourage you to teach your children everything you can teach them about the ways of God and to be a living example to them. Live in front of them the life you know God wants you to live, and pray that they will follow Him all the days of their life.

*Father, I appreciate all You have done in my life and I want my children to inherit what You have given me. I pray they will walk with You and that generations of my family will serve You.*

# GOD WILL DEAL WITH OUR ENEMIES

*I will clothe his enemies with shame, but his head will be adorned with a radiant crown.*

**PSALM 132:18**

We all have enemies, and our natural instinct is to seek revenge against them. But God promises to deal with our enemies and bless us if we will wait on Him and not try to take matters into our own hands. In today's scripture, God is speaking about David's enemies and says He will clothe them with shame.

God tells us to forgive our enemies, to bless them, and to pray for them—and this is exactly what we should do. Just this week, someone hurt me and falsely accused me, and I have been praying for that person every day and sometimes twice a day. I would much rather have God's justice than my own.

I encourage you to follow Jesus' commands in this area. Love your enemies and do good to them (Matthew 5:44; Luke 6:27). Don't stoop to their level by trying to get them back. God will be your Vindicator. He will defend you, bless you, and exalt you.

*Father, I want to live my life according to Your will. At times, it is hard for me to wait on You, especially in the area of dealing with my enemies. Help me to obey You. Help me to forgive, bless, and pray for those who hurt me. Thank You.*

# DO YOUR PART TO PROMOTE UNITY

*How good and pleasant it is when God's people live together in unity!*
**PSALM 133:1**

Our oldest son, David, and his wife once needed a place to live temporarily while their new house was under construction. My son and I are alike in many ways; we are both strong-willed, which does not always mix well in close quarters. Nothing negative had happened between us, but in anticipation of the move, my mind kept coming up with what-ifs.

I found myself regularly talking about negative things that could take place: "What if there is no hot water left for my shower in the morning after everyone else is finished? What if they leave messes for me to clean up?" David and his wife had not even moved in, and nothing bad had yet happened. But the enemy wanted me to criticize and say negative things about the situation in advance, which could have sabotaged the unity God wanted us to enjoy during a short, unique season with our son and daughter-in-law.

If the devil can get us to be negative, he can provide us with negative circumstances. Often, we call for our own problems. We call "into being that which does not exist" (Romans 4:17 AMP), only we do it in the negative sense by sowing negative seeds.

Our son and daughter-in-law did live with us for a month, and everything worked out fine.

Let me encourage you to promote unity by thinking and speaking positively about other people and your relationship with them.

*Help me, Lord, to promote unity and not to sabotage it in advance with my thoughts and words.*

# FREQUENT PRAISE

*Praise the Lord, all you servants of the Lord who minister by night in the house of the Lord.*

**PSALM 134:1**

Today's scripture is a good reminder to praise God, and we should praise Him frequently, for He is worthy of our praise. I encourage you to thank Him often for big things and little things. Don't waste your time meditating on foolish things that don't do you any good; instead, spend time praising and thanking God for His many blessings in your life.

The more thankful we are, the happier we will be. Thanksgiving brings us into the presence of God. We need more of God than we need of anything else. Paul said that his "determined purpose" was to know Christ and the power of His resurrection (Philippians 3:10 AMPC). We can be as close to God as we want to be, depending on how much time we are willing to invest in getting to know Him and His character.

Watch closely for His blessings in your life, and praise and thank Him for each one.

*Father, please help me to be aware of all that You do for me and then to remember to praise and thank You for it.*

# THE LORD IS GREAT

*I know that the Lord is great, that our Lord is greater than all gods. The Lord does whatever pleases him, in the heavens and on the earth, in the seas and all their depths.*

**PSALM 135:5-6**

It is always good for us to remind ourselves how great God is and to remember that He is greater than and above anything else. No problem we encounter is greater than our God. What are you dealing with right now in your life that seems to be an impossible situation? It is not impossible for God (Matthew 19:26).

Turn the things that you are tempted to worry about over to God and watch Him work and do miracles in your life. God wants to help us, but we need to ask and then let go, meaning that we are not to try to control the situation. Asking is easy, but letting go is sometimes difficult. We may let go of a problem but then take it back many times and try to fix it ourselves.

God does whatever pleases Him, and it pleases Him to help you and see you worry-free, enjoying your life. Put your trust in Him, and be sure to watch for His answer because it will come at just the right time.

*Father, I know that You are great and can do all things. Help me to turn my problems over to You and trust You to take care of me.*

# GOD IS OUR VINDICATOR

*Your name, Lord, endures forever, your renown, Lord, through all generations. For the Lord will vindicate his people and have compassion on his servants.*

**PSALM 135:13-14**

Today's scriptures assure us that God "will vindicate his people." To be *vindicated* means to be shown to be right or to be justified, or made right in the sight of God.

When we are treated unjustly or when someone hurts us, our natural instinct is to vindicate ourselves, but God wants to do it for us. He is our Vindicator, and He is a God of justice, which means that He makes wrong things right.

I recently dealt with someone who felt they had been treated unjustly. This person was angry, and the problem needed to be resolved, but they could not resolve it themselves. I urged them to forgive the person who hurt them and let God be their Vindicator, but they had a difficult time doing it. Sadly, they remained angry, and eventually it cost them their job and some valuable friendships.

If you have been mistreated, I pray you will turn the situation over to God and trust Him to be your Vindicator. His vindication may take time, but the wait will be worth it in the end. You can enjoy your life while God deals with your enemies.

*Father, help me to let go of the anger I feel toward those who have hurt me and treated me unjustly. I want to trust You to be my Vindicator.*

# GIVE THANKS TO THE LORD

*Give thanks to the Lord, for he is good. His love endures forever.*

**PSALM 136:1**

Psalm 136 has a total of twenty-six verses, each ending with "His love endures forever." The psalmist wasn't merely trying to be repetitive; he was making a point we should always remember.

God does so much for His people, and throughout this psalm, the writer states that God is good and His love is everlasting. It is important for us to always remember these two things. When we have trouble in life, God is still good and He still loves us. Meditating on these truths will help us get through difficult situations and not lose our faith.

God's timing isn't always what we would like it to be, but it is always perfect. If we have to wait longer than desired for Him to do something, there is a reason, even though we may not see it. All we need to remember is that God is good and His love endures forever. If you are facing something challenging right now, meditate on these truths, and they will strengthen your faith. Surely if God's Word says something twenty-six times, we should consider it important and believe it.

*Father, help me always to remember that You are good and that Your love endures forever. Help me never to doubt this, no matter how difficult my circumstances may be.*

# THE GREAT ACTS OF GOD

*Give thanks to the Lord of lords: his love endures forever. To him who alone does great wonders, his love endures forever.*

**PSALM 136:3-4**

Psalm 136 reminds us of many things God has done, and today's scriptures say that He "alone does great wonders." No one else can do what God does. This psalm says that He created the earth, the heavens, the moon, the sun, and the stars (vv. 5–9). He protected the Israelites while they were in Egypt; He delivered them from bondage by parting the Red Sea so they could pass through it on dry land (vv. 10–14), but He drowned the Egyptian army in the same sea (v. 15).

He led His people through the wilderness and killed mighty kings who wanted to harm them (vv. 16–20). He gave them their land, just as He had promised (vv. 21–22). He still frees us from our enemies (vv. 23–24) and gives food to all creatures (v. 25).

I watch a lot of television shows about nature and about animals. I am always amazed at how much variety God has created. I'm also amazed at how He gives each animal a way to protect itself and how He feeds it. Although some animals must hunt for their food, God always provides.

When we think of all the people and creatures on the earth and realize how God cares for each one, it is amazing. The more we think about the greatness of God, the easier it is to trust Him to take care of us and our problems. I encourage you to take time to think about these things.

*Father, the way You care for every living thing is amazing. You are great, and surely You do care for all of Your creation. Help me trust You to take care of me.*

# BE ACTIVELY AWARE OF GOD'S LOVE

*His faithful love endures forever.*

**PSALM 136:5 NLT**

When I began my ministry, as I was preparing for my first meeting, I asked the Lord what He wanted me to teach, and these words came to my heart: *Tell My people I love them.* My response was "They know that from Sunday school. I want to teach them something really powerful." The Lord reminded me that if people were actively aware of how much He loved them, as the psalmist was in Psalm 136, it would be powerful indeed, and they would act differently. If we knew how perfectly God loves us, it would cast fear out of our lives (1 John 4:18).

As I began to study the subject of receiving God's love, I realized I desperately needed the message personally. I had a subconscious, vague sort of understanding that God loved me, but I needed a deeper revelation of this life-changing truth. God's love is meant to be a powerful force in our lives, one that will take us through even the most difficult trials without our ever doubting His deep, unconditional, personal love for us.

If you need a deeper understanding of God's love for you, I recommend praying and asking Him to help you realize and experience His love on a personal level, and then studying and meditating on all the scriptures you can find about His love. This combination of prayer and God's Word is powerful.

*Thank You, God, for Your faithful love for me. Help me never to doubt it.*

# WE MUST NOT FORGET GOD

*If I forget you, Jerusalem, may my right hand forget its skill. May my tongue cling to the roof of my mouth if I do not remember you, if I do not consider Jerusalem my highest joy.*

**PSALM 137:5-6**

In today's scriptures, the psalmist emphasizes the importance of not forgetting God and His people. If they do forget, he prays they will lose their skills and that their tongue will cleave to the roof of their mouth, which I think would be very uncomfortable.

We often get busy and are guilty of forgetting God for long periods of time, but we should frequently think of Him, tell Him that we love Him, and thank Him for all He does for us. The more we think about God, the closer we will be to Him. Although He is always with us and has promised to never leave or forsake us (Deuteronomy 31:8), if we don't remember this truth, it won't benefit us.

God is with you right now, and He has a good plan for you. He is working on your behalf, and all He asks is that you don't forget Him. God is never more than one thought away from you. Simply thinking about Him brings you into His presence, so think of Him often.

*Father, help me not to forget You and to think of You often. You are good, and I know that You are with me. Thank You for all You do for me.*

# EMBOLDENED BY GOD

*When I called, you answered me; you greatly emboldened me.*

**PSALM 138:3**

In today's scripture, the psalmist David writes that God "greatly emboldened" him. When we call on the name of the Lord and pray to Him, He gives us great courage to face life and its difficulties. He helps us confront what we need to confront and deal with the situations that try to frighten us.

Second Timothy 1:7 says, "For God has not given us a spirit of fear, but of power and of love and of a sound mind" (NKJV). Fear is a terrible thing, and it is Satan's favorite tool to use against us. He doesn't want us to make any progress in life, and he uses fear to hold us back. But God will give us boldness when we pray and seek Him.

Be determined not to be fearful and timid in life, but instead to be bold and follow the leadership of the Holy Spirit. Step out boldly and do what He leads you to do. Don't be afraid to try new things, and always remember that if you fail at something, that doesn't make you a failure. Failure simply shows you that you may need to try again or that you should try something else. Live courageously. Face your fears and do what you want to do, even if you must do it afraid.

*Father, thank You for making me bold. With Your help, I refuse to bow down to the spirit of fear, because it is not from You. In Your name, Lord, I will do great things.*

# GOD WILL NOT ABANDON THE WORK OF HIS HANDS

*Though I walk in the midst of trouble, you preserve my life. You stretch out your hand against the anger of my foes; with your right hand you save me. The Lord will vindicate me; your love, Lord, endures forever—do not abandon the works of your hands.*

**PSALM 138:7–8**

As long as we live in this world, we "walk in the midst of trouble," as today's scriptures say. But God promises to preserve our life, deal with our enemies, and save us. You and I can relax and enjoy the life that Jesus made available to us when He died on the cross and was resurrected (1 Corinthians 15:3–4).

God loves us and will never abandon us. He will never leave us but will be with us always. I suggest that you stop what you are doing several times each day and simply say aloud "God is with me right now."

We do not have to be afraid of trouble, because the apostle Paul teaches us that in the midst of trouble, we are more than conquerors (Romans 8:37). Why? Because this world is not our home; we are merely passing through it on our way to our heavenly home. Jesus has already won the victory over Satan and given it to us. We receive it by faith now, and we will receive it in reality when our time on this earth is finished.

If we look past the troubles of this life, all we can see are good things that God has in store for us.

*Father, thank You that I don't have to worry, even though I live in the midst of trouble. I can relax and enjoy Your presence and the good life that You have prearranged for me to live.*

# GOD KNOWS YOU

*You have searched me, Lord, and you know me. You know when I sit and when I rise; you perceive my thoughts from afar. You discern my going out and my lying down; you are familiar with all my ways.*

**PSALM 139:1-3**

God knows us better than we know ourselves. He knows everything about us, even what we will do before we do it. The amazing thing is that even though He knows everything about us, even the sins that we will commit, He still loves us unconditionally.

God knows all our thoughts, and if you are anything like I am, all your thoughts are not good ones. God is familiar with all our ways, and many of these are not good either.

I have heard that true love is knowing everything about someone and loving them anyway, so we can certainly say that if no one else ever loves us so completely, God does.

God's love delivers us from fear. If we know that He is with us and that He loves us, we should also know that He will always take care of us. The apostle John writes that perfect love casts out fear, and that if we fear, we don't yet know God's perfect love (1 John 4:18). If you are struggling with fear, I suggest that instead of studying fear in God's Word, study His love and let it set you free from fear.

*Father, thank You that even though You know all about me, You still love me unconditionally. Help me understand the height, depth, and width of Your love for me so I can be totally free from fear.*

# GOD WILL HELP YOU FULFILL HIS PURPOSE

*Before a word is on my tongue you, Lord, know it completely. You hem me in behind and before, and you lay your hand upon me. Such knowledge is too wonderful for me, too lofty for me to attain.*

**PSALM 139:4-6**

God knows every word we will speak before it is even on our tongue, according to today's scriptures. It is hard to imagine that anyone can know us so completely, but God does. The psalmist David writes that God hems us in "behind and before." This means to me that God has us in places we cannot get away from so we can fulfill His purposes. He often wants to teach us lessons in situations we would run from unless He put us in a position where we could not escape.

Have you ever wanted to give up on something, but God wouldn't let you? I have. Often during the building of our ministry, I wanted to quit, but my heart was so full of passion to do what God had called me to do that even though I wanted to quit, He wouldn't let me. He had me in a place I could not get away from. It was uncomfortable at times, but in that place, He laid His hand on me and changed me.

We do not understand the ways of God. They are too wonderful and awesome for us to comprehend with our finite minds. Trying to understand God and His ways is a waste of time. It is too lofty for us, so why try? We should accept His ways without questioning them, believing they will always work out for our good.

*Father, help me to accept Your ways in my life without questioning them or struggling to understand them. I want to trust You completely.*

# WE CANNOT HIDE FROM GOD

*Where can I go from your Spirit? Where can I flee from your presence? If I go up to the heavens, you are there; if I make my bed in the depths, you are there. If I rise on the wings of the dawn, if I settle on the far side of the sea, even there your hand will guide me, your right hand will hold me fast.*

**PSALM 139:7-10**

God is omnipresent, meaning that He is everywhere all the time. No matter how long we meditate on this truth, we still have difficulty understanding it. We may try to hide from God, but no matter where we go, He will be there.

David hid in caves from King Saul, but God knew exactly where he was. Hagar ran to the wilderness to hide from Sarah, but God met her where she was because He was with her all the time (Genesis 16). We may try to hide our sin from God, but He knows what we will do before we do it.

It thrills me to think that everywhere I go, God is there. It is wonderful to meditate on His power and presence and to know that He loves us and is for us, not against us. You and I cannot hide from God, and we can be completely open with Him without shame or fear that He will find out what we have done, because He already knows.

God sees you and is with you right now, no matter where you are. If you are in a church, He is there with you. If you are in a nightclub or a bar, He is there with you. He will continue calling to you and drawing you to Him, no matter where you go. He has a plan for your life, and the sooner you surrender to it, the better your life will be.

*Father, the thought that You are everywhere I go is too great for me to understand. I find that I sometimes still try to hide from You, but I realize it is useless. Help me surrender to Your will and plan for my life.*

# EMBRACE YOUR UNIQUENESS

*For you created my inmost being; you knit me together in my mother's womb. I praise you because I am fearfully and wonderfully made; your works are wonderful, I know that full well.*

**PSALM 139:13-14**

In today's scriptures, the psalmist David is talking to God, and I think he is amazed at the way God uniquely crafted him. The Lord has uniquely crafted every human being who has ever lived, including you and me. I wonder, can you say with David, "I am fearfully and wonderfully made"? This is how God views you, and it represents how you should view yourself. The way you think God sees you and feels about you, and the way you see and feel about yourself, determine your quality of life. For this reason, it is vital for you to learn to see yourself as God sees you.

It's important to ask yourself what kind of relationship you have with *yourself*. Do you enjoy spending time alone? Are you able to forgive yourself (receive God's forgiveness) and give yourself grace when you make mistakes? Are you patient with yourself while God is changing you? Are you comfortable with yourself, and do you feel free to be the unique individual God created you to be?

When you answer these questions honestly, you can begin to understand what kind of relationship you have with yourself. If it needs improvement, God's Word will teach you how to love yourself in a balanced way, and you can always pray and ask Him to help you love yourself as He loves you.

*Thank You, Lord, for creating me in such a unique and special way. Help me to love myself as You would have me to, and show me how to have a good relationship with myself.*

# GOD THINKS ABOUT YOU

*My frame was not hidden from you when I was made in the secret place, when I was woven together in the depths of the earth. Your eyes saw my unformed body; all the days ordained for me were written in your book before one of them came to be. How precious to me are your thoughts, God! How vast is the sum of them! Were I to count them, they would outnumber the grains of sand—when I awake, I am still with you.*
**PSALM 139:15–18**

God saw us before we were even formed. In fact, He is the One who formed you with His own hands in your mother's womb. He also recorded every day of your life in His book before you ever lived a single one of them.

God's knowledge is so vast that we cannot understand it. He is omniscient, which means He knows everything. God thinks about us all the time, and that is quite humbling to David, who asks in Psalm 8:4, "What is mankind that you are mindful of them, human beings that you care for them?" How amazing. God is mindful of us.

Take time to actually think about what today's scriptures say. God's thoughts toward us are so vast that they would outnumber all the grains of sand on all the beaches and in all the oceans in the world.

Imagine trying to count the grains of sand and then realizing that God thinks about you more than that. His thoughts about you are all good. He believes in you even when you don't believe in yourself, and He has wonderful plans for you. Live with expectation.

*Father, I am grateful that You take time to think about me. When I feel lonely, help me remember that I am on Your mind and that You have wonderful plans for me.*

# INVITE GOD TO SEARCH YOU

*Search me, God, and know my heart; test me and know my anxious thoughts. See if there is any offensive way in me, and lead me in the way everlasting.*

**PSALM 139:23-24**

Would you be willing to ask God to search your heart and see if there is anything in you that is offensive to Him, even one anxious thought?

In order to invite God to search us, we must be confident in His love for us and should want His correction in any area that is not pleasing to Him. Before I understood how much God loves me, when the Holy Spirit convicted me of sin, I felt bad and guilty about what I had done. But now I welcome His conviction because I don't want to do anything that displeases Him. I realize that, even with my faults, He still loves me.

I also realize that God's correction is an act of love, not displeasure, toward me. I encourage you to invite God to examine your heart and let you know if anything needs to change. If so, repent, and ask Him to help you change it. Hebrews 12:6 says that the Lord disciplines those He loves, and Proverbs 3:12 says that "the Lord disciplines those he loves, as a father the son he delights in."

Never feel bad when God corrects you. Instead, thank Him that He loves you too much to leave you in your sin.

*Father, thank You for taking time to correct me when I sin and offend You. I am truly sorry for those times and I invite Your correction.*

# GOD RESCUES US

*Rescue me, Lord, from evildoers; protect me from the violent, who devise evil plans in their hearts and stir up war every day. They make their tongues as sharp as a serpent's; the poison of vipers is on their lips.*

**PSALM 140:1-3**

I love the boldness with which the psalmist David prays. He always leans on God to deliver him from his enemies, who were plentiful. David knew that God was his rescuer, according to today's passage, and He is our rescuer too. I am so glad that I don't have to be afraid of being left to fend for myself and not being taken care of.

When I was a child, my parents were abusive toward me, and I never felt safe. I always felt that I had to take care of myself. Not until I was born again years later and learned that God wanted to take care of me was I able to feel safe.

Perhaps you feel this way or have felt this way in the past, and today's message is good news for you. God is your rescuer. Cry out to Him as David did, and ask Him to rescue you from your enemies. You can rest in Him, knowing He has a plan for your deliverance.

*Father, thank You that You are my rescuer. Rescue me from my enemies, Lord, and teach me to trust You at all times.*

# BEWARE OF DECEPTION

*Keep me safe, Lord, from the hands of the wicked; protect me from the violent, who devise ways to trip my feet. The arrogant have hidden a snare for me; they have spread out the cords of their net and have set traps for me along my path.*

**PSALM 140:4–5**

Satan and those through whom he works are masters of deception. We should pray regularly to have discernment between good and evil and for God to protect us from deception.

Sometimes I think the devil seems to know us better than we know ourselves. He knows our weak points, and I often say that he sets us up to get us upset. One thing in which the devil delights is for us to lose our peace. For example, if having to spend money on repairs for your home makes you upset, the devil will make sure things break down. I can easily become frustrated and sometimes angry if a repairperson has an appointment to fix something in our home and doesn't show up or even bother to call to cancel. But getting upset does no good. It doesn't change anything except that it steals my peace and makes the devil happy.

You can see from our scriptures today that Satan sets traps for us, but we can avoid them if we are aware of his tactics. The Bible says we are to resist the devil at "his onset" (1 Peter 5:9 AMPC), meaning immediately when we realize he is working against us. He "roams around like a lion roaring [in fierce hunger], seeking someone to seize upon and devour" (1 Peter 5:8 AMPC). But you and I don't have to let him devour us. God will help us and teach us how to watch for the enemy's deception, and we should resist him immediately, knowing that God is on our side.

*Father, help me recognize the traps that the enemy sets for me, and give me discernment so I can avoid his wicked ways.*

# JUSTICE FOR THE POOR

*I know that the Lord secures justice for the poor and upholds the cause of the needy. Surely the righteous will praise your name, and the upright will live in your presence.*

**PSALM 140:12–13**

For God to give justice means that He makes wrong things right, and He promises justice for the poor and needy. We can be poor in many ways; financial lack is only one type of poverty. People can also be poor spiritually. They might not know the gospel and need someone to share truth with them. We should pray that God will send the perfect laborer to everyone who doesn't know Him.

People can also be poor physically. They may be sick or in chronic pain. I have been to places in the world where people don't even have access to an aspirin. When they break an arm or a leg, they have to let it heal in a crooked position, and then they are disabled for the rest of their life. I have seen people in almost unbearable pain because their teeth are decayed. Joyce Meyer Ministries, through the generous donations of our faithful partners, has been privileged to provide free medical and dental treatment to many of these people. We have conducted more than 130 medical mission outreaches, and I believe they are a great way to reach the lost with the gospel.

People can also be poor mentally. They have no education available to them, so they remain stuck in a pattern of poverty. Our ministry delights in building schools where needed around the world and watching people flourish as they begin to learn.

Pray that God will bring justice to the poor and needy, as He promises.

*Father, please bring justice to the poor and needy. Use me in any way You want to use me to make this happen.*

# OUR PRAYERS ARE
# LIKE INCENSE

*I call to you, Lord, come quickly to me; hear me when I call to you. May my prayer be set before you like incense; may the lifting up of my hands be like the evening sacrifice.*

**PSALM 141:1-2**

As we have seen in many of his psalms, David boldly tells God exactly what he wants. In Psalm 141, as in others, he not only wants and needs help from God, but he wants it quickly.

David asks that his prayer would come before God as incense. The burning of incense was symbolic of the prayers of the people rising to the Lord. As we lift up our prayers and our lives to God, they are offered as a sweet-smelling sacrifice.

In Revelation 5:8 and 8:3–4, we see that golden bowls were full of incense—the prayers of God's people. I like the imagery of my prayers going up to God as a sweet-smelling sacrifice, something that is pleasing to Him.

When we lift our hands in prayer, it is like an evening sacrifice to the Lord. Prayer is a privilege, and we can pray about anything, anytime, anywhere. Pray boldly, as David did, and know that God delights in your prayers.

*Father, thank You for the privilege of prayer. Delight in my prayers, Lord, and answer them quickly.*

# GOD'S WORD HAS POWER

*Set a guard over my mouth, Lord; keep watch over the door of my lips.*
**PSALM 141:3**

Reading, studying, and meditating on God's Word are all very important actions and will change your life. But do you know that speaking God's Word aloud, sometimes called "confessing" the Word, is also vital if you want to stay strong spiritually? Sometimes, the Word may not reflect how you feel about a situation, but if you will confess it and keep confessing it, your feelings will change. The Word is always right, and emotions are rarely right. Not only will speaking God's Word aloud help our feelings align with His truth, but His Word also brings comfort to us and quiets our distraught emotions.

In today's scripture, the psalmist David wants God to "set a guard" over his mouth and to "keep watch over the door" of his lips. In the Amplified Bible, for God to keep watch over the door of his lips means to keep him from speaking thoughtlessly.

According to Ecclesiastes 3:7, there is "a time to be silent and a time to speak." Sometimes the best thing we can do is to say nothing. When we do speak, we are wise to be intentional about what we say and to think about our words beforehand. Proverbs 18:21 teaches us that our words are filled with either life or death, and when we speak God's Word, we always speak life.

*Help me, Lord, to remember that Your Word has power and to speak it aloud often.*

# THE MERCY OF GOD

*I cry aloud to the Lord; I lift up my voice to the Lord for mercy. I pour out before him my complaint; before him I tell my trouble.*

**PSALM 142:1-2**

In today's scriptures, David cries out for mercy as he tells God his complaints and troubles. Let's consider Hebrews 4:15–16, which tells us how we can obtain God's great mercy: "For we do not have a high priest who is unable to empathize with our weaknesses, but we have one who has been tempted in every way, just as we are—yet he did not sin. Let us then approach God's throne of grace with confidence, so that we may receive mercy and find grace to help us in our time of need."

The prophet Jeremiah also writes of God's mercy, reminding us that without God's mercy, we would have been consumed (Lamentations 3:22 NKJV). His mercies are new every morning (Lamentations 3:23), and I, for one, am glad.

God wants us to ask for mercy, receive it for ourselves, and then extend it to others. This simply means that even though someone may deserve punishment, we can graciously show them mercy instead, just as God shows us.

Take time to breathe in God's mercy. Believe that He is giving mercy to you, as you have asked Him to do. He is a merciful God. Receive God's mercy today and do not waste your time feeling guilty about a past sin. Let God's mercy flow into you, and then let it flow out to others.

*Father, thank You so much for Your mercy. Help me be gracious to others and extend mercy to them as You have extended it to me.*

# GOD WATCHES OVER YOUR WAY

*When my spirit grows faint within me, it is you who watch over my way.*
**PSALM 142:3**

We sometimes have days when we feel strong, upbeat, and ready to take on the world. But we also have days or seasons of life when we feel weak, even times when our hearts are so discouraged or weary that we feel we cannot keep moving forward. I believe these experiences may be what the psalmist David refers to when he writes, "When my spirit grows faint within me." When that happens, he says to God, "it is you who watch over my way."

Today's scripture encourages us by letting us know that no matter how tired or discouraged we may feel at times, we are never alone or left to our own devices. God is always watching over us—not just in general, but watching over our "way," meaning that He is watching over the paths we take in life. He not only sees each step we take, but He lovingly watches over us and guides us, especially when we do not feel strong or confident and we are willing to lean on Him completely.

*Thank You, God, for sustaining me and for watching over me at all times, especially when I feel weak.*

# CRY OUT TO GOD IN DESPERATION

*Listen to my cry, for I am in desperate need; rescue me from those who pursue me, for they are too strong for me.*

PSALM 142:6

Now that you have read portions of almost all of the Book of Psalms, I'm sure you can see that David, who wrote more psalms than anyone else, was a person through whom deep emotions ran. In many ways, David teaches us through his psalms how to manage our emotions.

In Psalm 142, David feels overwhelmed, and in our scripture for today, he cries out to God, saying that he is in desperate need. He is hiding in a cave because King Saul wants to kill him, and he knows that King Saul and his troops are too strong for him.

His response to his feelings of depression and being "wrapped in darkness" (Psalm 142:3 AMP) was not to meditate on his problem. Instead, he dealt with his problem in this psalm by choosing to cry out to the Lord, his refuge and portion in the land of the living (v. 5). In other words, he thought about the Lord, his Deliverer, and it helped him to overcome desperation.

Perhaps you are in a desperate situation today. You may feel, as David did, that your enemies are too strong for you. Your enemies may not be people; they may be situations that cause you to feel alone, overwhelmed, depressed, frustrated, or confused. Whatever your circumstances, the same God who heard David's cry will hear you when you cry out to Him.

*Lord, teach me to manage my emotions. When my feelings are deep and intense, help me to cry out to You.*

# JESUS IS OUR RIGHTEOUSNESS

*No one living is righteous before you.*

PSALM 143:2

David looked forward to the Messiah's coming and to all the blessings He would bring, but he did not get to experience them. In today's verse, he says that no one living is righteous before God. This is also true for us today if we depend on our good works to make us righteous. But if we depend on Jesus for right standing with God, then because of our faith in Him, we can say something different from what David said. We can say that we are the righteousness of God in Jesus Christ (2 Corinthians 5:21).

No one is righteous, not even one person, if they depend on anything or anyone other than Jesus. He alone makes righteousness possible. We have right standing with God only through Christ, and this is good news! We no longer have to feel guilty and bad about ourselves if we look to Jesus for our forgiveness, mercy, grace, and righteousness.

Romans 3:20–22 teaches us that the law exists to make known God's righteousness, which comes only through faith in Jesus. And Romans 3:23–24 says: "All have sinned and fall short of the glory of God, and all are justified freely by his grace through the redemption that came by Christ Jesus." This is God's promise to everyone who puts their faith in Jesus.

*Father, I appreciate the right standing You have provided for me through Jesus. Help me to never forget that righteousness is mine through faith and faith alone. Amen.*

# THINK ABOUT GOD

*So my spirit grows faint within me; my heart within me is dismayed. I remember the days of long ago; I meditate on all your works and consider what your hands have done.*

**PSALM 143:4–5**

The psalmist David writes frequently about meditating on or thinking about all the wonderful works and mighty acts of the Lord. He thought about the name of the Lord, the mercy of God, the love of God, and many other such things.

I have mentioned before that David was bold in his honesty about how he felt. When he was joyful, he wrote about that, and when he was depressed, he wrote about that, as he did in today's scriptures. We see in these verses that his response was not to meditate on his problem. Instead, he actively came against the problem by choosing to remember the good times of past days. He deliberately pondered the doings of God and the works of His hands. In other words, David intentionally focused his thoughts on something good, and it helped him overcome depression.

Never forget this: Your mind plays an important role in your victory. Think thoughts that will add power to your life, not thoughts that drain your strength and energy.

*Help me, Lord, to choose to think thoughts that are positive, uplifting, and encouraging—thoughts about You, not thoughts about my problems.*

# CRY OUT TO GOD WHEN YOU NEED HELP

*I spread out my hands to you; I thirst for you like a parched land. Answer me quickly, Lord; my spirit fails. Do not hide your face from me or I will be like those who go down to the pit. Let the morning bring me word of your unfailing love, for I have put my trust in you. Show me the way I should go, for to you I entrust my life.*

**PSALM 143:6–8**

In today's scriptures, the psalmist David once again cries out to God for help, and I think it is good for us to see how often he does this. God never gets tired of hearing us cry out to Him or ask Him for help. He is always listening and ready to come to our aid.

When you and I find ourselves in need of God's help, we can follow David's example. We can spread forth our hands in prayer and supplication to Him. We can call upon Him to answer us quickly because we trust in Him. We can remember His unfailing love. We can lift up our souls, our inner beings, to Him, asking Him to show us the way to go and declaring once more that we trust Him.

These are all acts of faith, and the Lord responds to faith. If we are under a minor attack, His intervention may take only a few hours or days. But if we are under a major attack, it may take much longer. However long we need to wait on Him, we must stand firm and continue to cry out to God, receiving the help and encouragement that only He can give. The Lord will deliver us, just as He delivered David in every situation. We can be confident of this.

*Thank You, Lord, for being my deliverer. Help me stand firm as I wait for You to answer my cry. Amen.*

# EMOTIONAL STABILITY

*Rescue me from my enemies, Lord, for I hide myself in you. Teach me to do your will, for you are my God; may your good Spirit lead me on level ground.*

**PSALM 143:9–10**

David prays in today's scriptures that God will lead him on level ground. I have always thought of this as a request for God to keep him emotionally stable. David was being pursued by his enemies and declared that God was his hiding place. When I pray, I often ask God to hide me in Him. We are kept safe in Him.

David had many opportunities to become flustered and allow his emotions to affect him in negative ways, so he prayed that God would keep him level or stable. Emotional stability is very important. We all have emotions, but we should not let them have us. With God's help, we can learn to manage them instead of allowing them to manage us. We can live beyond our feelings by knowing and acting on God's Word rather than on the way we feel.

We cannot do this by willpower alone; we need God's grace. We need His help and power because emotions can be very strong, and without God's help, they will lead us in wrong directions. Have you been allowing your feelings to control you? If so, begin today to ask God to lead you on level ground.

*Father, I am sorry for letting my emotions lead me at times and I ask You to keep me stable and lead me on level ground.*

# WIN YOUR BATTLES GOD'S WAY

*Praise be to the Lord my Rock, who trains my hands for war, my fingers for battle. He is my loving God and my fortress, my stronghold and my deliverer, my shield, in whom I take refuge, who subdues peoples under me.*

**PSALM 144:1–2**

In today's scriptures, David says the Lord trains his "hands for war." I believe this refers to lifting his hands in praise to God. The Lord subdued those who came against him, but David also did what he needed to do. We must always remember that we are partners with God. God has a part, and we have a part. We cannot do God's part, and He will not do our part. This is the key to winning any kind of spiritual war the enemy wages against us—fear, discouragement, anger, jealousy, depression, and others. When such thoughts and emotions come to us, we can follow David's example. We can submit our struggle to the Lord, call upon Him for His help, and then fight it in the strength and power of the Holy Spirit.

We fight by spending time with God, by praying, and by speaking His Word. We also fight by lifting our eyes, heads, hands, and hearts to Him and offering the sacrifice of praise and thanksgiving to the Lord, our Rock and our fortress, the One who subdues those who come against us.

*Help me, Lord, to do my part when I fight a spiritual battle, knowing that You will do Your part to subdue anything that is against me.*

# GOD TAKES CARE OF YOU

*Lord, what are human beings that you care for them, mere mortals that you think of them? They are like a breath; their days are like a fleeting shadow.*

**PSALM 144:3–4**

The psalmist David was amazed that God took time to care for us mortals since He is so great and, apart from Him, we are so weak and fleeting. We, like David, should wonder about this; I think we have become so accustomed to God's care and help that we take them for granted instead of being amazed, as we should be.

Think of taking a can of aerosol spray and spraying it once into the air. Think of how quickly the spray disappears. David compares humans to that—fleeting and seemingly not worth God's thoughts and loving care. Yet God does care for us and thinks of us all the time because He loves us unconditionally. He considers us to be very important.

God created us because He wanted someone to fellowship with. He created us in His image because only two like beings can enjoy true fellowship and intimate relationship. We can only enjoy intimacy with other human beings and with God, because He has created us to have a deep, personal relationship with Him.

This is so wonderful that it is difficult to even know how to think about it properly, and it should amaze us as it amazed David.

*Father, the fact that I am created in Your image and that You desire a relationship with me is amazing and wonderful. Help me always to put my relationship with You before other less important things and to value it greatly.*

# THE POWER OF MUSIC

*I will sing a new song to you, my God; on the ten-stringed lyre I will make music to you.*

**PSALM 144:9**

Singing and the playing of musical instruments are mentioned often in Psalms, and we are encouraged to use both to lead us into worship and praise to God. Have you ever thought of just how amazing music is? I have briefly but not as deeply as I should have. Only God could take many different sounds and make them blend in such a beautiful way.

Yesterday I took about an hour to listen to the music app on my television and was amazed at how the music lifted my soul and provoked me to worship God. As I listened to the songs, I wanted to lift my arms in praise to God, and I did.

Thankfully, God tells us we can "make a joyful noise" to Him (Psalm 100:1 KJV), because not all of us have wonderful singing voices. However, God probably thinks our voices are beautiful, and we should use them to sing to Him. We can sing songs we know and even make up new ones that no one has ever heard. The psalms in the Book of Psalms were written not only as prayers, but often they were sung. These songs frequently revealed how the psalmist was feeling or they spoke of his enemies and his trust in God.

Music is amazing because it blends to make beautiful sounds that lift our souls into God's presence and cause us to worship Him. Sing frequently and enjoy listening to music because it can bring joy to your heart.

*Father, thank You for songs of praise and worship. They are wonderful gifts from You, and I want to sing and listen to music about You more than ever before.*

# CHOOSE GOOD THOUGHTS AND WORDS

*I will exalt you, my God the King; I will praise your name for ever and ever. Every day I will praise you and extol your name for ever and ever.*
**PSALM 145:1–2**

We don't know how David's day started out or how it was going when he wrote the words of today's scriptures. But we do see that he is praising God and is determined to praise His name "for ever and ever." He has set his mind ahead of time to use his words to praise and extol the Lord.

Words are wonderful when used with good intentions, as David used them. They can encourage, bless, comfort, affirm, and give confidence. When we understand the power of words and realize that we can choose what we think and speak, our lives can be transformed. Our words are not forced on us—they formulate in our thoughts, and then we speak them. We can learn to choose our thoughts, to resist the wrong ones, and to think on the good, healthy, right ones.

When you get up in the morning, if you need to do something you're not looking forward to, you can choose how to think and speak about it. You can say, "I dread this day," or you can speak as David spoke, saying, "I will exalt you, my God, the King.... Every day I will praise you and extol your name for ever and ever." If you choose to think and speak words of praise to God, He will give you the strength today to do whatever you need to do and to do it with joy.

*Lord, I choose today to exalt Your name and to praise You for ever and ever.*

# TRAINING THE NEXT GENERATION

*One generation commends your works to another; they tell of your mighty acts. They speak of the glorious splendor of your majesty—and I will meditate on your wonderful works.*

**PSALM 145:4-5**

In our Western culture, we tend to think only of the here and now—what is happening at the moment. But God also wants His people to teach the next generation His precepts and speak often of the great things He has done for them so they will know that they can trust Him to do the same for them.

Psalm 78:4 says, "We will tell the next generation the praise-worthy deeds of the Lord, his power, and the wonders he has done."

The Israelites were to make sure their children kept the traditional feasts year after year, because each feast celebrated something great that God had done. Those children were to tell it to their children and so on, throughout all generations.

I think today we may depend too much on churches or Sunday school to teach our children but fail to also do it ourselves. I encourage you to take your children to church, but even that is not as powerful as teaching them yourself. They need to know that what you tell them to do is also important to you, and they need to see you do what you tell them to do. It is urgent that we begin to train the next generation, because the longer we wait, the more will be lost.

*Father, help me remember how important it is for me to talk to my children about all the great and mighty things You have done. Remind me to encourage them to tell it to their children also.*

# BE SLOW TO ANGER

*The Lord is gracious and compassionate, slow to anger and rich in love.*
**PSALM 145:8**

We are to be slow to anger because anger does not promote the righteousness that God desires. It is our job as God's ambassadors in the earth to not only tell people what God is like, but to show them.

We cannot merely pray for anger to disappear from our lives, but we should also use discipline and self-control to deal with it, with God's help. Colossians 3:8 says, "But now you must also rid yourselves of all such things as these: anger, rage, malice, slander, and filthy language from your lips."

Proverbs 16:32 is one of my favorite scriptures about anger. It says, "Better a patient person than a warrior, one with self-control than one who takes a city."

This statement is very powerful. Think about it: If a person can control their anger, they are better than a person who could capture an entire city.

Anger grieves the Holy Spirit, according to Ephesians 4:26–31. This is something we should take seriously. We may feel anger, but we are not to allow it to stay in our heart. We should not let the sun go down on our anger, or we will give the devil a foothold in our lives.

Be quick to forgive. The devil gains more ground in the lives of believers through unforgiveness than through anything else. If you are angry at anyone or about anything, let it go now so you can be strong and free from the attacks of the devil.

*Father, help me to be obedient to Your commands regarding anger. Grant me the grace to let go of anger quickly and to walk in love.*

# GOD IS GOOD

*The Lord is good to all; he has compassion on all he has made.*

**PSALM 145:9**

God is good to everyone. He is compassionate, and the word for compassion in Greek refers to an emotion that is stronger than pity, one that compels us to take action.

We are to love all people. Jesus tells us to bless our enemies (Matthew 5:43–46), so obviously we are to show goodness and kindness to those who don't deserve it, remembering that we don't deserve the goodness and kindness God shows to us.

God is slow to anger and long-suffering; it is His goodness that leads people to repentance (Psalm 145:8; Romans 2:4). We don't know how long His patience will endure, but I believe He remains patient, even when He knows that a person will never accept Him.

God tries diligently to reach people through His goodness; however, His patience will eventually run out and the ungodly will see His wrath (Romans 1:18). Some people say, "I don't believe a loving God would send a person to hell," and they are right. He doesn't send people to hell; they choose it by refusing to believe in Him and obey Him. They finally meet with God's wrath because of their own unrighteousness.

Many people believe that because of God's grace, He overlooks all sin, but this is wrong. God says, "I have set before you life and death, blessings and curses. Now *choose* life, so that you and your children may live" (Deuteronomy 30:19; italics mine). We eventually reap the consequences of our choices. Choose God and His ways because the other choice is too wretched to even think about. Choose compassion.

*Father, help me to be patient, long-suffering, and compassionate toward people, just as You are. May all people choose You and experience the good life You have planned for them.*

# GOD IS TRUSTWORTHY

*Your kingdom is an everlasting kingdom, and your dominion endures through all generations. The Lord is trustworthy in all he promises and faithful in all he does.*

**PSALM 145:13**

These days, finding people we can trust completely seems to be more and more difficult. This is sad, but even if no one else we know is faithful, we can be sure that God is faithful. He does everything He says He will do.

God may not do everything exactly the way you want Him to, but if He doesn't give you or do for you what you asked for, He has something better in store. You might not see it right away, but eventually you will.

You may be weary of waiting on God, but I assure you that His timing is perfect. Everything is beautiful in its time (Ecclesiastes 3:11), but if it comes too early, it may not be healthy. God knows things that we do not know, and He knows the right time for everything. Know that God is faithful, and put your complete trust in Him. Don't worry or fret about anything, because even though He may not be early, He will not be late.

*Father, sometimes I do grow weary of waiting on You to answer my prayers, but I trust that Your timing is always better than mine. Your will be done.*

# GOD TAKES CARE OF EVERY LIVING THING

*The eyes of all look to you, and you give them their food at the proper time. You open your hand and satisfy the desires of every living thing.*

**PSALM 145:15-16**

If we meditate on what a job it must be to take care of not only all living people but all living things, it is beyond our comprehension. God feeds not only us but also all the animals in the entire world. He also waters and provides just enough sunshine for all the plants. The large amount and variety of plants and animals on earth number into the millions. What the world calls Mother Nature is truly amazing, but we know that all of creation is the design of Father God, not Mother Nature.

God satisfies the desires of every living thing, including you. What do you desire? God's Word says that if we delight ourselves in Him, He will give us the desires of our heart (Psalm 37:4). When we delight ourselves in God, we seek Him, which means we put Him first in all things. I have asked God for several things, but I have also told Him that if they are not right for me, please do not give them to me. I only want what God knows I can handle and still give Him first priority in my life. I know He will either give me what I have asked for or, if He doesn't, give me something better.

Put your trust in God and remember that He delights in you and wants you to have what you can handle while still keeping Him first in your life.

*Father, I love You and I appreciate Your generosity to me. Grant me the desires of my heart according to Your promise and help me be patient as I wait on You.*

# WILL YOU BE FAITHFUL?

*The Lord is righteous in all his ways and faithful in all he does.*

**PSALM 145:17**

According to today's scripture, "The Lord is righteous in all his ways," which means that everything He does is right. He is also "faithful in all he does," which means He will never, ever let us down. We can depend on Him completely. To know God is to know that He is perfectly faithful in every way.

It is important that you and I are faithful too. We will never be perfect, as God is perfect, as long as we are in our fleshly bodies. But we can set our hearts to be faithful in every way, and we can do our best every day. We can choose to be faithful in good times and in not-so-good times, faithful when we have plenty and when we are in need, and faithful to do what is right even when we seem to be the only ones doing it.

To be faithful is to be dependable, loyal, and devoted. Faithful people are worthy of others' trust. They are reliable, consistent, constant, steady, and steadfast, meaning they will stick with an assignment, an opportunity, or a relationship when sticking with it isn't easy. They will stay where God places them until He releases them, and they will be true to those people He has put in their lives.

You and I are to imitate God, and God is faithful.

*You are perfectly faithful, God, and I pray that I will be faithful too.*

# TRUST GOD MORE THAN ANYONE ELSE

*Do not put your trust in princes, in human beings, who cannot save.*

**PSALM 146:3**

Have you ever been hurt or disappointed by someone you trusted because they were not there for you when you needed them most? Or maybe you trusted them to help you in an important situation, but they didn't. I think we have all experienced this, but when we begin to think that any human being will never hurt or disappoint us, we set ourselves up to get hurt.

In John 2:24–25 (AMPC), Jesus says He did not entrust Himself to people because He knew them, "and He did not need anyone to bear witness concerning man...for He Himself knew what was in human nature. [He could read men's hearts.]"

It wasn't that Jesus didn't trust people, but He didn't *entrust* Himself to them. The difference is that He believed the best of them, but He also knew they could and probably would disappoint Him. He only totally entrusted Himself to Father God, because He is the only One who is totally trustworthy.

Peter disappointed Jesus (Matthew 26:33–35, 69–75), and Judas disappointed Him (Matthew 26:21–25, 47–49). Jesus' disciples disappointed Him because they fell asleep when He needed them to pray with Him in the Garden of Gethsemane (Matthew 26:31, 36–45). Paul discovered he couldn't trust those he had ministered to, because at his first trial, everyone deserted him (2 Timothy 4:16).

There are situations in which we should trust only God; He is the only One in whom we can put our entire trust. Trust people and don't be suspicious of them, but realize they are humans and may disappoint you.

*Father, help me put my total trust in You alone and not in anyone else.*

# HAVE HOPE

*Blessed are those whose help is the God of Jacob, whose hope is in the Lord their God.*

**PSALM 146:5**

Today is a day to be filled with hope. In fact, every day you walk with God can be filled with hope. All you have to do is choose hope over cynicism, hope over fear, and hope over all kinds of negativity. Hope will keep you positive, full of faith, and happy.

Most people who are unhappy in life are unhappy because they choose to focus on unhappy things. They see the worst in other people, they talk about what is wrong in their own lives, and they have a generally negative outlook. Hope does the opposite. Hope sees the best in others, it speaks about what is going well and declares good things, and it looks for the positive in the circumstances of life. Most of all, hope expects God to do something good in every situation. This is why hope makes us happy.

I urge you today to have a hopeful attitude. Like the psalmist, put your hope in the Lord your God—not in a job or a paycheck, not in a relationship, and not in another person. God is the giver of every good gift (James 1:17), and He wants to bless you. Expect Him to do something good in your life today.

*Today, Lord, I choose to hope in You. I'm expecting You to do something good!*

# SEEING TRUTH

*He upholds the cause of the oppressed and gives food to the hungry. The Lord sets prisoners free, the Lord gives sight to the blind, the Lord lifts up those who are bowed down, the Lord loves the righteous.*

**PSALM 146:7–8**

God does many wonderful things for us, but one of the most important is that He helps us see truth. Today's scriptures say He gives sight to the blind. Jesus did heal people who were physically blind, but He also heals those who are spiritually blind and cannot see truth.

People who are part of false religions or cults and those who are atheists are spiritually blind. Even those of us who are Christians are often spiritually blind in many areas of our lives. I was a Christian for many years, yet I believed lies the devil told me because I didn't know the truth of God's Word. Jesus said if we continue in His Word, we will know the truth, and the truth will make us free (John 8:31–32).

As I began to seriously study God's Word, I started learning truth that opened my spiritual eyes and set me free to live the life Jesus had died for me to enjoy. The same has happened, or can happen, to you.

Just one lesson I learned is that God loves me unconditionally. Before I knew this truth, I often felt that God was angry with me even after I had repented of sin. I felt guilty most of the time until I learned that there is no condemnation to those who are in Christ Jesus (Romans 8:1). I strongly encourage you to study God's Word and let Him open your blind eyes by showing you truth.

*Father, thank You for opening my blind eyes and teaching me truth through Your Word.*

# HOW TO TREAT THOSE WHO ARE LONELY

*The Lord watches over the foreigner and sustains the fatherless and the widow, but he frustrates the ways of the wicked.*

**PSALM 146:9**

God seems to have a special place in His heart for those who are lonely, and He wants us to be good to them. Psalm 68:6 says that He "sets the lonely in families." If you know someone who has no family, you can include them in some of your family functions. Invite them to your home for Thanksgiving dinner, a Fourth of July celebration, and other such events.

God gave the Israelites commands about how they were to include the foreigners and strangers among them (Deuteronomy 10:19; Leviticus 19:34). And Hebrews 13:2 instructs believers to show hospitality to strangers. We tend to gravitate toward people we know and are comfortable with, but God wants us to reach beyond our comfort zone and think about how it would feel to be alone so we will include the lonely in our lives.

The Lord mentions the fatherless and the widow frequently in Scripture and instructs us to be good to them and to help meet their needs. James writes that religion that is pure and undefiled is about visiting and helping to care for the widows and orphans in their distress (James 1:27).

Choose a widowed person in your church and show special attention to them. You can informally adopt them into your family. If you are going to lunch after church on Sunday, you can include them. There are many ways to minister to the lonely if we will just think about it, and when we do, it will put a smile on God's face.

*Father, help me remember how You feel about those who are lonely, and show me who I can minister to and help alleviate their loneliness.*

# GOD HEALS THE BROKENHEARTED

*The Lord builds up Jerusalem; he gathers the exiles of Israel. He heals the brokenhearted and binds up their wounds.*

**PSALM 147:2-3**

When people are brokenhearted, they are damaged or hurt in their soul; they are dysfunctional, especially in relationships. They don't think in healthy ways, and their emotions are wounded. Only God can heal the brokenhearted, because only He can reach into the soul of a person and touch them exactly where they hurt—at just the right time and in just the right way. I was once one of those brokenhearted people, and perhaps you were too. You may be brokenhearted right now. If so, let me assure you that God will heal you if you ask Him to and follow His lead.

People are often taught that God forgives their sins, but too often they are not taught that God can heal their wounded souls. They know they will go to heaven when they die, but they never enjoy their life on earth.

I suffered abuse and abandonment for many years of my early life. I didn't know what peace or joy was until I saw it in Dave's life and found that God could and would give it to me too.

I had to invite Him into the wounded areas of my soul, face the truth about what had happened to me, stop feeling sorry for myself, forgive those who had abused me, and do other things. But because I followed God's plan for restoration, I am no longer brokenhearted, and you don't have to be either. Let today be the day you step into your journey of healing if you need it.

*Father, I pray that You will heal all the broken places in my life. Teach me to submit to Your ways and help me not to give up until I am completely whole. Thank You.*

# THERE IS NOTHING THAT GOD CANNOT DO

*He determines the number of the stars and calls them each by name.*
*Great is our Lord and mighty in power; his understanding has no limit.*

**PSALM 147:4-5**

I read that, according to the people who study stars, the galaxy in which you and I live contains approximately 300 billion stars, and there are approximately 100 billion galaxies in the universe. I have no idea how anyone except God could count the galaxies, but let it suffice to say there are more than we can comprehend. Today's scriptures say that God is great and mighty in power, but to say that our God is great and mighty is an understatement because He is light-years beyond that. He is so amazing that I doubt we have a word that would even come close to describing Him.

In your wildest thoughts, could you imagine naming 300 billion stars in one galaxy—and still having 100 billion galaxies to go, all of which also include stars? I cannot find words to express what I feel when I think about this.

Not only does God count the stars, but He has given each one of them a name. I feel like laughing just trying to write this. Knowing that this same God cares about you and me gives me great joy.

I am sure that He can take care of whatever problems we might have, and there is no reason for us to worry. So, be at peace, because we serve a God with no limits.

*Father, I am amazed at Your creativity. Forgive me for ever making You too small in my thoughts. There is nothing You cannot do.*

# WHAT DELIGHTS GOD?

*His pleasure is not in the strength of the horse, nor his delight in the legs of the warrior; the Lord delights in those who fear him, who put their hope in his unfailing love.*

**PSALM 147:10–11**

No matter how strong we think we are, God does not delight in our strength. He delights in those who fear Him. The Word of God speaks frequently of the reverential fear of God, but we hear little about it in our churches or in the sermons we listen to. Why? Either people totally misunderstand what it means or they prefer to live life according to their own desires.

We are not to be afraid of God, but we are to have a reverential fear of Him, which means a deep respect that is strong enough to cause us to promptly obey Him. Reverential fear is a feeling of holy awe that says God is not to be trifled with (viewed as unimportant, without seriousness or respect).

For example, we should not take the Lord's name in vain, make jokes about holy things such the Holy Spirit or Scripture, walk out of church during an altar call for salvation, text on our phone during worship or preaching, do any act of disobedience, or have a casual attitude toward what is sacred.

Note also in today's scriptures that God delights in those who put their hope in His unfailing love. God wants us to trust Him and it honors Him when we do. Let's live to please and glorify God.

*Father, I am sorry for the times I have not shown You reverential fear. Help me understand more about what it means and help me to never dishonor You in any way.*

# LET ALL CREATED THINGS PRAISE THE LORD

*Praise the Lord. Praise the Lord from the heavens; praise him in the heights above. Praise him, all his angels; praise him, all his heavenly hosts. Praise him, sun and moon; praise him, all you shining stars. Praise him, you highest heavens and you waters above the skies. Let them praise the name of the Lord, for at his command they were created, and he established them for ever and ever—he issued a decree that will never pass away.*

**PSALM 148:1–6**

If all created things are to praise the Lord, how much more should you and I praise Him? To *praise* means to express approval of, to give adoration, to commend or extol, and to offer grateful homage to. I also read a definition of praise that said it is a tale or a narration. In other words, it is telling someone a story of what God has done for you or someone else.

The Bible is filled with scriptures instructing us to praise God. Psalm 100:4 instructs us to "enter his gates with thanksgiving and his courts with praise." I often think of this as I begin to pray. Too often, we begin our prayers with petitions or requests, but according to Psalm 100, the way to enter into God's presence is to first praise and thank Him for what He has done, what He is doing, and what He will do in the future.

Make a habit of beginning your prayers with praise and thanks. Praise God throughout the day and as often as possible.

*Father, You are truly worthy of praise from all created things. The earth and all that is in it belongs to You. I belong to You, and I give You praise, for You alone are worthy to receive it.*

# THE REDEMPTIVE
# NAMES OF GOD

*Let them praise the name of the Lord, for his name alone is exalted;
his splendor is above the earth and the heavens. And he has raised up
for his people a horn, the praise of all his faithful servants, of Israel, the
people close to his heart. Praise the Lord.*

**PSALM 148:13-14**

The Bible speaks of seven redemptive names of God. Each of
them represents something He does or is. His name, Yahweh, was
so holy that it was not even spoken aloud by the most religious
Israelites. They removed the two vowels, the English *a* and *e*, so
*YHWH* becomes a word that cannot be said. Yahweh is said to
mean "He brings into existence whatever exists."

The seven redemptive names of God, mentioned throughout
the Scripture, are
- *Jehovah-Jireh*, meaning the Lord our provider
- *Jehovah-Rapha*, meaning the Lord our healer
- *Jehovah-Shammah*, meaning the Lord (who) is present
- *Jehovah-Tsidkenu*, meaning the Lord our righteousness
- *Jehovah-Shalom*, meaning the Lord our peace
- *Jehovah-Ra'ah*, meaning the Lord our shepherd
- *Jehovah-Nissi*, meaning the Lord our banner (or refuge)

Jesus has been given the name above all other names (Philippians 2:9–11), and His name includes the power and work of the
seven redemptive names mentioned above. The names of God are
precious and should be respected at all times.

*Father, if I have misused Your name, forgive me and help me to
realize how important Your name is and to always to honor it.*

# THE HUMBLE GET HELP FROM GOD

*For the Lord takes delight in his people; he crowns the humble with victory.*

**PSALM 149:4**

The Bible says, "God resists the proud, but gives grace to the humble" (James 4:6 NKJV) and that if we will humble ourselves under His mighty hand, He will exalt us in due time (1 Peter 5:5–6). God hates pride, because proud people depend on themselves instead of on Him. They have an inflated opinion of themselves, and they think more highly of themselves than they ought to.

*Humble* in the original Greek language of the New Testament meant lowly or to make low. It means to make yourself lower than God and depend entirely on Him. We are often independent, which is the opposite of the way God wants us to be.

Jesus says that we are to abide in Him, and that apart from Him we can do nothing (John 15:5).

To *abide* means to live, dwell and remain; to depend on continuously. Because I didn't have anyone who really cared for me as a child, I became independent and repeatedly told myself that I could take care of myself and didn't need anyone. However, when I entered into a relationship with God through Jesus, I had to let Him break my independent attitude and learn to depend on Him.

I have discovered, as you will or may have already discovered, that life is much better when we humble ourselves and let God take the lead in our lives.

*Father, forgive me for the times when I proudly depend on myself instead of on You. Help me learn to always depend and rely on You for everything.*

# PRAISE DEFEATS THE ENEMY

*Let the saints be joyful in glory; let them sing aloud on their beds. Let the high praises of God be in their mouth, and a two-edged sword in their hand.*

**PSALM 149:5–6 NKJV**

Today's scriptures are filled with praise and keys to victory. In these verses, the psalmist gives us instruction about the position God's people should take against our enemies. He says that the "high praises of God" should be in our mouth and that we should have "a two-edged sword" (representing the Word of God, according to Ephesians 6:17) in our hand. In the remainder of Psalm 149, he says that the people of God take this position in order to defeat their enemies.

Sincere, heartfelt praise to God confuses the enemy and defeats him more quickly than any other battle plan. It also protects us from defeat and negativity in our minds. Genuine praise involves the Word of God. We praise God according to His Word and His character. As we praise God for Who He is and for His attributes, for His ability and might, we will see His power and attributes released on our behalf.

Do you feel that you are in some type of battle today? If so, use the weapon of praise. Begin to worship God and speak His Word. Stand firm in this position, and God will move in your situation, defeating the enemy and bringing victory to you.

God never loses a battle. He always wins, and when we praise Him, we win too.

*Thank You, God, that You never lose a battle. I praise and worship You today, and I believe that praise defeats the enemy.*

# LET EVERYTHING THAT HAS BREATH PRAISE THE LORD

*Praise the Lord. Praise God in his sanctuary; praise him in his mighty heavens. Praise him for his acts of power; praise him for his surpassing greatness. Praise him with the sounding of the trumpet, praise him with the harp and lyre, praise him with timbrel and dancing, praise him with the strings and pipe, praise him with the clash of cymbals, praise him with resounding cymbals. Let everything that has breath praise the Lord. Praise the Lord.*

**PSALM 150**

Psalm 150 is the final psalm in the Book of Psalms, and once again it reminds us to praise the Lord with all that we have. Praising God should go beyond the times we are in church; our lives should be filled with praise to God. Praise and thanksgiving are closely related, and I encourage you to let your days be filled with both.

We can see from all that is written in Psalms that God is worthy of our praise, and no matter how often we praise and thank Him, it can never be enough. Our God has done so many amazing and wonderful things that they could never be numbered. His greatness is beyond our understanding. Instead of trying to understand what God is doing in your life, just trust Him.

The more you trust God, the happier you will be. One of the fastest ways to relieve stress and anxiety in our lives is to depend on God and trust Him with everything that concerns us. Cast all your care on the Lord, because He cares for you (1 Peter 5:7). Remember that God sees you all the time, thinks about you all the time, and is with you all the time. Praise Him for who He is. Praise Him not only for all He has done in your life but also for all the good things He has planned for you.

*Father, thank You for the Book of Psalms and all the psalms have taught me. Help me remember what I have learned, especially the power of praise and gratitude.*

### *Do you have a real relationship with Jesus?*

God loves you! He created you to be a special, unique, one-of-a-kind individual, and He has a specific purpose and plan for your life. And through a personal relationship with your Creator—God—you can discover a way of life that will truly satisfy your soul.

No matter who you are, what you've done, or where you are in your life right now, God's love and grace are greater than your sin—your mistakes. Jesus willingly gave His life so you can receive forgiveness from God and have new life in Him. He's just waiting for you to invite Him to be your Savior and Lord.

If you are ready to commit your life to Jesus and follow Him, all you have to do is ask Him to forgive your sins and give you a fresh start in the life you are meant to live. Begin by praying this prayer . . .

*Lord Jesus, thank You for giving Your life for me and forgiving me of my sins so I can have a personal relationship with You. I am sincerely sorry for the mistakes I've made, and I know I need You to help me live right. Your Word says in Romans 10:9, "If you declare with your mouth, 'Jesus is Lord,' and believe in your heart that God raised him from the dead, you will be saved" (NIV).*

*I believe You are the Son of God
and confess You as my Savior and Lord.
Take me just as I am, and work in my heart,
making me the person You want me to be.
I want to live for You, Jesus, and I am so grateful
that You are giving me a fresh start in my
new life with You today.*

*I love You, Jesus!*

It's so amazing to know that God loves us so much! He wants to have a deep, intimate relationship with us that grows every day as we spend time with Him in prayer and Bible study. And we want to encourage you in your new life in Christ.

Please visit joycemeyer.org/salvation to request Joyce's book *A New Way of Living*, which is our gift to you. We also have other free resources online to help you make progress in pursuing everything God has for you.

Congratulations on your fresh start in your life in Christ! We hope to hear from you soon.

# ABOUT THE AUTHOR

Joyce Meyer is one of the world's leading practical Bible teachers. A *New York Times* bestselling author, Joyce's books have helped millions of people find hope and restoration through Jesus Christ. Joyce's program, *Enjoying Everyday Life*, airs around the world on television, radio, and online. Through Joyce Meyer Ministries, Joyce teaches internationally on a number of topics with a particular focus on how the Word of God applies to our everyday lives. Her candid communication style allows her to share openly and practically about her experiences so others can apply what she has learned to their lives.

Joyce has authored more than 135 books, which have been translated into more than 160 languages, and over 37 million of her books have been distributed free of charge worldwide. Bestsellers include *Power Thoughts*; *The Confident Woman*; *Look Great, Feel Great*; *Starting Your Day Right*; *Ending Your Day Right*; *Approval Addiction*; *How to Hear from God*; *Beauty for Ashes*; and *Battlefield of the Mind*.

Joyce's passion to help hurting people is foundational to the vision of Hand of Hope, the missions arm of Joyce Meyer Ministries. Hand of Hope provides millions of meals for the hungry and malnourished, installs freshwater wells in poor and remote areas, provides critical relief after natural disasters, rescues women and children from human trafficking, offers free medical and dental care to thousands through their hospitals and clinics worldwide, and much more—always sharing the love and gospel of Christ.

# JOYCE MEYER MINISTRIES

## U.S. & FOREIGN OFFICE ADDRESSES

**Joyce Meyer Ministries**
P.O. Box 655
Fenton, MO 63026
USA
(636) 349-0303

**Joyce Meyer Ministries—
Canada**
P.O. Box 7700
Vancouver, BC V6B 4E2
Canada
(800) 868-1002

**Joyce Meyer Ministries—
Australia**
Locked Bag 77
Mansfield Delivery Centre
Queensland 4122
Australia
(07) 3349 1200

**Joyce Meyer Ministries—
England**
P.O. Box 1549
Windsor SL4 1GT
United Kingdom
01753 831102

**Joyce Meyer Ministries—
South Africa**
P.O. Box 5
Cape Town 8000
South Africa
(27) 21-701-1056

**Joyce Meyer Ministries—
Francophonie**
29 avenue Maurice Chevalier
77330 Ozoir la Ferriere
France

**Joyce Meyer Ministries—
Germany**
Postfach 761001
22060 Hamburg
Germany
+49 (0)40 / 88 88 4 11 11

**Joyce Meyer Ministries—
Netherlands**
Lorenzlaan 14
7002 HB Doetinchem
+31 657 555 9789

**Joyce Meyer Ministries—
Russia**
P.O. Box 789
Moscow 101000
Russia
+7 (495) 727-14-68

# Other Books by Joyce Meyer

The Power of Simple Prayer
Power Thoughts
Power Thoughts Devotional
Powerful Thinking
Quiet Times with God Devotional
Reduce Me to Love
The Secret Power of Speaking
God's Word
The Secrets of Spiritual Power
The Secret to True Happiness
Seven Things That Steal Your Joy
Start Your New Life Today
Starting Your Day Right
Straight Talk
Teenagers Are People Too!
Trusting God Day by Day
The Word, the Name, the Blood
Woman to Woman
You Can Begin Again
Your Battles Belong to the Lord *

**Joyce Meyer Spanish Titles**
Auténtica y única (Authentically,
Uniquely You)
Belleza en lugar de cenizas (Beauty for
Ashes)
Buena salud, buena vida (Good Health,
Good Life)
Cambia tus palabras, cambia tu vida
(Change Your Words, Change Your Life)
El campo de batalla de la mente
(Battlefield of the Mind)
Cómo envejecer sin avejentarse
(How to Age without Getting Old)
Como formar buenos habitos y romper
malos habitos (Making Good Habits,
Breaking Bad Habits)
La conexión de la mente
(The Mind Connection)

Dios no está enojado contigo
(God Is Not Mad at You)
La dosis de aprobación
(The Approval Fix)
Efesios: Comentario bíblico
(Ephesians: Biblical Commentary)
Empezando tu día bien
(Starting Your Day Right)
Hágalo con miedo (Do It Afraid)
Hazte un favor a ti mismo...perdona
(Do Yourself a Favor...Forgive)
Madre segura de sí misma
(The Confident Mom)
Momentos de quietud con Dios
(Quiet Times with God Devotional)
Pensamientos de poder
(Power Thoughts)
Sanidad para el alma de una mujer
(Healing the Soul of a Woman)
Santiago: Comentario bíblico
(James: Biblical Commentary)
Sobrecarga (Overload)*
Sus batallas son del señor
(Your Battles Belong to the Lord)
Termina bien tu día
(Ending Your Day Right)
Usted puede comenzar de nuevo
(You Can Begin Again)
Viva valientemente
(Living Courageously)

* Study Guide available for this title

**Books by Dave Meyer**
Life Lines